£1-29
BRS
45

KT-418-188

Peter Biddlecombe is a businessman who has travelled all
His first book, *French Lessons in Africa*,
briefcase as his companion) throug
popular and critical acclaim. This was
Briefcase, a delightfully funny account
Zürich. His most recent book, *I Came, I Saw, I Lost My Luggage,* is published in hardback by Little, Brown in 1996.

Around the World
– on Expenses

I Came, I Saw, I Lost My Luggage

PETER BIDDLECOMBE

An *Abacus* Book

First published in Great Britain in 1995
by Little, Brown and Company
This edition published by Abacus in 1996

A CIP catalogue record for this book
is available from the British Library.

ISBN: 0 349 10684 3

Typeset by Solidus (Bristol) Limited
Printed and bound in Great Britain by
Clays Ltd, St Ives plc

Abacus
A Division of
Little, Brown and Company (UK)
Brettenham House
Lancaster Place
London WC2E 7EN

Contents

Introduction

Don't you just hate the professional traveller?

'Oh my dear, if you haven't seen the gorillas in Upper Volta you just haven't lived.'

'Been to Florence? Not been to the Prado? Oh, how could you?'

'That sunshine. In Reykjavik. In Japan. In December. Exquisite.'

The poor dears, smeared with equal portions of Jungle Cream and artificial suntan, with an empty pith helmet full of travel knowledge culled from a lifetime flicking through the magazines on the middle shelves of W.H. Smith. You come across them all the time: in offices; in bars; falling asleep in their immaculately pressed tropical suits in airport lounges with their suitcases held together with elastoplast and every tourist board sticker you can imagine. At dinners; at receptions; and, God help me, at practically every cocktail party it's ever been my misfortune to attend. Misfortune, that is, until I've had a couple of drinks. Then in retaliation I can bore for any country in the world as well as the rest of them.

'Not seen the Niah Caves in Borneo! What have you been doing with yourself?'

'That volcano in Mexico – what's it called? – the Paricutin. Earth-moving.'

Have I been there myself? Of course not. But that's not the point. As I see it, the role of the professional traveller is to put

1

you off travelling, as much as the job of the professional travel writer is to put you off travel books. And what about travel writers. Are they serious?

First, there's the twin-set-and-pearls golly-gosh travel writer who does nothing but complain about emerging from planes and boats and trains dragging designer suitcases heavy with books and typewriters to an apartment lent to them for the duration by the Countess of somewhere or other, where they will sit on the balcony for months on end going into ecstasies about the local drains. Anyone they bump into in a bar wearing a club tie and a blue blazer they immediately label a savage cannibal who has eaten no less than twenty-seven people, when you can bet your life he is actually a failed property developer who is now making a living giving exclusive interviews one week to David Attenborough and the next to Michael Palin.

For the rest of their stay, the poor luvvies try to go exploring on their own but get nervous if they stray more than three feet from their typewriter. In desperation, they then lock themselves in their bedroom and write big rambling descriptions about what's on the local television. Heavens above! I'm reading a travel book in the first place because the last thing I want to know about is what's on television here, let alone in other countries.

Then there is the hobnail-boot travel writer who has to make a big fuss about everything. They're in the middle of the Amazon jungle. They're running out of rations. They're facing starvation. What do they do? They eat their pet dog. I ask you! If it is so rough in the Amazon jungle how come they took their pet dog with them in the first place? Then just because they forgot to pack a couple of extra tins of Spam how come the poor dog has to pay for it?

My favourite story of a hobnail-boot travel writer is about a certain great Chinese-egg-eating aesthete who was invited to visit Westonbirt Arboretum, 500 acres of trees, trees and nothing but trees in Gloucestershire. Could he catch the train

2

or drive down there like everybody else and spend a pleasant afternoon wandering around enjoying the scenery? Could he hell. He couldn't possibly, he insisted, go there on foot. He could only go there on horseback. Can you imagine the fuss and bother that caused? Within twenty minutes of clambering into the saddle he had to dismount to stretch his poor tired aching legs, when the horse – good for him – promptly galloped off into the sunset.

Then, best of all, there is the solitary travel writer who scours the world for meaningful experiences accompanied by a television cameraman, a sound recordist, an electrician, his personal doctor and a make-up girl, presumably to make-up to him in the evenings. If he is not joining a queue of thirty-seven other lone travellers taking it in turns to be photographed alone at the top of Everest, he is shuffling along the Silk Road where, I'm told, the first words a Kashmiri baby learns are, 'So which television channel are you working for?'

And the way they go on about wherever it is they are. I mean, if you or I go somewhere it's no big deal. I tell you the things I saw. You tell me what you saw. End of story. We go and have a drink.

Not these guys. Great travellers can't seem to go anywhere without having great thoughts, experiencing great experiences and then throwing up great chunks of Roget's *Thesaurus* to tell us all about it. They go on and on about the prelapsarian unawareness, the miraculous lightness of wherever they are, the self-consciousness, awe and condescension they feel in spite of the baleful remedies of forced egalitarianism they had to suffer to get there.

What about the poor unprofessional business traveller who probably covers more ground in an afternoon than they do in a lifetime? Does he go on about the prelapsarian unawareness of chauffeurs who fail to turn up on time; the miraculous lightness of his wallet after a dinner in Tokyo; or the forced egalitarianism he has to display meeting politicians, government ministers and even presidents? Of course not. The difference is that after God knows how many tons of plastic airline food and too many years of staring out of empty hotel bedrooms at the traffic lights changing in the rain, for him the mere thought of studying a grain of sand becomes more and more attractive.

In *Travels with my Briefcase*, I tried to describe the awful agonies and hardships the presumably postlapsarian aware, miraculously heavy and naturally egalitarian business traveller has to suffer staggering from one end of the world to the other. *Around the World – on Expenses* continues the sorry saga of how again and again we risk our lives checking in at French airports while the local riot police are baton-charging strikers; how we have to contend with the hordes as we battle our way through Rome during the school holidays; and the trials of eating our way through a *Good Food Guide* in one of the poorest countries of the world.

If *Travels* warranted a twinge of compassion, *Around the World* will have you gritting your teeth, wringing your hankie and howling in sympathy. For it proves yet again, I believe, that the professional traveller, let alone the professional travel writer, knows nothing about the real world. They're just gimmick tourists. The only true traveller is the business traveller.

Peter Biddlecombe
(On a one-eyed Irish reindeer going backwards down an up escalator in Yunnan Province, South East China)

Dublin

'Let it stand. Let it settle. Treat it with reverence, ye must. 'Tis not a drink ye be drinkin . . . .'

Glory be to God. 'Tis not just the Guinness and the countryside that makes Ireland the Lord's own country (though I was once told by an old County Clare farmer it was in desperate need of repair). It's the talk. For heaven help us, the poor tired old English language suddenly becomes mighty, fine, glorious, romantic music in the hands of themselves. The simplest, most straightforward throwaway remarks become pure magic.

Get a cab from the airport.

'So how far is it to the Westbury?'

''Tis about twelve miles. But for you, eight.'

It's pouring with rain.

'It's a soft day,' they sigh, before plunging into a raging force-nine gale.

At six o'clock in the morning, the Lord have mercy on me, I've stood in creameries in County Clare with the local farmers.

'Ye see this pipe?' I nod respectfully. 'I'll tell ye now. This pipe I've had for fifty years. This very same pipe.' I nod even more respectfully. 'Though I'll admit the bowl's been changed three times and the stem five – once when it was eaten by a goat and the other two times by a sheep. But I tell ye now 'tis the very same pipe. Fifty years. You can't say that about many things today.'

At eleven o'clock in the morning I've gone to the end of the world to be in offices in Limerick.

'The files are so full I cannot be getting another postage stamp in them. Can I be throwing some of them away?' says the secretary.

'To be sure,' says himself, the high and mighty boss. 'But make sure you photocopy them first.'

The secretary, God bless her, doesn't bat an eyelid. 'To be sure. It's not stupid I am.' She turns to me. 'Do you go to abroad very often?' she smiles.

I go into a bank in Tipperary to change my pounds into punts.

'So it's some hard currency you'll be after, is it?' says the cashier. I nod sheepishly. 'It's pockets in your shroud ye'll be needing to spend that lot here.'

With all this glorious music going on around me, far more fun and far more rewarding than all your Bach and Beethoven and Barry Manilow, I asked an Irish politician, 'But how on earth do you understand what people actually mean?'

'If you're not confused, you haven't been listening,' he replied.

For me Ireland is unlike anywhere else on earth for the talk, the wonderful, glorious, non-stop talk. Or 'the crack', as they say in Ballynacally, just outside Ennis, where my mother comes from. There, I've admitted it. I'm half Irish myself. A mongrel, as they say. But does that mean I'm biased? Not on your life.

The Irish will tell ye, I mean you, that the streets of London are paved with gold. But if they are, the highways and byways of Ireland are paved with poetry. Pure, beautiful poetry. Joyce, Shaw, Yeats, Wilde, O'Casey, Synge, Swift, Goldsmith, Sheridan, Beckett, Somerville and Ross . . . . If I could take just one book with me on a desert island it would be *The Experiences of an Irish RM.* I think it's the most wonderful book I've ever read, re-read and re-read again. Remember the fuss when Lord Armstrong came out with his comment about

6

being 'economical with the truth'? Everyone thought this was some clever new Whitehall jargon. Nonsense. It's in the *Irish RM*, where Flurry was not shrinking from being economical with Mrs Knox over the case of Trinket's colt.

My idea of heaven would be careering across country in the morning with the Galway Blazers, spending the afternoon at the Dublin Horse Show, the evening drinking and talking the night away in any bar you care to name in County Clare and finishing a chapter of the *Irish RM* before lights out. Ireland must be the most literate and literary country in the world. It probably has more great writers, or book eejits as an old aunt of mine used to say, per head of population than anywhere else on earth.

Trevor, O'Brian, Seamus Heaney . . . .

Computer programmers, works managers, even boring old accountants are more interested in discussing the relative merits of Joyce and Yeats than whether there's a blip in the bought ledger account. Taxi drivers in Dublin talk about Joyce as if they've just dropped him outside his home in Eccles Street. Even the homeless begging in Grafton Street don't hustle you with out-of-date copies of the *Big Issue*. Instead, for half the price of nothing they recite your favourite Irish poems with all the passion and interest of a Flurry Knox being economical with the truth with Mrs Knox over the case of Trinket's colt.

Everybody you meet, talk to, bump into, have a glass of Guinness with, is a real live Joyce, Shaw, Wilde or O'Casey.

It's lunchtime. I'm in this enormous tiny little bar of a place somewhere in Galway, no more than a corner at the end of the boreen. I go into the grocer's for a drink. Outside Dublin, grocer's are bars. And all bars are grocer's. There is a curtain across the middle of the room.

'What's the curtain for?'

''Tis for Father O'Malley.'

'You mean for confessions?'

'Not at all. 'Tis his way of making sure that when he comes

7

in here nobody sees him drinking.'

'But everybody sees him come in.'

'To be sure they do. He's been coming in now every day for the last thirty-seven years. 'Tis an institution he is.'

'Then why does he have the curtain?'

''Tis discretion. He doesn't like the parish to know.'

It's the middle of winter. I'm clambering over dry-stone walls, falling in ditches, fighting my way barehanded through impenetrable brambles, gorse, blackthorn and stinging nettles in the pouring rain, in the moonlight, in the middle of the night, to get to the nearest bar for a bottle of Guinness, or a sergeant as they call them in County Clare, to ward off the threat of a cold.

'This dark silence is so noisy,' says himself as soon as we get to the bar.

'Sure and can't I hear it meself,' says another.

I'm in a bar in Dublin. I've just had a bottle of red burgundy and gorgonzola sandwiches – Leopold Bloom's favourite dish. I want to go to the Abbey Theatre. I go up to the cash desk.

'To be sure we're sold out, we are. But not to worry. We still have some tickets left,' the old lady behind the desk tells me.

And if they're not real live Joyces, Shaws, Wildes and all the other book eejits, they are to a man experts on something far, far, more important still: horses. I say to a man because all women in Ireland are men. Providing, of course, they are 'a gas, a real gas'. If not, they're ignored; they don't exist.

'Young Mary,' they say. 'One of the finest lads you'll find this side of Galway. If she loses her virginity someone is sure to find it and give it back to her before her mother finds out.'

And if they go racing, with or without their virginity, they don't go as women. They go as one of the lads.

'There's no danger in them. They're drinking and gambling. There'll be no mischief in them,' old farmers will tell you.

It's the priests who have the mischief. Especially those from the horsey counties of Kildare, Carlow, Tipperary, Neath and, of course, Galway. They know as much, if not more, about

horseflesh as they do about the four gospels, the life of the
Little Flower or how to pour a decent glass of Guinness with
exactly the right level of pure white froth, or dog collar as they
call it.

Go to a horse show or a horse race anywhere in Ireland and
the ground will be black with priests' coats and jackets and
hats. I've spent years watching horses scrambling over banks,
leaping over ditches as wide as the Atlantic or hedges as high
as the Empire State Building, and there have always been as
many priests in the crowd as children and widows at Mass on
Sunday morning.

Some people seem to think priests are only interested in
saving your soul. Not the ones I know. They are only
interested in saving your skin.

''Tis a fine jumper, he is. Sails over them fences. Glory be to
God he's the finest beast in creation,' they exclaim. The
trouble is, they say that about every horse. You take their
advice, you put your money on. But win or lose, it doesn't
matter; the priest's faith is as unshakeable as it is in the
Apostles' creed, the four last things and the medicinal value of
a drop of Jamesons after a day at the races. ''Tis saving himself
he is for the next one. Now you mark my words, the next time,
he'll fly over the . . . .'

If he wins, the sky, as they say, is black with priests' hats
celebrating your victory. If he loses, the sky will be just as
black. They'll still be cheering. In the pubs afterwards they'll
be in the middle of the bar, crawling around on all fours, knee
deep in Guinness, reliving the race and jumping make-believe
ditches twice the size of the Atlantic.

One priest I know, who has brains to burn, is as earnest and
dedicated about taking his parishioners to Cheltenham for
Gold Cup Week as he is organizing pilgrimages to Lourdes or
seeing the Holy Father.

''Tis with my flock I must be. That's been my vow for forty
years. I'm not going to be breaking it now,' he says.

So concerned is he for the salvation of his flock that he not only goes racing with them, he also sits up all night with them playing poker, then heads them all off to church in the morning, where he says Mass and gets them to put their winnings in the plate so he can give it back to the losers so they can carry on gambling through the following night.

Forget Bishop Casey. The biggest moral dilemma faced by the clergy in Ireland is whether, when they slip off to the races or to watch the golf, they should wear their clerical collars. I've been in Irish bars where there's been as much debate over spotting the clerical collar or the clockwork television set as spotting the winner.

'Bedad and there's another.'

'And another. Bless me, over there behind the tree.'

'Quick. Quick. There. In the front next to the young thing in the big hat . . . . '

Some priests say they should wear a scarf on top of their collars so as not to cause scandal among the faithful, who would no doubt be hard at work while they were out enjoying themselves. Others say no. One priest assured me, over a sergeant in Mrs Mollony's bar in Newmarket-on-Fergus, that they should wear the collar. There was no doubt about it. Not to wear the collar was to 'deny their divine calling', he said, 'as horsemen.' All I know is, if you are ever watching the racing or the golf from Ireland on a hot summer's day and the screen is full of people wearing scarves you can bet an Irish halfpenny to a barrel of Guinness they are all priests.

Some cities are for getting away from. They're filthy; they're crowded; they're so noisy you can't hear yourself drink. Dublin, that soft morning city in which the Irish will tell you they see France in the quays, Naples in Dublin Bay, a touch of Hanover around Trinity and heaven itself in a glass of Guinness, is for staying in. For talking in. For drinking in.

''Tis the mightiest city in the world for a crack,' they say. Glory be to God, what cracks there are. From the moment you tumble off the plane as a blow-in – the Irish way of describing a visitor – to when you reluctantly drag yourself away from another bar, fall into a taxi and race like a bat out of hell back to the airport, every second is spent talking. And drinking. And talking and drinking. And . . . .

Wander along Parnell Street; outside the headquarters of the Vintners, Grocers and Allied Trades Assistants Union is a plaque dedicated to all the barmen who died during the troubles fighting the British.

''Tis crazy the way they insist barmen serve a five-year apprenticeship,' I say.

'Not at all. Are ye some kind of eejit? They've cut it to three years.'

I'm the eejit! And this is the country:

– where banks go on strike for weeks on end and everybody is forced to cash their cheques at local bars
– where police lock up suspects in prison cells containing enough ammunition to re-start World War One
– where bogs, not towns, are twinned with other bogs in different parts of the world
– where walking pigs backwards and forwards across the border earns you more in a week than the Brussels bureaucrats who dreamt up the eejit scheme earn in a year.

In *The Risen People*, James Plunket says that if you're fat, you're a Catholic. If you have a long face and a sharp nose you're a Protestant. If somebody has a long face and a nondescript sort of nose then that's a Catholic trying to look like a Protestant. Stroll through the brick-paved pedestrian precinct off Grafton Street, linking Trinity College and St Stephen's Green, and you hear them, fat and thin, Catholics and Protestants and Catholics trying to look like Protestants.

'When will the electricity come back on again?'

'Between six and nine.'

11

'You mean tonight or tomorrow morning?'

'To be sure.'

I knew an old lady once in Dublin, a Protestant, who dried her hair in the oven because she said she couldn't rely on the electricity.

The best cracks, of course, are heard through the bottom of a glass of Guinness in one of the 600 bars during happy hour, which in Dublin lasts from 7.30–9.00 every weekday evening.

'What'll ye be having?'

'No thank you, I've—'

'Come on now. A sergeant. It'll be a sergeant, will it?'

'No. It's okay—'

'Michael, will ye give this man a sergeant.'

'Well. No. I mean, thank you very much.'

Now normally I don't drink Guinness. Usually I give it to the horses especially after a long hard day out riding. They're covered sweat and caked in mud. On the way home I stop at the local pub.

'Two pints of Guinness.'

'Mugs or glasses?'

'Bottles, please. They're not for me, they're for the horses.'

Then I get a funny look, as if I'm some kind of horse eejit. That's in England. But not in Dublin. In Dublin I drink the Guinness. Because in Dublin Guinness, the famously homely brew, bebattled by bottle as Joyce described it in *Finnegans Wake*, is unlike Guinness anywhere else in the world. It's richer, creamier, thicker. It has a beautiful, gentle, dark, roasted barley aroma with a slight fruity finish. Sometimes it's so thick you can stand a spoon upright in it. Or, if you take the word of my old uncle, John Gavin, a mouse could run across the top of it.

Let it stand. Let it settle. Treat it with reverence. Immediately in any bar in the land you'll be welcomed into the most exclusive society.

I was once in a bar in County Galway waiting for my Guinness to settle. An old man in a thick tweed jacket with battered thornproof trousers is sitting opposite me. He is still wearing his greasy black trilby and holding an old blackthorn stick. He leans across to me. ''Tis one hundred and two years old I am,' he smiles quietly. 'One hundred and two years it is if I'm a day.'

I smile, suitably impressed. He reminds me of one of my old Irish uncles who, like him, always but always kept his hat on, no matter where he went or to whom he was speaking. When he was ill towards the end, I remember seeing him once sitting nodding by the fire. His hat was beside him on the corner of the table. His face was brown and leathery, burnt by the elements of a lifetime in the open country. His forehead, which had remained hidden under his hat, was white: icy white and as soft as a newborn baby's.

I smile at the old man. 'And to what do you owe your great age?' I ask.

'To a printer's error,' he says quietly.

I buy him another Guinness.

If you can't see Dublin, the fine, grand, competent city, through the bottom of a glass of Guinness, the next best way is from seven miles away on top of a hill in the middle of Courtsdown Forest from where you can also see the Bay.

The last time I deserted my Guinness for the hills, I had just got past the Garden of Remembrance for the Dead of the Civil War when an old lady came rushing up to me.

'I've lost my Dobermann,' she sobbed. 'Did you see it?'

'Glory be, but you didn't leave your keys in it?' exclaimed my Irish colleague.

The compromise, of course, is to avoid fresh air and lost dobermanns – or should it be dobermenn? – altogether and stagger around Dublin instead. From bar. To bar. Through the inner cordon, the city centre which covers seven-and-a-half square miles and is bounded on three sides by two canals and, of course, the River Liffey and twenty-seven bridges. Down Grafton Street with its statue of Molly Malone and her wheelbarrow – known among the Murphia as the Tart with the Cart. Along the magnificent terraces of charming eighteenth-century Georgian houses and elegant garden squares. Around Christ Church Cathedral, by Dublin Castle, along Fleet Street, into Poolbeg Street, across into Lower Bridge Street and all along Duke Street.

Everywhere everybody is talking and talking and talking. Along the Quay, by the Liffey with its Customs House and Four Courts, which has twice been destroyed this century; first in 1921 when the Republicans set it on fire in order to destroy all British records, and again the following year when de Valera's anti-Free Staters seized it at the start of the Civil War.

'The Lord save us and guard us,' a fat Catholic old lady is protesting. 'I went to the theatre the other night. Can I remember what I saw? I cannot. But it was the experience itself.'

An opinion polster stops a thin Protestant old lady and asks if she will vote yes or no for Maastricht.

'To be sure, I'll be voting maybe,' she says.

Wandering around Dublin listening to them talking is one thing. Working with them is something else. For years I worked with engineering and electronic companies outside Dublin. It wasn't easy. Not because they were Irish. But because they were in business. I'm sorry, somehow I just can't accept the Irish as businessmen. Priests and barmen, or curates as they are sometimes called: doctors, nurses, farmers; that I can accept. But serious businessmen running engineering and electronic companies. No way. What's more I'm sure they don't see themselves as serious businessmen either.

Go to a planning meeting which for the third time has failed to produce the figures we agreed at the previous two meetings should be produced for the German company interested in buying them.

'Trouble is it's always mañana,' I murmured gently. I couldn't remember the German for mañana.

'I'm sorry, sir,' said the director responsible, who has his copy of *Fox's Book of Martyrs* on top of his papers on the

14

boardroom table. 'I don't think in this country we have a word which quite expresses that sense of urgency.'

Go to a business conference attended by government ministers. The place is full of plain clothes policemen. How do I know they are plain clothes policemen? They are all wearing security badges – with photographs of themselves in police uniform, including hats.

Go to an annual meeting. The chairman welcomes shareholders 'to this island of saints and scholars'.

The Irish, I know, are the greatest literary nation on earth, but sometimes I feel even they go too far. One chairman regaled his AGM with a long story about how their balance sheet 'exemplifies in almost Disney fashion how you can apparently get wealthier as you expand' and went on about how, in spite of earnings being down and spending being up, the net value of the company had soared.

'This kind of contradiction, which,' he said, 'so baffles bunnies, is airborne by the magic carpet of cashflow.'

I pick up the *Irish Times*. 'A typographical error resulted in a sentence which read, "The annual rate of Irishmen travelling abroad to have an abortion is higher now than in 1983. This should, of course, have read . . . ."'

I get back to my hotel for dinner. Outside, I notice, on the lamppost is a sign saying that illegal dog fouling of the footpath is forbidden. Legal fouling, presumably, is okay. I switch on the television; Gay Byrne is on the Late Late Show. A man from Limerick is describing a domestic foot disinfector he has invented for people who want to disinfect their feet.

To the true Irishman, the only food anybody ever needs is Guinness. I'm only half Irish so I need to eat as well as drink. In the old days I can remember not only was it virtually impossible to find anywhere to eat in Ireland, but before you even tried you had to hang a roast potato in a sock around your neck and rub goose fat onto your chest to stop yourself from catching cold from all the holy water that would be poured over you before you set out. Then if you were lucky enough to find anywhere it was usually closed for lunch to save costs. But it would still be full of people ordering one tea – and two cups.

On one visit to an elderly bachelor cousin in County Clare, in desperation I grabbed myself a cucumber sandwich off the plate only to discover a caterpillar curled up fast asleep underneath it. Come to think of it, I can also remember sitting under a hedge by the side of a boreen outside Newmarket on Shannon cracking open bags of oysters with a pair of pliers and eating them with great hunks of soda bread because the restaurants were all closed.

And of course there was black pudding. One of my Irish uncles used to make black pudding so delicious it would make an angel renounce his vows. He'd go out in the yard, grab a pig, hit it between the eyes with a hammer to kill it, sling it up on a hook in the kitchen, slit it open from top to bottom then let the blood drip into a bucket underneath. The following morning, the blood had dried. My aunt then fried it up over the open hearth fire. Glory be to God was it the most delicious taste known to man himself.

Today it's different. Irish salmon caught off Dinish Island, off the magnificent coast of Kerry, and smoked over Irish peat, is the best you'll find in the world. The clams and scallops as well as oysters – grapes of stone, the Irish call them – served in many famous Swiss, German and even French restaurants now come from Ireland. So good have the Irish become at producing oysters, and so clear is the sea, that they are now producing the deep-shelled gigas or Pacific oysters as well. In Killybegs in County Donegal they are even shipping off the small, boney, common-or-garden horse mackerel to Tokyo where it is hailed, would you believe it, as an unbelievable delicacy.

There are also plenty of fabulous restaurants which now even stay open for not only lunch but dinner as well: Cliffords in Cork; the Park Hotel, Kenmare; Aheiner's in Youghal in County Cork, famous for its sensational cod; the Park Restaurant and the Wine Espergne, both in Dublin.

But wherever I go I don't normally suffer from the after-effects of an Irish meal. Irish hangovers are nowhere near as bad as, say, Yugoslav, Russian or even Finnish hangovers, which can make you look twenty-five years older overnight and take three weeks to recover from. After one particularly enthusiastic session with a group of Finns in London, I was frightened to drive a car for a month.

One export manager I know solves the problem of hangovers by not sleeping. After a heavy dinner, let alone a full night's drinking, for the sake of British exports, he just heads for the nearest sauna and sweats the alcohol out of his system. He claims it saves him a fortune on hotel bills, bumps up his expenses and enables him to run two gundogs and go shooting nearly every weekend during the season.

Once in Ireland, however, I felt as though there were a couple of dozen Kilkenny cats inside my head fighting to get out. It wasn't the Guinness. Knowing my luck it was probably the fine, weighty black pudding I'd had the previous evening in some fancy restaurant out towards Blackrock where I remember thinking, at least during the early part of the evening, that the floor was deceptively level. Instead of pig's blood, it was sheep's blood, mixed with bacon and lard and heaps of thyme and garlic and served with apples and calvados. Obviously the thyme had not agreed with me.

Me, I don't believe in saunas. My mother must have been frightened by the only Calvinist to have set foot in County Clare. I find the best cure is to carry on working. I locked myself in my hotel room, put the 'Do Not Disturb' sign outside the door and settled down to sober myself up writing reports and proposals for clients who would turn them down before they even read them.

But Ireland being Ireland, I kept being disturbed. First by the housekeeper. She had to check the room had been made up. Next by room service. They wanted to restock the mini-bar. Then came an engineer who'd had complaints about the room's air-conditioning and wanted to test it. Then security.

They came because they were suspicious so many people were going into a room reception had told them was empty.

'Now look,' I finally began to simmer, 'what's the point of me putting "Do Not Disturb" on my door if you do nothing all day but disturb me?'

'To be sure,' the girl at reception said, 'but how can we be certain you have everything you want if we don't disturb you?'

'But I have everything!'

'In that case,' she purred, 'you have my assurance we'll not be disturbing you again.'

'Thank you very much.'

'Not at all.'

Two minutes later a lady came to measure for new curtains. Then the plumber. Then I fled back to the bar. What else could I do?

Inevitably, there was the German businessman who was interested in acquiring one of the engineering companies. He was sitting by himself. Maybe it was because he was drinking gin and tonic and not Guinness.

'Zay say ziss Dublin has six hundert pups. We visit zem all. Komm,' he said as I sat down opposite.

For the sake of the deal, I agreed. 'But first,' I said, 'you must drink Guinness. You can't drink gin and tonic in Ireland. First nicht möglich.'

'Nein danke. Always trinke ich gin and tonic. Never I drink das schwartzes Bier.'

'But . . . .'

'Nein.'

Then he muttered something like:

> 'Wasser macht weise
> Fröhlich der Wein
> Darum trinken beides
> Um beides zu sein.'

Which apparently is some famous poem by Goethe about

water making you wise, wine making you happy, but too much of either making you wet your pants.

Eventually, of course, he gave in. Gently the barman poured the glass. With the utmost reverence. He put it on the bar. Slowly he then topped it up. Delicately he scraped the thick white froth off the top of the glass. Slowly, again he topped it up. Delicately again he scraped the thick white froth off the top of the glass. He placed it solemnly in front of the German, who eyed it suspiciously for a second. His arm then shot out to grab it.

'Nein,' I screamed. 'Not yet. Let it stand. Let it settle. To be sure you must. Treat it with reverence.

'To be sure,' whispered the barman.

The German looked at me suspiciously. 'But in Deutschland—'

'But this is Guinness,' I said. 'It's not just beer. It's – it's – Guinness.'

We let it stand. We waited for it to settle. We looked at it with all the reverence in the world. Finally it was ready. I nodded solemnly. The barman smiled. The German lifted it to his lips.

'Ist gut,' he whispered. 'Sehr gut.'

'Okay,' I said. 'Now I'll take you round the pubs.'

I don't exactly know every one of the six hundred pubs in Dublin, but for me the best are the small, airless bars with oak-panelled varnished interiors, thick lincrust, and yellow ceilings aged with tobacco smoke. They are decorated with spit and sawdust and ancient posters of the days before the Troubles, and as full of alcoholic fumes as the back of a church at midnight Mass on Christmas Eve.

I thought of going along Leeson Street off St Stephen's Green where, underneath the Institute of Professional Valuers, the Sacred Heart Messenger and the Apostleship of Prayer, are all the basement clubs such as Chaos, Money Business, or even Screwy Lui where entry is free but a bottle of wine costs you £25 or a glass of orange £2. But it didn't seem quite right. Instead I made for St Stephen's Green and the Horseshoe bar in the Shelbourne Hotel, where between rounds the Irish constitution was drafted in 1922, and which is still supposed to be the centre of Dublin social life. We ordered our Guinness. We let it stand. We waited for it to settle. We treated it with reverence.

'Here they must be trying to rationalize, create larger units to compete in single European market,' he began as he took his first sip. Then another. And another. And another. 'In spite of zoo many small farmers producing as little as 100–150 gallons in a world where average European farms are producing 100-150 million gallons a year,' he continued as he sank a second pint.

We graduated to whiskey. Irish whiskey, with an e, with its mix of malted and unmalted barley which adds to the flavour, unlike Scotch. On top of that it's triple distilled, which makes it less smokey and more velvety. With the whiskey, he became more Irish and less German.

'More than thirty-five food companies in Europe have sales of more than 1R £1 billion. The top ten account for almost sixty per cent of their total turnover. Not one of them is Irish. Why is dat? Please to . . . .' he was going on.

After I don't know how long, as we staggered out full of Guinness and Jamesons, he said, 'To you must I tell my secret.'

The Lord guard me and save me, I thought. The last thing I want to know is his secret. Anyone's secret. Especially if they're bombed out of their minds, away from home, in Dublin.

'Are you ready?' He wagged his finger at me like Germans do at EC meetings in Brussels.

I nodded a little uneasily.

'I am a Joyce-lehrer,' he gasped. And sank slowly to the ground. But that's not what amazed me. What amazed me was that he sat on the ground without first putting a towel down to reserve the space.

With the help of some passers-by I got him into a taxi.

'Now you take me,' he gasped. 'Will you come where I want to go?'

Heaven help me, I thought. Not Nachstadt. The last thing I wanted was getting up to some schenanigan in Nachstadt mit einem Deutscher. Especially a sehr drunk Deutscher.

'I want to see alles Joyce,' he grunted in a bass-band tone of voice.

Gott sei dank, I thought. It could have been ein hundert thousand times worse. I took him to a Moralische Kneipe. It wasn't Davy Byrne's, but he didn't know.

Over I can't remember what or how many, served by a cracked looking-glass of a barman, he told me he had studied the *Odyssey* at university. He had recently discovered James Joyce. Now he wanted to visit all the places Bloom, ein jüdischer Werbekaufmann, had visited on Bloomstag.

'Dublin rejoyced. Dublin mit Joyce,' he kept repeating. 'Können sie mir bitte hilfen?'

What could I lisp? He was interested in buying the engineering company. If he bought it, it would solve lots of problems.

'Natürlich,' I mumbled.

He told me he wanted to translate *Ulysses* into German.

Not only is history a nightmare, I thought. What's the German for 'snotgreen, scrotumtightening sea'? 'Natürlich,' I mumbled.

I took him back to the hotel and dumped him in a chair in reception. We agreed to meet for lunch. I suggested the Barley in Duke Street. The front door of number 7 Eccles Street where Leopold Bloom lived is on display there, along with Michael Collins's revolver. It seemed as good a place as any to start.

The following morning he was there when I arrived. He didn't say a word about *Ulysses*, Joyce, or what had happened the previous evening. He just kept staring at the Guinness on the table in front of him.

'One must let it standt. One must let it settle. To be sure,' he was whispering to himself. 'Treat it mit reverence . . . . '

Athens

In theory I should love Athens. It should be my favourite city. For I have known it for nearly 3,000 years. What I mean is, I've known its history for nearly 3,000 years.

Most children nowadays are brought up in a carefree environment of declining moral standards, sexual abuse, violence and death. I was brought up on the strict moral standards of Euripides' *Medea*, Sophocles' *Oedipus* and the *Iliad*, Homer's untruths from abroad. To me it was normal to have long leisurely discussions about everything under the sun; encourage old men to commit suicide and if you didn't hate your father and love your mother there was something wrong with you. Everybody outside the gates who wasn't Greek or studying Greek, was a barbarian. Or if not a barbarian a shadow on the wall.

While every other kid in the street was studying the *Beano* and Desperate Dan, I was marching with Xenophon and the ten thousand all the way through Persia to the southern shores of the Black Sea. While they were all at Saturday morning pictures screaming at Superman not to save the world – I came from that kind of area – I was agonizing with good old Sophocles on the relationship between man and the state and whether it was worth saving or not.

While the whole world was worrying abut the Cup Final and talking about Pan as if he was a paperback, I was studying the entrails, puzzling over the sacrificial marks on the sheep's shoulderblades and losing sleep trying to master Aristotle's *Nicomachean Ethics*.

I was so steeped in Greek literature – Homer Sweet Homer – that until I was thirteen I honestly thought losing your marbles had something to do with Lord Elgin, and that women 'of many skills' were valued in terms of oxen and awarded as second prizes in wrestling matches. Now, of course, I know that is untrue. They are only awarded as third prizes after the television rights and the sponsorship deals.

For me, give or take the odd eye operation, death in the family or slow journey home, the Greeks were the most organized, civilized, rational and logical human beings in the world and Athens the pinnacle of civilization. When I finally got here, however, Athens was a mezz. It was definitely not organized or civilized and the Greeks were most certainly neither rational nor logical. The gods of order had been usurped by the gods of inadequacy, inefficiency and chaos. They couldn't even organize plate-smashing in a taverna any more. I was only glad that, unlike Nietzsche, I didn't have to wait until I had syphilis and was going mad before I discovered the mistakes of my youth.

Edinburgh keeps calling itself the Athens of the north. They're crazy. My guess is, knowing how free the Scots are with their money, that none of them have taken even a weekend package trip to Athens since Socrates drank his wee dram to find out what it's really like. If they did they would change their slogan. The only connection I can think of between Edinburgh and Athens is that not so long ago the men of both cities walked around without trousers on.

Melina Mercouri calls Athens (the Edinburgh of the south) 'an ugly woman with great charm'. She forgot to mention the gasmask. On a clear day, you're supposed to be able to see forever. Not in Athens. On a clear day in Athens – cough, cough – you can't see the glasses on the end of your nose let alone how ugly she is. As for the charm, it's safer to forget the whole idea, stay indoors, practise your irregular Greek verbs or read about the glory that once was Athens, than go outside and try to find it.

'You want fresh air ın Athens, you close the window,' a Greek banker told me. For the fog, no *nefos* – cough, cough – is thick, heavy, sulphurous, streaky and yellow. It's not like your ordinary smog. This is a classical Greek smog. It's hot as well. Sometimes as much as 35°C – even 40°C. It makes your eyes smart. You start sneezing. You are gasping for breath. Then when you breathe you wish you hadn't. It's so thick, people get lost rushing from their hotel to a taxi. Just a few feet above ground level, planes disappear into thick billowing clouds before they've even taken off. Up there, high above the streets somewhere, is the Parthenon. Somewhere – is it that direction or that direction? – is the Saronic Gulf.

Everybody complains of headaches and nausea and dizzy spells and the cost of being treated for respiratory problems. In the old days the Greeks claimed they had the sea in their blood. Today they have *nefos* in their blood. If they have any blood left. Through the *nefos* – cough, cough – you hear ambulances, lights on in the middle of the day, desperately trying to rush another victim with heart and breathing problems to hospital. Aristotle maintained the world was comprised of four elements: earth, air, fire and water. If he were alive today, he would add a fifth: smog. Your average Athenian in the street, if he can find the street in the *nefos* – cough, cough – says its a million times worse than the tear gas used by the police against strikers who nowadays seem to spend more time and effort working against the government than they spend working at their full-time jobs.

My old Greek master, who tried to envelope everything in his own special kind of *nefos* – 'Please, sir, why does Jason want to leave his wife?' – would have said it was as thick and as poisonous and as sulphureous as the Styx, the river of hate that enclosed the Underworld (but he still wouldn't tell us why Jason wanted to leave his wife). To me, however, the *nefos* – cough, cough – is as impenetrable as the thick, goo-ey prose of – dare I say it? – Patrick Leigh Fermor.

The first time I arrived in Athens I was full of ouzo and Patrick Leigh Fermor. One of the great and uncovenanted delights of Greece, he was saying, was 'a pre-coming of age, a direct and immediate link, friendly and equal on either side, between human beings, something which melts barriers of hierarchy and background and money and . . . .'

Within seconds of landing the only direct and immediate link I experienced was a sharp jab in the ribs as a modern day Hermes tried to snatch my briefcase. The friendliness and equality didn't extend to the police on duty at the gates to the arrivals hall. And they certainly didn't look upon me as if I was even as civilized as a barbarian.

Undaunted by either Leigh Fermor or a sore rib, I was still convinced Athens was the Athens of my dreams, that everybody I saw through the *nefos* – cough, cough – would look like either a Greek god with a gold breastplate and a short leather jacket, or something out of Sophocles or Euripides or Homer.

The following morning, at a meeting at Alpha France, a Greek merchant bank in what I think was the centre of Athens, the woman at reception was obviously another Medea; the type of woman who creates an awful fuss just because her husband wants to ditch her and run off and marry someone who is going to be more useful to him in his job. The director I had arranged to meet was obviously a modern Odysseus. He wasn't there. He was still travelling. Nobody knew when he would be back. That was the end of meeting number one.

I couldn't even see the road to try and get a taxi so I strolled back passed the Royal Palace. At least I think it was the Royal Palace. I swear I bumped into – the *nefos*, again – Admetus. Well if it wasn't, he looked as though he had just persuaded his wife to die in his place so he could marry an air hostess. Along Academias Street, one of the grimiest areas in the city, I was surrounded by a twelve-strong black-clad chorus wailing at me in hideous blank verse.

According to Leigh Fermor, this would presumably be one of the great and uncovenanted delights of Greece. 'It is not a thing which functions in the teeth of convention, but in almost prelapsarian unawareness of its existence. Self-consciousness, awe and . . . .' That means he likes it, doesn't it?

I crossed into Syntagma Square, Athens' central square where, incidentally, you can always buy cheap, but very cheap, air tickets to Cairo. Prometheus was still there pushing his cart. On one trip I was so worried about my 'almost prelapsarian unawareness' that I was frightened to go into the Hotel George V on the corner, which had remained virtually untouched since it was built in the thirties. I was convinced the head receptionist was another Hecuba looking for an excuse to go around murdering more innocent people. One evening I was there plucking up courage to ask for the key to my room when an imperious British foreign office type complete with umbrella, who looked as though the nearest he'd ever been to Greece was the Athenaeum, barged passed me.

'Evening, George,' he barked at her. 'My key, please,' and disappeared into the bar.

The Athenians are nothing like Pausanias says in his *Descriptions of Greece*, the oldest travel book ever written. Having marched with Xenophon, they would, I imagined, have solved the problems of transport by now. Having agonized with Sophocles, I thought they would have the most efficient government machine in the world. Having philosophized with Aristotle, I was certain they would be cool, calm, rational.

Not on your life. The Greeks may have invented the word for *civilization* but they don't know the meaning of it. They are disorganized, unreasonable, stubborn, absolutely impossible to deal with; the kind of people who invent philosophy, democracy, theatre, and then turn any drama into a tragedy. The home of Pericles, I'd forgotten, had also invented the word for chaos. And questions. If this was the prelapsarian unawareness, self-consciousness, condescension that Leigh Fermor kept on about, he could keep it. Maybe he was talking about another Greece.

Then gradually the *nefos*, if not Patrick Leigh Fermor, clears. What do you see? The descendants of Alexander are living in a huge, faceless, nineteenth-century sprawl of ugly concrete buildings, blocks of modern flats and great chunks of Hellenic bric-à-brac. Nothing like Rome, the Eternal City, with its basilicas and churches, and those fabulous plazas and glorious fountains on every street corner. It's not even as pretty as Algiers. On a foggy day. During Ramadan. In the middle of the fundamentalist riot season. It's like a giant housing estate designed by a committee chaired by Attila the Hun and built by the Bulgarians.

Sure, it sits on three hills: Lycabettus, the highest, which has borne the brunt of Athens' rapid expansion; Phyx, the smallest, where Kleisthenes invented democracy in the market place – the joys of a classical education! – and, of course, the Acropolis with the Parthenon, the temple of Athena on top. Of course the Venetians should not have blasted away fourteen of its columns, even though it does give it a certain lived-in feeling. Of course Lord Elgin should not have scooped up their marbles. But it is still stunning. For my two drachmas' worth it should be one of the wonders of the world.

Wait a minute. Kleisthenes invented democracy? Sure. He was a scheming wheeler-dealer who 2,500 years ago wanted to outmanoeuvre his enemies. The only way he could think of doing it was by setting up a string of different electoral areas who would each elect a representative to sit on the central council. This he did – and, the ultimate example of doing the right thing for the wrong reason, *demokratia* was born.

Want to make a Greek lose his marbles? For the second time, ask him why there aren't any statues of Kleisthenes in Athens.

'Who?' they squirm.

'Kleisthenes. The founder of democracy.'

They look at you.

"You've never heard of him?'

A blank stare. My only reward for all those years studying Greek.

I once flew into Athens early in the evening. The plane was late, again. Don't ask me which airline. As we swooped down low you could see the Parthenon floodlit in the distance. An elderly couple in front of me started arguing about taking a photograph of it.

'Quick, quick, the camera,' he hustled her. 'Give me the camera.'

'That? You want to take a photograph of that thing?' she exclaimed.

'Of course. It's the Parthenon,' he said. 'The cradle of Western civilization. Quick.'

She dithered and dithered, looked in one bag, then another.

'Quick, quick,' he kept whispering.

Finally she gave him the camera. He snapped it and it disappeared into the night below us.

'Of course it won't come out,' she announced to the whole cabin in that voice women use when they know they're right. 'You didn't fix the flash to it.'

Athens might have the Parthenon, but it has less green space per inhabitant than any other city in Europe, which is probably why they also have the *nefos* – cough, cough. Other reasons, of course, are the heat and the traffic. Buses from the Trojan Wars chug along belching out clouds of soot. The rest of the traffic does the same, although more often than not it's at a standstill. If the buses are on strike the streets are jammed because everyone is using their car, motorbike or pony-and-cart to try not to get to the office. If the buses are not on strike, it's still at a standstill because everyone is using their second car, motorbike or pony-and-cart not to get to the office. And I mean second car, because in order to reduce the *nefos* –

cough, cough – and the amount of traffic in Athens, the authorities, instead of insisting that everybody wore winged sandals, decided to ban cars with odd numbers on one day and even numbers the next. What happened? Exactly the same as in Lagos when they tried to introduce a similar scheme. Everyone bought a second car, which was invariably older and, therefore, pumped out even more thick black clouds then their first car. Now you know why it took Ulysses ten years to find his way home. He got stuck in the Athens traffic. As if it isn't bad enough battling through the traffic, most drivers behave as if they only have one eye in the middle of their head. I always feel as if I need eyes all around my head, and I'm just sitting in the back of a cab.

If they ever get home, *hoi aristoi*, especially in fashionable Kifissia to the north, as opposed to *hoi oligoi* in the suburbs, also have to suffer the coughing and spluttering of the Cerberuses and Arguses bought to protect their homes during the *nefos* – cough, cough. Trouble is, the descendants of Achilles and Alexander forgot that dogs are also affected by smog. Most dogs in Athens would probably be happier working as live mine detectors in Afghanistan.

And cats. I've never been anywhere in the world where there are so many cats running about. Most of them are mangy and flea-ridden; most of them are wild; and most of them are waiting to be rescued by well-meaning, innocent British tourists. Go to a nut-cutlet dinner party in Hampstead and I bet you all England to a glass of ouzo one of them will have brought a stray cat home from Athens.

The only part of Athens which seems even to acknowledge the problem of animals is singleminded Hydra, a tiny island away from the *nefos* – cough, cough – in the Saronic Gulf just outside the city. There they have decided to tax not the cars but the donkeys and mules which clog and especially foul up the streets. If you have a donkey on Hydra, you pay US$100 a year tax. I doubt whether even Kleisthenes could get any other towns to agree.

Greece itself, like *nefos* – cough, cough – to the Athenians, is a tragedy to practically everyone else. It should be the cultural centre of the Mediterranean, or at least the south-east corner. It should be the link between east and west. Greek businessmen should be key players on the world stage. Doing business with the Greeks should be as easy as building a wooden horse and being welcomed in the city centre with open arms. Instead it's like trying to end the Trojan Wars.

There is no greater Greek tragedy today than Greece itself. And in typical Greek fashion they have brought it on themselves – with a vengeance. In fact, in many ways it's a shame Athens survived. Had Alexander, the Great Macedonian, destroyed it as he did Thebes, or had it been devastated by an earthquake, or just disappeared off the face of the map, it would have maintained its reputation. Today Greece is seen as just another poor Balkan country wrecked by one financial scandal after another. The gap between Greece and the rest of Europe – and the Greeks, don't forget, invented the word – is widening, not narrowing as it is with other countries.

Looking at the economy is like peering into a bottomless eye socket. Inflation is running at 17.4 percent. Unemployment is 10 percent, probably more. The budget deficit is 17.2 percent of GDP and growing. It is not in the Exchange Rate Mechanism, and probably won't be for years to come. It seems completely uninterested in meeting its goals for full economic and monetary union with the EC. It refuses, admittedly very subtly, even to think about that country of which Ankara is the capital. It promised the EC it would negotiate a friendship and co-operation agreement with you-know-who, but what has it done? Nothing. The EC, as a result, can't begin talks with Turkey. Neither can it even think of letting Cyprus into the club. When Greece is granted massive loans for restructuring it ignores the commitments it solemnly undertakes. It has one of the most antiquated banking systems in Europe – so bad that every week many businesses cash a single cheque at their local branch and carry the money out in bags to deposit in another branch rather than risk making transfers bank to bank.

'In the old days everyone wanted to marry a girl who had National Bank shares for a dowry. Now everybody treats them as if they were Harpies,' a Greek stockbroker told me.

Telecommunications are as reliable as the oracle at Delphi. The civil service is a bloated Aeschylean web of blood, destruction, revenge and retribution. There are power black-outs all the time. The streets are piled high with rubbish. Houses are overrun with rats. Crossing the road you are likely to catch a disease; just look at a glass of water and you're a dead man.

'Do you know, in Crete they had toilets 3,000 years ago.'

'Yes, but where are they now? When I was there, they had nothing. You think France is bad. Let me tell you . . . .'

Go to a dinner party in Chiswick, let alone Highgate, and you hear nothing but the last thing you want to hear at a dinner party. Even in Chiswick.

'We were sitting at this pretty café by the harbour, and what happened? Along came this tanker and emptied all this sewage, raw sewage I tell you. You could see everything, and I mean everything. Right into the harbour. Right in front of us.'

'That's nothing. I was in this hotel. The kitchen was right next to the sewage tanks, and they were leaking. You could see . . . .'

Maybe this is what Leigh Fermor was talking about when he said that 'all the gloomy factors which limit the range of life and de-oxygenise the art of Western Europe, are absent'. Or maybe it wasn't.

As for the law, there are more lawyers in Athens than in the whole of France. For every cough, splutter and nod of the head, therefore, there are a thousand lawyers to argue your point of view. If you want to add weight to your case you simply hire more lawyers. If you look as though you're going to lose, you hang on until the next legal strike; they come along as regularly as bus strikes, when special legal pickets stop illegal legal people from going about their legal activities. Which makes many Greeks wonder if democracy is such a good thing after all. Plato and Aristotle didn't reckon it. Just because the majority say yes, it doesn't mean they're right. Right is right regardless of how many say yes or how many say no. To me, Democracy, as I keep telling my friends in Africa, is the freedom to make mistakes.

If you're between strikes, however, you have no worries. The Greeks have such a high philosophical respect for the law that they don't believe it should be tarnished in any way by being put into practice.

Athenians, like Parisians, park everywhere: on pavements; on traffic islands; on double yellow lines; in the middle of the road; in front of no parking signs. Especially in front of no parking signs. They get a parking ticket – so what? The administration is so bad they'll probably never have to pay it. If they do they can probably pay for it over ten years. What the Hades!

The result is that the law is either ignored or, if it is in danger of actually being respected, the lawyers immediately go on strike to ensure it remains untarnished. Unless, of course, you are a teenager handing out leaflets labelling Alexander the Great a war criminal. Then you are immediately charged as a common criminal and sent to prison for twelve months.

But tax evasion is something different. It's not a crime, it's a way of life. A traditional way of avoiding paying sales tax is to pay cash. To crack down on the system the finance ministry decided to fire anybody leaving a shop or restaurant without a receipt up to 100,000 drachmas. What happened? Tax inspectors were ordered to stand guard outside restaurants frequented by *hoi polloi* during the *nefos* – cough, cough – when nobody can see their hand in front of their face let alone a senior member of government racing for his Mercedes without a receipt in his pocket.

Following the success of this policy, the government came up with what, even for the Greeks, was a novel way of dealing with tax evaders. They should be arrested, they decreed, and thrown, not into prison, but into a luxury hotel. The government found they had so many empty state hotels on their hands and so many crowded prisons that they thought – *eureka!* – the only logical thing to do was to put all the tax evaders into the luxury hotels.

For the tax evader the problem now is whether to stop evading and be forced to spend the rest of their life not only at home put paying for it as well, or to continue, get caught and be thrown into a luxury hotel where they can see out the rest of their days at the state's expense. My own problem, on checking into a Greek hotel, is that I can never tell, from the building itself or from the standard of service, whether I'm in a luxury hotel or a prison.

As for doing business, the Greeks believe that commerce and thievery are the same thing. As a result, Greek business is highly creative.

I was in Athens when Yannis Alafonzos, ship owner and rising media baron, was given permission to build a single-megavolt radio transmitter on top of Mount Hymetus overlooking Athens for his private sky radio station. What did he do? He built a 30-megavolt transmitter. 'But surely that was against the law,' I said innocently. Nobody seemed to worry.

Over a leisurely lunch in fashionable Kolonaki Square where the Athenian chattering, as opposed to coughing, classes drink too much ouzo and brag about chasing bored British housewives, I turned to Leigh Fermor for enlightenment. '. . . self consciousness, awe and condescension (and their baleful remedy of forced egalitarianism) and the feudal hangover and the post Talk-of-the-Bastille flicker . . .' I would willingly have sacrificed a whole herd of black bulls on the seashore if Poseidon would have explained what on earth he was talking about. Now I know what he was saying. Nothing.

In my own simple state of prelapsarian unawareness, it

seems to me the only thing Athenians take seriously is the Parthenon. Coca-Cola Italy came out with an advertisement replacing the pillars with cases of Coke. There was uproar. The Greek Minister of Culture, Madame Psanouda-Benaki, sent letters to the EC denouncing the Italians and calling for a special meeting to investigate the affair. The Italians apologized. Which amazed everyone. Because nobody thought the Greek post office could even deliver a letter, let alone find Brussels. What's more, they cancelled the ads. Probably because they didn't want to overburden the Greek postman.

I was too busy with the Ancient Greeks to hang around Annabel's when I was young, so I didn't meet my first real life modern Athenian until almost twenty years later. He had been a minister in the days before the Colonels, and was living in an enormous, sumptuous apartment in Queensway in London. He looked as though he sent his washing to Paris, held parties for his grandchildren in Baden-Baden and every evening dug his spoon into the caviar without it hitting the bottom.

His office looked as if he had lifted it straight out of the Elysée. The walls were dripping with paintings. Empty bottles of Dom Perignon and Croze Hermitage were always on the corner of his desk. On the floor by his desk was a carry-cot overflowing with soft, yellow blankets, and curled up in the middle of the blankets was a Chihuahua, a mini-pocket-handkerchief Cerberus.

In another corner were three telex machines spewing out paper non-stop. Mr Croesus spent all day every day wheeling and dealing round the world. One machine did nothing but contact company after company asking what they wanted, the price they were prepared to pay and when they wanted delivery. The second machine sent message after message to his worldwide network of contacts and suppliers telling them what he wanted, what he was prepared to pay and when he wanted delivery. The third machine was for doing the deals, opening up credit facilities with one bank after another, arranging shipping and transport.

Trying to telephone him was impossible. 'He will call you later back,' his secretary kept saying.

His turnover in a year, he told me, was anything between US$5 and 10 million. Maybe more. His profit? He would just grin.

A small, dark, swarthy man who always wore the most expensive suits – he looked as though he could have been one of Xenophon's generals – he reckoned he doubled or even tripled his turnover in the famous cement rush into Nigeria, in the good old bad old days when everybody and his secretary were sending ship after ship into Port Harcourt loaded down with cement. Or, at least, trying to. So great was the rush that most ships had to queue for maybe weeks on end to get into the harbour. When they got in, they found the cement had set rock solid and had to be taken back out to sea again and dumped. But nobody was worried. Everybody had been paid in advance and the huge commissions were already stashed away in Switzerland. The only losers were the poor, desperate Nigerians who did not get the schools and clinics and hospital buildings they were expecting.

At that time I was travelling all over West Africa, and I can remember seeing the ships queuing up. It was the same across the Nigerian border in Benin, where the port worked overtime trying to handle the non-cement ships which were seriously trying to get in. And even worse further along the coast in Lomé, Togo, where the port was working twenty-four hours a day, seven days a week handling the overspill. Roads in and out of the port were choked with trucks queuing to take everything into Nigeria, which was either four or five hours, or four or five days away by road, depending on what arrangements you had made with the customs authorities along the way.

Now and then I would see Mr Croesus in London: occasionally in the City; now and then at embassy receptions and dinners. Wherever it was, the carrycot with its pile of yellow blankets was always in the corner of the room with him, little Cerberus curled up in the middle. Once I even saw him carrying it along Old Bond Street, shopping for jewellery.

He is also one of the few Athenians I have actually met in Athens. In the old days I found it was easy to tell a Greek, although you could never tell him much. He was smooth. He looked as though he had been marinated in retsina and left out to dry in the *nefos* too long. And he not only knew all the answers, he knew the answers to questions nobody had ever thought of asking. Today it's much harder, because there are fewer Greeks in Athens than ever before.

Gypsies, for example, with necklaces of garlic, have taken over Monastriki, the old Turkish bazaar which is always packed on Sundays. Russians are selling linen and textiles along the way to Anafiotika, the Cycladic village halfway down the Acropolis.

'So how can I tell who are the Greeks?' I once asked a taxi driver.

'They are the ones who are not Albanians, Kurds, Turks, Iraqis, Iranians, Pakistanis, Asians or even Africans,' he said.

Statistics are difficult to obtain, partly because the Greeks say they have been stolen by the Albanians. Or the Kurds. Or the Turks, or whoever. To me it doesn't make any difference. Whenever I go to Athens I find the place haunted by ancient Greeks. It's animated Robert Graves.

One evening, I was due to meet Mr Croesus at the Athens Inter-Continental. I'd just been to see a company which published telephone directories in third world countries, and which wanted to move into Africa. I had been introduced to them by a Greek businessman I knew in Birmingham who was importing gunpowder from Poland and producing shells for clay-pigeon shooting. The gunpowder was cheap and, therefore, unreliable. But what difference did it make? The shells were only being fired at clay pigeons and if they failed to explode nobody worried. The last time I saw him, he had outgrown the broken down farmhouse he lived in and was moving into a twelve-bedroom mansion just outside Glouce-ster.

A cousin wanted him to invest in the company. They had big plans. They were planning to move into Africa. They were going to make a lot of money. When I arrived there nobody wanted to talk about anything except Constantin Psaris, an Orthodox priest in Farsalla in the centre of Greece, who had just upped and left not only his wife and two children, but also his mistress, also with two children.

'But in Africa there's no way you can find out who's got a telephone and who hasn't,' I eventually got round to telling the president director-general, who looked as though his only pleasure in life was picking the wax out of his ears.

'Not important,' he said, 'we make it up.'

I thought I knew all the tricks being pulled in Africa. But this was a new one.

'Sure,' he grinned. 'Nobody knows who has telephone, or who hasn't. If you have telephone they change the number or cut the line. It's not important.'

'So what's the point?'

'The advertising. We make money on the advertising.'

On my way back along Xenokratous Street I swear I spotted Jason outside the Dexameni Café, still wondering how to break the news to his wife.

While I was waiting at the hotel for Mr Croesus the same foreign office type, complete with umbrella, came in and went up to reception. 'Morning, George,' he said to Aphrodite behind the desk. 'My key, please.'

'George?' I gasped. 'How can she be called George?'

'Call 'em all George,' he grunted. 'Makes life easier. Don't have to remember their names, what?'

When Mr Croesus arrived he told me he had been playing the metal markets. He'd been buying as much lead as he could because he was convinced the price was going to increase. Instead it looked as though it was going to crash. He was getting worried. Not about losing his home, or his reputation, but in case he couldn't afford to look after Cerberus in the manner to which it had obviously grown accustomed. To try to get his money back he was going to start dealing again. In cement. He wanted to buy more. Not that Nigeria needed it. Luckily Port Harcourt had cleared the backlog otherwise they would be buried in the stuff. It was just that another of his telex dealers wanted to buy more and he was eager to make the sale. He had heard that a German dealer was also in Athens and that he had some cement to sell. He asked me to go with him.

We drove out towards Corinth. On the way I swear I spotted Agamemnon riding through the traffic on a magnificent white charger. Croesus said it was a Mr Nikis Apostolides, one of Athens' modern eccentrics who rides around all day dressed as a crusader, carrying a huge silver cross and warning *hoi polloi* that the end of the world is nigh. I didn't believe him.

The meeting was brisk. They discussed qualities, quantities and shipment dates. The German wanted to know if he could trust Croesus. How much was he worth? What were his assets? Did he have any bankers' references? Croesus picked up his briefcase, pulled out a single sheet of white paper and buried the German in figures. As soon as he paused for breath the German agreed everything.

Instead of heading back to the Inter-Continental we made for Syntagma. Wherever you go, New York, Paris, Milan, even Madrid, there seem to be fantastic bars and bistros and restaurants everywhere. But since, to me, Greek food is to food what Greek music is to music, I'm not unhappy that all the restaurants in Athens are mercifully squeezed between the Parthenon and Syntagma Square.

In one area the size of Soho there must be as many restaurants as there were snakes on the head of the Medusa.

The cheap and cheerful ones are called Kostas. The more upmarket, smarter ones are called Oyzeric, which are just as likely to golden fleece you as the cheaper Kostis. But whatever restaurant you enter, you know you're going to be honoured with the same wide, rich selection of traditional Greek dishes: day-glo taramasalata, which was responsible for launching 1,000 Greek tavernas in West London alone; the ubiquitous horaitiki salad and moussaka and chips. All washed down with gallons of retsina.

When you think the Greek gods were quite happy smashing people's heads together, tearing them limb from limb and crunching their bones for dinner, it's probably not surprising that the best thing about eating in a Greek restaurant is smashing the plates afterwards. My guess is, the Greek pottery industry realized long ago that, given the state of Greek cookery, they would never make a fortune supplying china to new Greek restaurants. So one morning a marketing Plato came up with the idea of getting people to smash plates after each meal. Which you must admit is a pretty novel concept.

As for retsina, most people swear it should be mixed with twenty measures of water like the wine Maron, the last surviving priest in Thrace, offered Ulysses, before you can even think of drinking it. Even then it takes the enamel off your teeth. Not me. I think it's fabulous. I'm convinced it was produced originally for Prometheus. You just have to know your liver is automatically going to be renewed again and again before you even get the cork out of the bottle.

If I have a decent bottle of wine anywhere else in the world everybody wants a glass. With retsina I'm left to drink the bottle by myself. Trouble is, afterwards I feel as though that damned rock is inside my head and I have a thousand eagles flying about inside my stomach trying to get out.

Over non-stop ouzos from the remote island of Lesvos, served by a black-coated waiter who I swear was a second cousin of Thanatos, and non-stop bouzouki music, I tried asking Croesus about the figures he had quoted the German.

'I didn't know you controlled that many companies with that kind of turnover,' I mumbled. 'And those kind of profits.'

He picked up his briefcase, opened it and handed me the piece of paper. It was blank.

'But why?'

'I did it for—'

'Cerberus,' I said.

'Yes.' He smiled.

'So that's how you made so much money so quickly,' I said.

'No, not that way,' he said. 'I bribed the wayhouse keeper at the Suez Canal. Everything I ship through the Canal I give him a percentage. In return he cuts my rates.'

So much for Leigh Fermor's prelapsarian blah blah.

'Dorolipsia,' he smiled.

'Do-ro-lip-sia,' I repeated.

My 3,000 years of classical Greek had not equipped me for this modern Greek world.

Milan

Mama mia, what can I say about Milan?

I can't say a word about Milan, I can wave my hands in the air about Milan. Everybody in Milan waves their hands in the air. They also do other things with their hands, like using imaginary toothpicks; like pulling down the corner of their eye; like holding forefinger and thumb together in the shape of a circle; like a thousand other things, only half of which I wish to know about.

Speaking the Italian language must be wonderful. It's so musical, so lively, so *fantastico*. Whenever I come back from an Italian trip, I find I am thinking in an Italian accent. I am reading in an Italian accent. *Mama mia*, I have to keep stopping myself from speakin in a da Italian accent.

If, as the experts say, there are over 700,000 different gestures that one human being can use to another, the Italians are masters of all 700,001 of them. The extra one is so individual to the Italians that nobody dares refer to it, let alone understand what it means.

Somebody cuts you up on the motorway from the airport into Milan where they invented the chariot-race school of driving, which means everyone drives wheel-to-wheel, bumper-to-bumper at three times the speed of light. The driver gives you the legendary Ben Hur *digitus impudicus*, the Italian one-finger salute which my old Latin master would only admit most definitely does not mean, I'll have a Martini.

41

To him and to all us Latin scholars, you see, Martini is the plural of Martinus. So to hold up one finger for two drinks is impossible. *Comprende?*

You're in a meeting. Somebody asks for your honest opinion. You give it, only to be greeted by a barrage of forefingers and thumbs held together not in a circle but as flat together as they can make it. What do they mean? They mean what they mean when they flick their thumbnails backwards and forwards under their top set of teeth. What do you think they mean?

Scratch your ear during a meeting. Do it one way and you're just scratching your ear. Do it another way and you'll be marched straight back to the airport. Do it yet another way, and you might well be invited back to the chairman's flat for dinner and God knows what afterwards.

Flick your cheek with your forefinger during lunch and you could either be making a pitch for the girl opposite or telling your guest he's crazy. Shake hands the wrong way and you could either be making aspersions about your client's mother's mother or telling the world that you are not only a Mason but the head of the Blackfriars Bridge branch of P2.

When I first went to Milan life was simple. Italian waiters were Italian. Milan was Italian. And Italian businessmen were impossible to deal with. Now, Italian waiters are Egyptian, Tunisian, Yugoslav, or even Albanian. Milan wants to break away from Rome and, probably without thinking of what it sounds like in English, set up their own sovereign republic of Po. And Italian businessmen are still impossible to deal with.

But everything's changed. Rome is still beautiful. Florence is still magical. Venice is still sinking. And Naples is still lying and cheating and stealing whatever it can lay its hands on. Italy is still the black hole of Europe. Its national debt is still greater than for the rest of Europe put together. Theft and corruption are still the order of the day, if the order of the day hasn't also been stolen. The EC sent £100 million to the Italian government for another big office project just outside Milan.

It disappeared. Disappeared! Can you imagine that? The whole lot. Into thin air.

Still nothing works. The post office takes six days to send a letter from Rome to Naples. Buses and trains run if and when the driver feels like it. The government doesn't govern. The legislature doesn't legislate. Judges do not judge and most of the administration do not leave early to play *il golfo*. They don't even bother to come in.

With the whole country in the biggest mess of all time, you'd have thought the ordinary Italian would by now have taken to the piazzas. Not on your life. The amazing thing is, nobody cares. So many people have been crying *lupo* about Italy for so long, they don't take any notice. They just carry on the same old Italian way. Years ago when Michelangelo's mama was still lecturing him about going out and getting a decent job with the Mafia that would mean he wouldn't have to spend half his life on his back but the people with whom he came in contact would, I was looking for an Italian agent. Not being a fully paid up member of Opus Dei, I was forced to do it the hard way: by post and by telephone.

After years of letterwriting and months of inconclusive telephone calls I'd identified our man. He owned a big engineering company north of Milan and was associated with a string of companies throughout Italy. Whenever I managed to reach him on the phone he sounded enthusiastic. I'd sent him a draft agreement which he said he was prepared to sign without alterations. What could be better?

'Okay' I said down the 'phone, 'I'll come across next Friday morning. We can sort out any last minute problems. Then we can sign the agreement. Okay?'

'Okay,' he said. 'No problem.'

I booked myself on the usual first flight out and last flight back. Friday morning I was in Milan, the richest city in Italy and home of Armani, Benetton, Maserati and all the other glitteratti. But it didn't look it. Which surprised me. It didn't feel like Italy either: no crowds, no chaos, no arguing, no shouting. Everybody seemed determined to go about their business, head down, serious; when that's finished, get on to the next job.

Milan makes it, they say, Rome spends it. According to the European Commission, Milan and the surrounding Lombardy region is the richest part of Europe. It has La Scala, duomo and the Galleria Vittorio Emanuele, and a nice little trattoria at the back of the railway station which serves the best tiramisu I've ever tasted. It also has more financiers, bankers and business-men than any other part of the country. Sometimes I think it also has more widows hobbling along in shapeless black dresses.

Visiting most parts of the world is just a matter of racing to the airport, dashing to a plane and falling out the other end. Before I visited Rome I'd spent my whole life preparing for it. I felt I knew it inside out. Five years studying Latin and being hammered into the *terra firma* by irregular verbs makes you feel like that. I knew its history, I knew all the important landmarks: St Peter's; the Colosseum where Charlton Heston performed some of his greatest feats; the Appian Way; the catacombs; Babington's tea rooms by the Spanish steps, opposite the house where Keats died; the Hotel Excelsior on the Via Veneto where the old paparazzi used to hang out between invasions; even Mussolini's typewriter, the enormous monument to Vittoria Emanuel. Not to mention the Caffé Colombiana on the Piazza Navona where they serve the second-best tiramisu I've ever tasted.

What I hadn't appreciated was the sheer size and scale of everything. I thought Rome was going to be like Verulaneum but a bit bigger. No way. Everything was colossal on a colossal scale including the Colosseum. St Peter's, I thought, would be big. But not as big as it is, and certainly not as spectacular and as new-looking. The Sistine Chapel is worth a crick in the neck any day. Neither did I realize how much of it had been preserved. The occasional fallen pillar here or the remains of a house there, I can handle. But in Rome there are as many ruins as there are pickpockets. The only time I've ever had anything stolen, touch wood, was coming out of St Peter's on a Sunday morning. In the crush at the door somebody grabbed my folding umbrella. When I got outside all I had left was the strap around my wrist. And it wasn't even raining.

A lot of cities are infectious. But Rome is infectious in its own way. Some people say it has turned decadence into an art form. Not me. However many times I visit Rome, I still come away wanting to go back. I could visit it a million times, still not see everything, still not go everywhere and still not be bored.

On the other hand Naples, the *rectum mundi*, as my old Latin master once generously described it, is also infectious, but in a different way, of course. Like the kasbah of Marseilles or even Moss Side, Manchester, especially the stretch between the leisure centre and the precinct laundry, it makes me feel dis-eased, as my old English master, a French priest with a magical grasp of the English language, used to say. More than any other city I've been to in Europe, it really does feel like a third world country. Close your eyes, and on a hot summer's day the stench alone makes you feel you're in Lagos. Just drive very quickly through parts of the Scampia area of Second-igliano Sanit, Piscinola San Giovanni, or Poggioreale with its blocks of flats and back alleys, and you could be in Cairo.

The Vicaria is like or maybe worse than the Forbidden City in Hong Kong with, I was told, three or even four families living in a single room, often below ground, without heat, electricity or running water. Although, fair's fair, I must admit I didn't see any pigs on any balconies. The people also scare me – well, maybe not as much as they do in Manchester. Just walking through the station you get the impression Italy emptied all its mental hospitals and lunatic asylums straight into the centre of Naples. I know I don't always bring out the best in people, but why is everyone giving me crazy grins and inane smiles? I have heard some maniacal catcalls, stomach-turning screams and howls of despair in my time, but they were always at annual meetings, sales conferences, or the occasional lunch attended by Mrs Thatcher. The screams and howls you hear in Naples are like something from the depths of Dante's Inferno. In fact, the whole city could have come out of Dante's Inferno.

Every kid or bimbo you see hanging around the streets seems to have a packet of Marlboro inside his shirt or under his jacket. Thanks to the Italian state monopoly on cigarette sales, Naples is Marlboro country, the world capital of cigarette smuggling, where less than one cigarette in five is sold at official licensed outlets at official prices. Contraband sales are well over £100 million a year. This is Camorra territory, the Naples branch of the Mafia. They apparently have it all sewn up. The big guys have big stakes. The medium and the baby Camorras or gangs of teenagers all have their own mini-territories. Like their elders and betters they will think nothing of killing each other to protect their own mini drugs, cigarette and protection rackets. How do they do it? The Camorra way: a bullet through the back of the neck straight into the brain.

Take your life into your hands and wander round the harbour any time of the day and you'll see them hard at it in their pretty little boats, ploughing backwards and forwards shipping in more and more loads of cigarettes. Live dangerously and race from your bulletproof car – what do you mean you don't have a bulletproof car in Naples? – into any restaurant and at the next table but two you'll hear strange words like grass, crack, heroin, cocaine. But whatever you do, don't let them know you heard what they were saying otherwise it won't be your heart but your kneecap you'll be leaving behind in Naples. *Capito?*

When the Italian gypsy comes round serenading you – you never, never hear Frank Sinatra singing in any restaurant in Naples – pretend, especially if he's tapping the side of his nose, that as far as you're concerned it's the most natural thing in the world for him to put his foot on the table to balance his guitar and for you to pay the equivalent of three months' salary for him to very kindly and courteously take it off again so that you can continue with what's left of your meal.

Venice – la Serenissima – and Florence just couldn't be more different. Venice with all its old, corrupt and decadent churches I could happily visit for ever and ever in spite of having to listen all the time to my more sophisticated fellow countrymen asking for a cornetto. In Venezia, whatever they say on television, a cornetto does not mean what you think it means. It means a green bean. So put that in your cornet and lick it. Admittedly the Rialto Bridge is no longer crammed with jewellers and gold and silversmiths; instead there are cheap stalls and shops. But it is still spectacular. *Mama mia*, I even like the bit up by the Arsenal and the other side of the Park.

I used to feel the same about Florence. The Piazza del Duomo is fantastic. So is the Uffizi Palace and all around the Piazza della Signoria. Pure magic. Trouble is, on one quick visit I got stuck with a group of Americans who didn't know their art from their elbow and kept complaining about sensory overkill. Except for one old Daughter of the Revolution.

'Florence,' she drooled all over me. 'I always come to Florence to buy curtains for my apartment in New York.'

Now, may Michelangelo forgive me, whenever I think of Florence I think of her damned curtains in New York.

But whether you're in Milan, Rome, Naples, Venice or Florence – there! I've thought of those curtains again – or even Pisa, the Italians are superb at leaning on other people. They are always, but always, late for meetings. No matter whether the meeting is at their place or yours. No matter what time of day or night. It's as if they are constitutionally incapable of getting to a meeting on time. Maybe it's in their blood. They just feel everybody should wait for them. Maybe they happened to spot a shirt in Batistone's in the Via Condotti or a tie in Carlo Palazzi's in the via Borgonona. Or maybe they are just wandering up and down the street murmuring 'Ciao, bella' at every woman in sight. And if they are late for meetings, they are equally late at supplying or doing anything at all. Proposals by the end of the month? Maybe two months. Costs and estimates in two weeks? Whistle for them. An order to purchase? Don't believe it until you see it. Italy has its own form of efficiency.

'I'll fix it,' they say, whatever the problem. 'I know his brother.' Or his sister or his wife's uncle's cousin's third auntie twice removed. Italian business, like Italian bureaucracy, is like a great ball of spaghetti. You've got no idea where it begins, no idea where it ends. All you know is, it's there and all beautifully wrapped in glorious Botticelli.

Like Dante's *Divine Comedy* and everything Italian, there seem to be three layers. Well, three layers that I know of. First, the top heavenly public layer of a thriving, prosperous country about to overtake the UK; a country of big, successful international companies, virtually run by the *salotto buono*, an intricate web of giant family-owned holding companies; laws on everything down to selling bread rolls; regulations which insist that even for sale signs in shop windows must have their own postage stamps; and a strict judiciary which will not only send fourteen-year-old boys to prison for playing football on beaches where ball games are prohibited but will also fine Paul 'Gazza' Gascoigne $13,000 for belching during a television interview.

The second layer is sheer purgatory for anyone who comes into contact with it. It is the world where everybody believes they have the right to bypass all the rules; the world of seriously avoiding serious taxes; of embezzlement of public funds; nepotism; doctoring wine, you name it. They can wave their hands in the air about it and ignore it. It is the world of wheeler-dealers, of civil servants making fortunes from overtime by working twenty-nine hours a day, of fakes, of forgeries, including forgeries of official anti-forgery government forgery stamps, and of annual reports and accounts and statistics that nobody believes, not even, I suspect, the Pope himself. We make jokes about Italian companies having three sets of figures: one for the shareholders, one for the taxman and one for the owners. But even when they show you the real one you can't believe it.

An Italian businessman once told me his company was 63.7 percent profitable.

'Sixty-three point . . .' I gasped.

'Sure, sure,' he said. 'Sixty-three percent of the business is on the point of being profitable and seven percent is profitable.'

It's enough to make you weep into your Armani handkerchief – if, that is, you could afford to buy another one.

The third layer, of course, is hell. It is the Inferno, the world of il racket which some experts believe accounts for 17 percent of Italy's GNP and that the first and second worlds probably know about in all too much sordid detail but, probably for the sake of their families, wish to ignore.

Again, the amazing thing is that they get away with it. Everything is slow. Everything is late. Yet still they get the business and, over the last few years, more and more business.

Is Europe a single market? *Si.* Are companies supposed to compete fairly throughout the whole continent from the Atlantic to the Urals? *Si.* So what do the Machiavellian Italians do? Take the electronics industry, for example. Confrontation is too crude. Opposition is futile. Instead they have three different electrical voltages operating throughout the country: 230 volts in town, 160 volts in the villages and 130 volts up in the mountains. Apart from playing hell with your electric razor – after three days touring Italy even I am beginning to look like Nigel Kennedy – it makes foreign companies switch off. No way can they afford to supply equipment in three different voltages for a single country. As a result, Italy remains a preserve of Italian electronics companies.

In Africa, they seem to land one big contract after another. Perhaps it's because their casual approach appeals to Africans. They don't feel inhibited by tight deadlines, strict deliveries, impossible schedules. Perhaps the Italians have better production, better prices, better services. Or perhaps the Italians are more persuasive . . .

So when I landed in Milan half of me expected my agent-to-be not to be there. The British half. Half of me expected him to be there. The Italian half. The rest of me wasn't worried because I'd always wanted to visit the Pinacoteca di Brera round the back of Laura Ashley in the via Brera, one of Italy's greatest art collections which was, again typically Italian, always closed whenever I'd been there in the past. At the time the city centre was a battlefield. The left was in deadly conflict with the right. Everybody, especially if they had two lira to rub together, was terrified of being kidnapped, having a finger torn off and sent in the post to their family. It seemed as good a time as any to try again.

But he was there, waiting for me, which was not what I really expected – neither the British nor the Italian half. Except he didn't look as I expected. Our agent, who knew everybody from the Pope to Pavarotti, who was going to increase our sales dramatically and make us as famous in Italy as Giorgio Armani, was definitely not one of the *loggionisti* who dress up in all their fuss and finery to howl abuse at the latest productions at La Scala. He looked more like a car mechanic. He was wearing blue overalls, a beret and carrying a definitely non-Italian-style army backpack.

Formalities over, I said, 'Okay, where can we go to talk?'

'Talk?' He grabbed my arms. 'First we make friends. *Avanti!*'

Over £100,000-worth of Lamborghini was parked immediately outside the airport guarded by two policemen.

'How can we do business unless we are friends?' he chuckled as I tried to squeeze myself and my briefcase into the tiniest space imaginable. 'When we are friends, we do business.'

For a split second, as the Lamborghini leapt forward at the speed of sound and with an enormous roar rocketed towards the sky, I thought we were going to be friends until death did us part. Along the edge of the airport, I swear, we were going faster than the jets on the runway. Including, especially including, those taking off.

Even in those days Milan was known for having the worst traffic jams in Italy. Now the hold-ups are made even worse by hundreds of little African boys, usually from Senegal, sometimes even from Ethiopia, as well as lots of medium and large ones, who descend upon you in waves if you slow down to as little as 20–30 kilometres an hour. Between the trucks and cars they come selling everything from wooden masks and *les lieux saints de l'Islam* to lavatory cleaners and toilet rolls. They will even dash in front of the cars if they get the slightest vibration of anyone thinking of spending as much as 100 lira. Open your wallet – no, just think of opening your wallet – and I swear you'll be buried alive. This time, however – a world record – I didn't see any. I hardly saw any cars either, we were so close to the ground. All I could hear was the roar of jet engines under the bonnet. All I could see were dots on the horizon and then smudgy blurs as I guessed we overtook police cars cruising at 150 kilometres an hour to maintain the so-called strict Italian speed limit. If Dante was writing his *Comedia* today, he would have to add one ring or circuit for Italian sportscars.

Around corners we skidded. On long narrow stretches we overtook everything in our blurred vision. Never cross the road in Italy, they say, if the traffic lights are green. You'll be knocked down. I can believe it. The speed we were doing we never saw any traffic lights of any colour. Gradually, however, I sensed we were either climbing a mountainside or taking off for New York. The atmosphere was either getting rarer or I was getting more scared than I dared let myself think. Then with a violent jolt we shrieked to a halt.

'And now we celebrate.' The car mechanic turned supersonic pilot was out of the cockpit before I could begin breathing again. Slowly I unfolded myself out of his supersonic sardine tin, gave thanks for my survival and stumbled after him. He was sitting, like a king in all his glory, in a tiny typical Italian family restaurant within, I guessed, twenty-three light years of Milan. On the table were typical Italian bottles of campari, typical Italian bottles of mineral water and typical Italian bottles of grappa, the rough home-made Italian brandy. In the corner was a typical Italian pram and inside it a typical Italian *bamboletto*. '*Come sei bello*,' he was purring. '*Ma sei davvero piccolo. Ma piccino. Un veno . . .*' I couldn't understand a word. But I knew what he was saying.

'Now, amico,' he said turning to me, 'we make friends.'

For the next three or four hours we ate mountains of typical Italian food, we drank gallons of typical Italian wine and we made friends.

'Okay,' I kept saying, 'the agreement. We must discuss the agreement.'

'Agreement. How can we discuss agreement?' he kept waving his hands in the air and shrugging his shoulders at the same time. 'We cannot discuss agreement until we are friends. Have another drink.'

Then more salad, drowned in 'extra virgin olive oil'. Only the Italians could come up with a concept like extra virgin. Then more salami and pasta and bottles of deep red dusty Italian wine. Then more cheese and bread and glasses of grappa.

Then suddenly it was 3 o'clock. I didn't know where I was, but my automatic clock was still working. This was the time to start heading back to the airport.

'Look, I've got to go,' I said. 'My plane leaves at . . . We must . . .'

'But my friend,' he waved his hands and shrugged his shoulders, 'we are just becoming friends. You cannot go now.'

'But I must,' I said. 'I promised I'd be back . . .'

'Change it.'

'I can't change it. I've . . .'

'Why not?' He leant across the table. 'Our agreement is not important?'

'Well of course it's important. It's just that . . .'

He clapped his hands. More food was unloaded onto the table. More wine flowed into our glasses.

'Look, can't I get a taxi?' I was still fighting back. 'You stay here, I'll—'

'Taxi,' he exploded all over the restaurant. 'You listen to this man. This – this – this – Englishman,' he called out to the restaurant as a whole. Everybody put down their forks and spoons and hands. This was creating a storm in a cappuccino if ever I drank one. 'A taxi,' he shouted. 'He wants a taxi.'

Everybody else began shrieking; then slowly, one by one, they began standing up and staggering across the restaurant napkins in hand to hug and kiss each other. As they hugged and kissed the shrieking ebbed and flowed. Call me a popera fan if you must, but I swear it sounded like the chorus of the Hebrew Slaves. For the want of a taxi, I was the slave unable to escape.

'He wants taxi,' they all kept shrieking.

'Mama! Mama!' he howled at the kitchens. 'Come quickly, pronto, pronto.' Mama came out. She was as big as the dome of St Peter's. 'Have your heard? This man wants . . .'

By now the whole village was around the table. The laughter would have lifted the dome off the top of St Peter's. The tears would have submerged Venice for ever. I felt like one of the gladiators awaiting the verdict.

So did I catch my flight? Of course I didn't. Did we discuss the agreement? Of course not, although at one point, through the haze of too many extra virgins, too many camparis and mineral water, too many bottles of wine and heaven knows how many grappas, I can remember discussing commissions.

'So what commission do you . . .?'

'Half past 15 per cent,' he said.

We talked about London and all his favourite places there: Gucci, Armani, Valentino, Versace and everything else even slightly Italian in and around Bond Street. I've never met an Italian who talks about the Tower of London, the Tate Gallery, the Science Museum. It's always Bond Street.

We talked about serious things, such as Italian politics. 'We're socialist,' he laughed. 'But we are like capitalists.'

He told me about index-linked wages, jobs for life, enormous pensions, discounts, subsidies.

'So, how do you earn your money,' I asked him, 'if you have all these problems?'

'Free electricity.' He banged his hand on the table. 'Free electricity. We bypassare the system.'

We went on to talk about frivolous things such as company accounts, balance sheets and, the biggest laugh of all, annual accounts.

'In Italy,' he confided, 'we make company inter-sales. Four times inter-sale between company. Four times we write sale. Four times we write profit. But,' he grabbed the edge of the table, 'only once do we make the sale. One time. Only. Only one time. Only . . .'

I thought for a moment he was going to crash off the chair onto the floor, but he didn't. Ordering another bottle of grappa seemed to sober him up.

I met his brother, his aunt's cousin, his nephews and nieces, his grand-bambini and practically every living Italian creature who's ever heard of Chianti or swallowed the tiniest portion of pasta.

'Ciao, ciao,' I kept muttering. 'Va bene.'

He held his hand out, but somehow the thumb and little finger were sticking out. The three middle fingers were curled up together in his fist. I didn't know whether to shake it. In the end, what-a-da-hell, I did.

One of the brothers – or was it a cousin? Hell, it was probably his mama. Anyhow, one of them told me they made a fortune selling bulletproof Mercedes, complete with 500 lb of bulletproof glass and enough steel to stop an Exocet, to African dictators at US$500,000 a time.

Another brother or cousin or whatever came in. I thrust my hand out. My thumb and little finger were sticking out. The three middle fingers were curled up inside my fist.

'Hullo old chap,' he said giving me a funny look. Instead of shaking hands he just gave me an anaemic little wave with his fingers. It was my friend's UK agent. Great, I thought. Now at least I'll be able to get some sense about ... But he disappeared almost immediately, through a door behind the bar.

'Ciao.'

We moved on to cheese; great heavy boulders of mozzarella, and still more wine. With more vino came more relations. An aunt, a cousin, *la bellocia* herself or maybe it was the *bamboletto* in the pram, leant across the table: 'You know how he made his money?'

'Mada his money? Witta d'machina tools?' I slurred back.

'Witta d'machina tools and da slabs of toppa da quality marble.'

'Da toppa da quality marble?'

'Da toppa da quality marble packed insida da boxes for da ballesta.'

The man in the black suit in da corner, I mean the corner, then started telling me about the family firms. Tiny contributions from newspaper sellers are known as *pizzo*. Stallholders give what is known as a *busterella*. Shops such as the grocers you find on every street corner give a *spintarella*. If I'm after a big contract and you know who can fix it then they get a *mazzetta*. For the real big stuff, the big boys deal in a *tangente*.

'In Sicily we have the Mafia. In Sardinia we have the Ndrangheta. In Naples we have the Camorra.'

'And in Milano?'

'In Milano, everything is set in concreta.'

To him there was nothing sinister or wrong about it. It was the system. It was tradition. Everybody knew somebody who was selling cigarettes ...

Suddenly, halfway through a serious in-depth discussion on the new FRS3 accounting standards for reporting financial performance, or were we talking football about which I know nothing, my new agent grabbed my arms again. 'Now we are friends,' he said.

'Great,' I burbled. 'The agreement. Let's—'

He stood up, grabbing the table for support. 'Now we visit da factory. I show you my church, my basilica. We go.'

I followed him out of the restaurant. He was pouring himself gently into his Lambo . . . into the car. I tried to follow suit. We took off like a jet bomber on red alert. Down mountain passes, around h-h-hair pin bends, along co-coun-country l-l-lanes.

In those days there were no drink-driving laws. Well, I say no laws. There were Italian drink-driving laws. If you were lying dead drunk, or just dead, in the middle of the road for two days they would begin to think about bringing charges. On the other hand, they might not. It all depended on . . . on you-know-what. Today it's all changed. They book you after one day. Maybe.

Italians, we all know, ooze style. Italian offices always look as though they have come straight out of *Vogue*. They are always housed in discreet little courtyards and everyone in them looks as though they have just got back from Acapulco. My agent's, I mean my friend's factory was exactly the same, but a million times better.

Visit any British engineering company anywhere in the world and, if it's still in business, it's like visiting a cross between a Victorian workhouse and Strangeways. During the riot. This, however, was like the headquarters of the European Bank for Reconstruction and Development. Old Jacques Attali would have immediately felt he was in a position to help the poor of Eastern Europe.

In reception there was a long bar serving any drink you tried to pronounce whatever the time of day.

'We like to look after our customers.'

Too hot? 'I'll turn up the air-conditioning. We like to keep our customers happy.' Still hot? 'Try the swimming pool. It's through the door at the end.'

These guys had their own company swimming pool. For customers. Complete with floating bar. 'We like to keep our customers happy.' You bet your life they do.

The factory itself was like a church. No, it was a million times better than most churches I've every seen, even in Italy. It was tall and bright. The walls were painted white, with giant murals at either end. In between were huge sweeps and swirls of colour. And the floor had mosaic tiles, just like – no, better than – St Peter's itself. In most factories, whether in Britain, France, the US or wherever, you can't tell what's on the floor it's so covered in grease and dirt and a thousand years of rubbish. But here it was bright and clean and sparkling. So was the machinery. You could see the paintwork. You could even read the name of the manufacturer.

In one British company I worked for a million years ago the machinery was so old nobody could remember when it had been bought, yet we claimed to be using the best, most accurate, most technically advanced components in the world. I remember one Saturday morning, I had big problems. I was negotiating an enormous deal with a Swedish entrepreneur. Everything was agreed: the price, delivery, service. Then he said he wanted to visit the factory. I went cold. The factory was so bad we had all agreed that absolutely nobody should be allowed in. If anyone came near the place we knew we would lose any chance of getting business. When the bank manager insisted on walking through the works to satisfy himself everything was in order before he authorized yet another disastrous loan for the already disastrously over-extended company, we managed to hide the worst areas and the most clapped-out machines on which we were supposed to be beating the Japanese hands down, by blocking them off with screens and dust-sheets and strips of tarpaulin.

'What happens if he asks to have a look?' the works director asked me.

Tell him we're working on a big contract. Ministry of Defence. Sensitive. Top secret. That kind of stuff.'

He never even asked. He obviously thought it the most natural thing in the world for a world-beating British company to have its machines draped in dust-sheets. He even gave us more money than we were asking for. Unfortunately.

The Swedish businessman, however, knew what it was all about. He was in his late sixties, tall, still athletic-looking, silver-grey hair. He'd been in engineering all his life. I tried the usual lame excuses: no keys; security guards not allowed to let anyone in; insurance implications; fire risk. No way. He wanted in. I was trapped. If I said no, I'd lose the order. If I said yes, I'd probably still lose it. But I might not.

We got to the factory. The car park was full of rubbish. It looked like the day after a prison riot. The glass door to reception was smudged and greasy. The 'closed' sign said 'open' and was hanging by a corner. As I opened the door, it fell off and clattered across the black and not-so-black tiles. Friday's post was still sitting on the reception desk. Lipstick and powder compacts were by the switchboard. The telephone was off the hook.

'It's the same all over the world,' I grinned weakly. 'You just can't get the . . .'

'Shall we go in?' he said.

I walked across to the factory door like a doomed man to the gallows. It was jammed. I kicked it open. The Swede rushed in. My past business life began to flash before—

'What wonderful machines,' he shouted back at me. 'Wonderful.'

Wonderful? Our clapped-out . . . Have I missed something in translation? Is this a Swedish joke?

'Wonderful,' he cried, slipping and sliding across the grease and stains and trying one after another like a child not knowing which toy to play with first on Christmas morning.

He ran back to me. 'Wonderful,' he grinned. 'Wonderful.'

I looked at him as casually as I could.

He put his arm around my shoulder. 'Would you believe?' he grinned so wide his stainless steel glasses almost fell off his face. 'These are the very machines I trained on as a boy over fifty years ago.' I didn't know whether to laugh or cry. 'Tell you what.' He slapped my back. 'For old times' sake, you have the business.'

If those machines got me the Swedish business, these Italian machines could have got me the world's business.

'And now, my friend, I show you our secret.' My friend pulled down the corner of his right eye.

We walked across the mosaics from the Lady Chapel and the big robots, across the nave where the enormous cutters were lined up like a row of bishops, to the corner of the Sacred Heart Chapel.

'This', he whispered over a row of computer-controlled machines that I had never seen before, 'is where we make our money.'

'These?' I said slowly. 'Just these few machines? But what about . . .?'

'Ammunition,' he whispered. 'Here we make ammunition for da guns.'

'But are you allowed?' I whispered back, so convinced was I that we really were in church. 'I thought there were strict . . .'

'Shhh,' he said still tugging at his eye. 'Shhhhh.'

It was like going into greenhouses in Holland and spotting, behind the tomatoes, clumps of marijuana growing away merrily on all that cheap Dutch gas. What he was doing, he told me later in another restaurant, run by another fifty-three members of his family, was bringing in bags of cheap, granulated gunpowder from Poland, mixing it with better quality gunpowder he bought in Belgium, and producing cartridges for Russian- and Romanian-made rifles and shot-guns.

'And machine guns?'

'Shhh', he said. 'You tell no one. If I don't forget, I will remember I told you. You are my friend.'

'But how do you sell—?'

'Shhh.'

'Are you certain it's only used for—?'

'Shh.'

A bottle of grappa later I gathered he was only responsible for the manufacturing. Somebody else supplied the materials. Somebody else again was responsible for selling. And yet another somebody else took care of the authorities. Well, it was Italy.

'What about VAT and tax and wages and overheads and . . .?'

'Shh,' he said, tapping the side of his nose. 'It is secret. You are my friend.'

All over Italy, he told me, making small circles in the air with the *digitus impudicus* of his right hand, it was the same. The Italians are fantastic. They have their own rules, their own laws, their own interpretation of their own laws. They twist, they turn, they will do a double back somersault before your eyes and convince you they didn't bat an eyelid. What's more they practically make you apologize for doubting them.

That evening I still couldn't get back. I was in the zuppa Milanese. I spent the night in the Grand Hôtel des Iles Borromées, Frederick Henry's refuge in *A Farewell to Arms*, a glorious, dusty, faded wedding cake of an hotel, appropriately enough in Stresso, one of the prettiest towns, if not the prettiest, on Lake Maggiore. Along the corridors I expected to bump into retired and/or exiled South American dictators. In the downstairs bar I expected to see Zeldas flinging themselves through windows because their Scott Fitzgerald husbands had knelt at the feet of Isadora Duncans in the lounge. Instead I saw three elderly house widows all in black who obviously lived in the hotel. Each came in separately. Each sat at her special table. Each ordered exactly the same meal. Each drank the same half bottle of the same Piedmont red wine.

Each then signed her own receipts, and shuffled out without saying a word to anyone.

The waiter, who was a bit like an elderly Sacristan himself, saw me looking at them. 'Pazzo,' he said gently, patting his forehead with the palm of his hand. Old ladies and old Italian hotels seem to go well together.

The following morning, I actually managed to get a taxi – not a Lamborghini, not a Maserati, just an ordinary Fiat. At the airport, there was nobody at the Alitalia check-in desk. There was nobody checking tickets. There was nobody on passport control. I wandered into the departure lounge. Nobody stopped me. Still no Alitalia staff. I wandered back again. Still nobody around. I switched my flight to good old boring, reliable British Airways.

Did we ever sign the agreement? *Mama mia!* As my Italian friend would say, better never than late.

Belgrade

Poor old Yugoslavia. It's falling apart now. What's happened to the people and the places I used to visit, I don't know. Sometimes I spot the odd building on television or in the papers which I think I recognize. More often, they all look as though they have been shot to bits.

Like many people, I've got lots of happy memories of Yugoslavia. It was in Belgrade, in fact, that I was present at one of the great events in the history of the world: the opening of the very first McDonald's in the country. With a couple of thousand other people. I was doing a lot of work with Yugoslaviapublic, the big Yugoslav advertising and marketing organization which was based in Knez Mihailova, with all its cafés and restaurants and bookstores, in the heart of old Belgrade.

'You like hamburgers?' the director asked me. 'I remember you are always eating hamburgers. Tonight we eat hamburgers here. In Belgrade.'

What could I say?

I had organized a big Yugoslav mission to London. I had arranged meetings, seminars and an exhibition. I was rushing from Whitehall to Westminster and from the City to Olympia. Somehow there never seemed time for anything else but hamburgers, hamburgers and still more hamburgers. When the Yugoslavs came through arrivals at Heathrow, I had just grabbed a hamburger for breakfast. When they turned up to inspect the exhibition stands, I was halfway through one of Olympia's less than tasty imitation burgers. For dinner at the hotel, I only had time for another quick burger in the coffee shop before rushing back to the telephone.

The previous night we had drunk more than enough going from one café to another in Skadarlija, the so-called artists' quarters, sampling the local beers and wines and, of course, tasting much too much Serbian plum brandy.

Belgrade I always enjoyed visiting. One of the oldest inhabited cities in Europe, it is – or rather was – a glorious unlovely mish-mash of a capital city of a mish-mash of a country. It was European. It was Slav. It was Austrian. It was Asian. And, of course, more than anything, it was Serbian, steeped in the Ottoman tradition, heavily influenced by years of Turkish occupation, although it seems to have been ruled by everybody: the Romans, the Bulgarians, the Byzantines, the Hungarians and the Austrians.

It's part exciting and modern. One of the most spectacular inside-out buildings I've ever seen anywhere in the world, where the courtyard and trees were in the middle and the offices were on the outside, was in Belgrade. The head office of Energoprojekt, a big Yugoslav Construction Company, was a revelation. Somehow they had managed to combine the flair of the Italians for design with their own definite, almost plodding practicality.

But Belgrade is also drab; brown and black and grey. You feel it in the cobblestones. Its bureaucracy is crippling. You've only got to go into any office and it hits you between the eyes. In triplicate. It is also like the Serbs themselves – dark and brooding. It is really an understudy of a city. It's like turning up expecting to see the star and instead seeing the understudy. On a bad night. In the middle of winter.

Tonight, however, it was carnival time. The sight of hundreds of serious Serbs queuing up for their first Big Mac and Triple Chocolate Milk Shakes was enough to make Josip Broz Tito turn in his grave. First to the left. Then back again quickly to the right. Just as he did all the time he was alive. Over my first Yugoslav Big Macski, the director, another brooding Serb, was telling me his latest project.

'Watch out,' he said suddenly as a great, bearded Davy Crockett figure shuffled towards our plastic table. 'A mountain man.'

'A mountain man?'

'A Montenegran.'

The director's cousin had just taken over a shoe factory. He wanted to start exporting to Russia. He wanted to help him with the marketing. He showed me some rough photocopied drawings of various shoes.

'What do you think?' he asked, desperately struggling to open his first plastic sachet of capitalist ketchup. 'This is what they are doing at present.'

They were terrible. They looked as though they had been sketched in a Siberian snowstorm and reproduced on a photocopier run by gas. You could barely see the outline of a shoe anywhere.

'Well, the first thing I would do is improve the pictures,' I said. 'You don't know whether you are buying a load of . . .' His ketchup squirted across the table, hit the Montenegran in the face, then dripped slowly down on to his sweater. Neither said a word.

'. . . or a pair of shoes,' I continued.

'You mean photographs?'

'Sure. Show the customer what he's buying. Then he'll go out and buy. How can he buy without seeing what he's spending his money on?'

'Even the Russians?'

'Sure. Even the Russians. Why not?'

We finished our first Big Mac.

'So do you want another one? Or do you want to go and have a couple of slivovitz in Skadarlija?'

I won't tell you what we did. Except that the big Montenegran watched us, mopping his sweater as we went out.

Doing business with the Yugoslavs is – was – well, always tricky. You never quite knew who you were dealing with; what the rules were – if, in fact, there were any rules. It was a bit like arranging the deck chairs on the *Titanic*. Sooner or later you knew it was going to explode. Tension was built into the fabric of the country. With five languages, five alphabets, three religions, twelve ethnic groups, the whole country, of course, was politics. Nobody ever said Yes or No. There was always a reason for not taking a decision. Either they had to consult someone else, wait for the budgets to be drawn up, arrange their allocation of foreign exchange or they were just plain thirsty and wanted to have lunch. They also never seemed to be able to tackle the problem in front of them. They always somehow saw an implication or motive behind the situation which they had to solve first. Then they said they would tackle the main problem.

The first problem was always trying to decide how much business they actually wanted to do. Many businessmen running state companies were very professional managers of state companies. Many others, however, were very professional managers of state companies as well as very successful private businessmen in their own right. Some state managers would always negotiate and buy at the best possible price for their state-owned company. Many others would negotiate and buy at the best possible price on behalf of their own private company which would then resell to the state company they managed. Some more far-sighted or criminal managers, depending on your point of view, used to buy and pay for their own machines which they then hired out to the companies they were managing.

'Isn't that wrong?' I asked one manager who ran a big Yugoslav company exporting furniture to companies like John Lewis.

'Why?' he replied, as if I had grossly insulted him. 'If I didn't buy the machinery myself the company couldn't operate. If the company couldn't operate we couldn't employ people and we couldn't earn foreign exchange. What am I doing that is wrong?'

It was the same with Yugoslavs in London. At one time I organized and ran the Yugoslav Wine Information Bureau to promote Yugoslav wines in the UK. The trouble was none of the UK Yugoslav wine importers wanted to import any more wine.

'We're already importing enough. Why import more? It will lower the price,' I kept being told.

The Yugoslavs, on the other hand, just wanted to shift the wine. They weren't worried about any subtleties. They wanted hard currency – and the foreign trips.

Whenever I was among Yugoslavs, I noticed the Serbs always told you they were Serbs. Everybody else told you the Serbs were Serbs. And the Montenegrans told you they were the real Serbs.

Iskra, the big Yugoslav electronics and electrical goods company – they are like Philips – had asked me to prepare an advertising campaign to promote their wide range of electrical goods. I was in their luxury modern offices in Belgrade for the presentation.

'You wanted a campaign to promote all your consumer products?' I began.

'Yes,' they said.

'You want it to highlight the wide range of products you have?'

'Yes,' they said.

'You want to show that anybody can buy these products?'

'Yes,' they said.

'You want one single slogan?'

'Yes,' they said.

'There you are,' I said, turning over the flip chart. 'The slogan for your new campaign: Power to the People.'

'No,' they said. Altogether. All at once. In one voice. Although I swear the big Montenegran didn't say it as loudly as the others. It was the first time I ever got a single, definite decision out of the Yugoslavs.

On another trip, I arrived in poor old Sarajevo, with an Egyptian radio producer. The two of us made up the 'top international range of speakers' for Yugoslavia's first big conference on advertising financial services. Muslim, Ortho-dox, Oriental, Sarajevo was covered in snow. It was bitterly cold. The big Gazi Husrev Bey Mosque was buried. Old Sarajevo with its narrow streets and alleys and the upper market were a sea of slush. Walking around – even just peeping through the frosted hotel windows – you got the feeling this was a frontier town; a frontier between Christians and Muslims, between Rome and Constantinople, between East and West.

Inside the hotel – a modern, faceless, quick-built, identikit hotel – it was boiling hot. It felt as though the air conditioning had jammed on about 120 degrees. Yet somehow it still felt chilly. Largely because it was practically full of Russian factory workers who'd beaten all their production targets and been rewarded with two weeks' holiday in sunny Sarajevo. It wasn't so much that they were all Russians. It was that they all looked and behaved the way we expected Russians to look and behave in those days. They were all five foot three inches tall, and about thirteen stone. Including the women. They all had that heavy, jowled, sagging look. Including the women. And they all moved around in packs. Including the women. If one came in for breakfast, they all came in. In one great never-ending crocodile. If one ordered fruit juice, they all ordered fruit juice. As soon as one wanted to leave, they all left. Together. Including the women.

The conference was like a conference anywhere in the world. Speaker after speaker drawled on and on. Normally at conferences I swap my name badge for somebody else's and disappear into the bar. This time I couldn't do it. Not for the obvious reasons. But because, somehow, I knew I wouldn't feel happy wandering around wearing a badge saying Zotan Ivanovski or Zdravko Rittgasser, or even Slobodan Zaric. Instead, I kept being introduced to people. I met the winner

of the Yugoslav Ad of the Year Competition. It was for a fly
spray called 'Bum'.

'Bum?' I said to the winner.

'Bum,' he said.

'But why Bum?' I wondered.

'You point at fly. You press button. Bum. He's dead,' he
replied.

I was supposed to be giving the key-note address. It was the
first time they had had a presentation on financial advertising
and public relations.

'. . . and finally I would like to introduce . . .' The chairman
shuffled his notes looking for my name. '. . . like to . . . great
honour . . . first time . . . erh, erh . . . Thank you,' he mumbled
with enthusiasm.

I got up and walked to the microphone. I looked at the
chairman. I turned to the audience. I ostentatiously shuffled
my papers.

'It is a great honour to be here,' I began nervously. 'It is a
great privilege to be invited here by Mr erh, erh, erh erh . . .'

An obvious trick. But it brought the dacha down. A Russian
in the front row practically fell out of his seat. All the
Yugoslavs, especially the Slovenes, Croatians and Montenegrans, kept jumping up and slapping each other, which
probably meant I had insulted a Serb. The Bum award winner
jumped up and down in the middle of the audience, spraying
imaginary flies with his spray. The Serbs grinned fiercely at
everybody.

I'm sure nobody listened to a word I said afterwards. In fact,
I know nobody listened to a word I said. For the rest of the
conference people kept coming up to me and saying, 'Erh,
Erh'. Especially the Slovenes, the Croatians and the Montenegrans, which was probably not surprising. To me, Slovenia
and Croatia are certainly far more Western than the rest of the
country. Slovenia is certainly more Italian or Austrian, with its
sloping red roofs and high-spired Catholic churches. Which is
probably why most bars and restaurants accept Austrian

schilling or deutschmarks. It was also much richer than other parts of the country. Its per capita income was more than double that of the rest of the country. It was also more export-oriented. The language they speak, I'm told, is related to the Slovak of Czechoslovakia.

One Slovenian I met at the conference was tall, thin, very elegant. He wore a wide, floppy black hat, a slightly tired velvet jacket, large grey-checked trousers. Everywhere he went he carried an ivory-topped walking stick. He looked as if he had just drifted in from the opera. An Italian opera. He was from near Trieste, the Italian border town just forty miles from Venice, which he said was Mecca to every Yugoslav who had two kopeks to rub together.

'Giovanni's,' he sighed. 'You should see Giovanni's on a Saturday morning. It's more like Yugoslavia than Italy. Slovenes, Serbs, Croats, Montenegrans. Everybody. Everywhere.' Giovanni's is apparently a huge department store piled high with Western goods. To the Yugoslavs it was Mecca. 'Toilet rolls,' he told me wistfully. 'They sell them by the lorryload.' He then drifted off to another opera.

Croatians seem to me to be westerners with a conscience. Very Catholic, very right-wing – some Serbs will tell you that Croatians backed Tito on condition that he didn't de-Nazify them too much. They are the businessmen of Yugoslavia. The big shipbuilding industry is all along their 1,000-kilometre of Adriatic coastline. Most of the main tourism is there. Or rather was there. Half of them say they are part of the West and must work with the West. The other half say they are Croatians and they must devote every waking second of every waking day to building up their own infrastructure. They talk of Croatia being the south-eastern hub of Greater Europe. They imagine a vast highway linking Munich and Zagreb, their capital; railway lines running from Budapest, Prague and even Berlin to the Mediterranean coming through Croatia. But there is only one thing wrong with Croatia as far as I'm concerned. That's Grk. Pronounced Grrkk.

One evening I was in poor old Dubrovnick, which to me is kind and gentle. Almost romantic. Definitely more Italian in style, architecture, atmosphere, than Yugoslav. Or was. I was sitting on a rooftop restaurant in the old town overlooking the bay. I ordered a bottle of wine. The waiter brought me a bottle of Grk. Pronounced Grrkk. The sun was beginning to set. I picked up the glass and took a sip. It virtually made what little hair I have left stand on end and my teeth drop out. Somehow it scrapes the stain off the inside of your mouth, destroys your palate for a moment, then blows your top off. All at the same time. It's the only wine in the world which I'm convinced is made specially for people who smoke Turkish cigarettes. About 1,000 a day.

I never managed to get as far as Macedonia down in the south-east with its mountains and villages. But I've driven all over Montenegro, which seems to be everything to all men. Mediterranean; low, flat, fertile countryside; river valleys and lakes; and, of course, mountains. Life there always seemed simple, uncomplicated, unhurried. The capital, Cetinje, seemed more like a frontier town than a capital of a major regional area of Europe. Old King Nikolas's Palace looked as though it would have had trouble even being considered by the National Trust.

Afterwards I visited what must be the biggest vineyard in the world. It covered 3,000 hectares and ran right up to the Albanian border. It's the only vineyard I've ever visited which had its own landing strip. It was so big all the spraying had to be done by its own fleet of planes. Whenever any pruning or picking had to be done, all the soldiers stationed in the region were given two weeks' holiday – to work in the vineyard.

Walking just a fraction of the way along one of the rows of vines, it seemed as if the vineyard was the size of Albania itself. Except the vineyard was a million times more exciting. When I finally got back to the tiny little vineyard office I asked the director who owned it.

'The World Bank,' he said. It was established entirely with

World Bank money to try and stimulate development in the area. 'The World Bank,' he said, 'is the biggest wine producer in the world.'

After the conference was over, back at the hotel, I spotted, over the heads of all the fat, little Russian delegates swarming in and out of the dining room like a demented swarm of bees, one of the executives working for Yugoslaviapublic. I asked about the Serb with whom I'd discussed selling shoes to the Russians.

'He's been promoted,' he said.

'Where to?' I shouted across another swarm of Russians heading from the dining room to the lounge.

'To Teheran,' he said.

'Teheran?' I said. 'That's not promotion.'

'He's got to organize the Yugoslav stand at the Teheran International Trade Fair.' These were the days when the Ayatollah's revolution was pushing up from third into fourth gear.

'So what happened?'

He told me about the shoe campaign.

'So did it work? Did they like the photographs?'

'No,' he said bluntly. 'A disaster. A big disaster. That's why he was sent to Teheran.'

I couldn't believe it. 'But you took good photographs?'

'The best.'

'They were properly printed?'

'Of course.'

'The right . . .?'

'Naturally.'

'So what went wrong?'

'The photographs,' he said, 'were too good.'

'Too good? How could . . .?'

'They were so good the Russians could count every single stitch on every shoe.'

'So . . .'

'So when we delivered the shoes and they didn't have

exactly the same number of stitches as they had in the photographs, the Russians rejected them. They said we were not supplying as specified.'

'But that's . . .'

'Of course it is. But what could we do? We had to take them back. It cost us a lot of money, I can tell you.'

'So what did you do about the photographs?'

'We scrapped them. We've gone back to the old-fashioned drawings. That way the Russians can't count the stitches.'

'And the director?'

He shrugged his shoulders.

In the car to the airport I met the other star of the conference, the Egyptian radio producer whom I had not seen since my arrival. Nor, come to think of it, had anybody else.

'So where have you been?' I asked guardedly.

He had spent the whole conference locked up in his room at the hotel because his suitcase had not arrived from Cairo.

'So why didn't you tell the organizers?' I gasped.

'They didn't ask me,' he said.

'But you should have.'

'I didn't want to embarrass them,' he mumbled.

Years later, after Iran settled down again, I met the director of the agency. I was in Belgrade visiting a construction company that was doing a lot of work in Zambia. I bumped into him outside McDonald's. We spoke about the conference in Sarajevo.

'Erh, Erh,' he kept nudging me. He had obviously been well briefed. The elegant Italian with the floppy hat and ivory-topped walking stick, he told me, had just committed suicide. 'He could never get over the fact he was Yugoslav and not Italian,' he said.

I asked him about the Russians.

'Your idea,' he said. 'It got me the sack.'

I started to explain.

'Don't worry,' he said. 'I always wanted to visit Teheran. Especially during a Revolution.'

I started again to . . .

'Don't worry,' he said. He invited me back to his flat for a drink. 'You never had time in London,' he said. 'In Belgrade you have plenty of time.'

We strolled back across Knez Mihailova. We stopped outside what looked like Lubjanka Prison in Moscow. The great oak door creaked open. Inside it was pitch black. I followed his voice into the void. I heard clanking and banging. We were now inside what I imagined was a tiny metal lift. We cranked our way up three or thirty-three storeys. Probably three storeys, as this was Belgrade. Then fell out on to a tiny landing. The director was trying to get the key in the lock. The door swung open, revealing an elegant, modern, flat; an Italian-style flat. The fruits of all those years travelling the world. Or perhaps it was just a couple of weeks at Giovanni's.

I collapsed in the middle of an enormous soft leather sofa.

'Now,' he muttered, 'we have zupper.'

He put an iced bottle of vodka on the ultramodern coffee table.

'But I haven't got any hamburgers,' he said as we staggered across to the fridge. 'I'm afraid all I've got is . . .' He threw open the fridge door, '. . . caviar.'

The whole fridge was packed from the floor to practically eye-level with caviar. Not your cheap Danish imitation caviar. The real 100 per cent caviar from the Caspian Sea which the Russians have started eating as there are no longer any sturgeon left in the Volga.

'I never got paid the whole time I was in Teheran,' he said. 'The only thing they gave me was caviar, caviar and still more caviar. I'm sick of it.'

By the time I staggered back to my hotel, I was dreaming of hamburgers.

Toronto

Quick – oops, I mean *vite*. Go to Canada while it's still there. I don't mean it's going to disappear; it's just that I'm convinced the whole idea of something called Canada is going to disappear, even though the United Nations for some reason reckons it's the best place to live in the whole world. Although I suppose if like the United Nations you've been concentrating on struggling to survive in Sarajevo and Somalia, Canada's bound to have some attractions.

You think that's being unkind, you should hear what typical Canadians say about Canada.

'We're like Belgium,' a Turkish waiter told me one evening in a French restaurant in Benvenute Place, in Toronto. 'The Americans treat us the same way the French treat the Belgians.'

'Vichyssoise, that's what this country is,' a Hong Kong Chinese secretary told me one day while I was waiting to go into a meeting with a Lebanese banker in the Spanish part of the city.

'You mean because you supported Vichy France during the last war?'

'No, because it's cold, tasteless, half French and impossible to stir.'

All the same, during the last war French Canadians threw in their Davy Crockett hats with Marshal Pétain, although nobody seems to have told de Gaulle, or no doubt he wouldn't have gone around supporting them as much as he did. Or maybe we all got it horriblement wrong, and when he was shouting 'Vive Quebec' from the rooftops he was really saying, 'Put some life into this God forsaken dump. Loosen up. Live a little.'

It seems to me that every day Canada is becoming more like the US, and/or France, depending on where you come from and which bit you're in. God knows, whichever bit you're in has got precious little in common with any of the other bits. The Western provinces resent the Central provinces. The hoe-downers in the Central provinces resent the Western and Eastern provinces. The Eastern provinces resent the Western and Central provinces. The anglophones, or rather non-Québecois, resent the Québecois, and the French for encouraging them. The Québecois resent everybody under the soleil except each other. The only thing that seems to unite them is that none of them wants to be American.

The country stretches from cold, to very cold, to wait-a-minute-what's-happened-to-my-foot? Just 400 miles to the north of Quebec city, you're in the Arctic. Another 400 miles and the only means of transport is sledge. After that? Nothing. The landscape as far as I can tell is dense forests covered with snow, dense towns covered with snow and dense Québecois covered with snow. In some parts of Canada it gets so cold that motorists drive to work across lakes and along rivers, which is probably why over 90 percent of the population is huddled together for warmth in the south. The other 10 percent of the territory, roughly the size of Greece, is occupied by the Inuit, or Eskimos. They have been there for 4,000 years, give or take a frozen 1,000, and are staying put hoping that, if Quebec gets its independence, what's good enough for Jean, Jacques and Rousseau will be good enough for them. Which shows you that they are not only isolated but out of touch as well. So it's no wonder Canadians cannot agree on what Canada is or isn't.

Take Toronto, for example, on the far north-west corner of

Lake Ontario. To me, on the odd one or two days I've been there when it hasn't been snowing, it looks more like New York than New York – at least the New York that New Yorkers think New York is like. Not the New York that non-New Yorkers know New York is not like. If you don't see what I mean. Bits of the Eaton Center look like Fifth Avenue. Stand on one leg in Nathan Phillips Square, near Bay Street, put one hand over your left eye, and I swear you can see bits of Wall Street. Parts of Yonge Street – this I cannot believe – are supposed to be like Greenwich Village. But I can't see it. Every time I go there, however, apart from the wind that comes howling across the lake, the place seems full of New York film and television crews making yet another blockbuster about how dangerous it is living on the front line in New York, because New York is too dangerous for New Yorkers to make films there about how dangerous New York is. They prefer the safety of anonymous, leafy, tranquil Vichyssoise Canada.

'We say it's New York run by the Swiss,' an Irishman in one of the thousand bars along Yonge Street told me one evening.

'So why did you come here?' I asked him.

'To drink Canada dry,' he grinned.

In the United States, goody-goodies slip away to Vegas for the weekend to break out. In Canada they go to Toronto. It's the kind of straight-down-the-line, harmless, anonymous city where Baptist ministers sneak off during the week hoping to visit the straight-down-the-line, harmless, anony-mous strip clubs without being recognized. And they always are, by other Baptist ministers who've also sneaked off for a safe frisson of danger. Virtually founded – that is the correct phrase – by Scottish and Irish Protestants, and run by teetotal Methodists, at least in the early days, you can bet your life everyone in Toronto sits up straight at table, eats their greens, never speaks with anything in their mouth and says thank you afterwards. Laugh at table and I bet it's a capital offence.

'Know what Toronto would be called if it was in Russia?' an

Italian taxi driver asked me as we sailed down Yonge Street. 'Retrograd.'

A Chicagoan I know, on the other side of the lake, calls it a sanctimonious icebox.

To many people, however, Toronto is one of the nicest cities in North America. It's waspy. It's reserved. It's politeness itself. They're the kind of people who genuinely believe that the only way to reduce what little crime they have is to reduce the number of criminal offences.

I was told that if Torontonians decide they want to break out in the deep inner privacy of their own homes, they will think about having mirrors fitted on the dining-room ceiling. The Reichman Brothers of Canary Wharf fame apparently have a glass-ceilinged home in North Toronto.

To me it's Goody-Two-Shoes country, where the middle class of any nation you care to name – most of them are in Toronto – immediately feel at home, and accepted by all the other middle classes in town. The only problem is that, like so much that is middle class, it's boring, boring, yawn. After 10.15 in the morning there's nothing to do. Why 10.15? Because it takes Torontonians that long every day to realize that there's nothing to do. When 500,000 Torontonians took to the streets to celebrate their local baseball team, the Blue Jays, becoming the first non-American team to win the World Series in 1992, there wasn't one arrest, not one broken bottle and probably not one voice raised in anger. And they call that celebrating. To try and liven things up they have the only television service in the world which not only enables you to watch a good, clean game of football but somehow makes the camera focus on particular players, so that you can see close up what a good, clean game they are playing.

It's not just the people, it's the buildings as well. Toronto has lots of nice, friendly office blocks; lots of nice, friendly shopping centres; the world's largest and nicest free-standing structure, the CN Tower, all 1,815 feet 5 inches of it; a million miles of nice underground tunnels – it's possible to walk from one end of the city to the other without getting snow on your boots – and the largest and nicest igloo in the world, the Toronto SkyDome, complete with retractable roof and a television screen three storeys high by nine storeys across which can house 50,000 nice people. Then there are lots of lovely industrial buildings on the outskirts put up by the Reichman Brothers before they became rich, put mirrors on the ceiling of their dining room and lost the lot. There's a moral there somewhere, especially if you're a teetotal Methodist with mirrors on your dining-room ceiling. But I'm not sure the Torontonians would understand it.

It is also, I was told very proudly by a Montenegrin computer scientist who fled Belgrade University because of the troubles, the only town in North America which does not believe in air-mailing.

'Air-mailing; what's air-mailing?' I said.

'Throwing your garbage out of the window into the street.'

Of course, of course. We do it all the time where I come from. How unusual.

I know some people, however, who love Toronto so much they pop over for the weekend. They leave London on Friday. The flight takes six hours. Take into account the time difference and you can be back in London by Monday morning after at least two and a half days. You're knackered, but it's probably worth it.

Most Torontonians are not Torontonians. Over 55 percent of the 3.5 million population comes from outside Canada. Every cab I get seems to be driven by a reformed Lebanese freedom fighter, only too happy to regale me with tales of the good old days when all he did was drink champagne on the terrace of the St George Hotel with Gerry Loughran. Not even their pride and joy, the world famous Blue Jays (at least to everyone in Toronto they're world famous) are from Toronto. They're all from the States or Dominica. They're only in Toronto, I'm sure, because of the nice people, the absence of air-mailing and, of course, the money. Toronto boasts a little

Italy, a little Portugal, a Greek Street and three Chinatowns. It's also the only place I know where Italian restaurants are run by Portuguese and Greeks, with Chinese cooks. There are even offices which close way before sunset on Friday evenings to allow their employees to get home in time for the Sabbath.

Toronto has so many different groups that if everyone wanted to run their own show the place would splinter into a thousand pieces. That's not to mention the red setters. Every Canadian yuppy seems to have a red setter. If they start demanding their independence as well . . .

On the other hand, Montreal, famous for its gothic-style Notre Dame Basilica, the oldest church in the city, for la Place des Arthropoda, the biggest insectarium in the world, and for the bidet once used by Robert Maxwell in the Carlton Ritz Hotel, every jour becomes more and more comme la France. Whatever anyone says, it's happening; sur la terre, dans les bars, under the snow, partout.

After nearly thirty years of campaigning for its indé-pendance, ten years of being run by their own parti Québe-cois and le Dieu knows how many threats, Quebec, which is bigger than Alaska and twice the size of Texas, is admittedly still Canadian – en principe. But with more than a distant whiff of garlic. The Québecois see themselves as a race, a nation, a people set apart. Everybody else is just Canadian, including the Indians, who everybody, including the wolves, coyotes, beavers, eagles, bear and moose, but not the French, agrees were there first and even gave their name to the place.

The name Quebec comes from the old Algonquin Indian word, kebec, meaning the place where the river – not the mind – narrows. In fact so rich in history is the whole area – Bell Telephones and Quebec Hydro have their own staff archaeologists – that if a Québecois gets his gardener to turn over a tiny patch of soil, it will throw up a mass of antiques. The top archaeologist with Parks Canada claims that the best place to start looking for them is – typical French – in the old latrines. 'The lack of air in the fine silt does a beautiful job of preserving ceramics, leather shoes, even animals,' he says.

His name? You're not going to believe this, take a seat, monsieur – Pierre Bidet.

Voltaire once described Canada as 'so many useless acres of snow not worth fighting over with the English.' Charles Dickens, after a quick swing through in 1842, did not have great expectations for the place either. Quebec, he said, was 'a place not to be forgotten'. To this day, however, every homme, femme and enfant in Quebec is convinced that was a compliment. Obviously a tale of two languages.

Québecois, or Quebeckers, to maintain the linguistic balance, enjoy more control over their own affairs than any other minority in the country. They think this is wrong; so does the rest of the country. But for different reasons, naturellement.

'All the English speakers are leaving,' I kept being told by English speakers. 'We're the next.'

To which the French speakers invariably reply, 'Nobody speaks English anyway. Their ancestors didn't speak English. Why should they?'

In some countries, all I ever see are industrial estates; in others, banking parlours or government departments. In Canada, all I ever visited was shopping centres. Small-town shopping centres; city-centre shopping centres; huge, sprawling out-of-town shopping centres like Eaton Place in Toronto, the world's largest – so big that by the time you walk from one end to the other a thousand sheep have been sheared, their wool turned into Blue Jay sweaters, hung up on racks and sold to visiting tourists.

At the time I was retained by one of those massive British property groups which was growing so fast it just didn't know what it had in its bag. It hardly knew which companies it had acquired either. I'm not saying they didn't know they owned a string of shopping centres throughout North America, the UK and Europe. They had all the glossy photographs in their annual report to prove it. What they didn't know was the detail. Times were good, acquisitions were being made all the time, the money kept pouring in. The annual reports got bigger and bigger and the photographs of the chairman showed him getting younger and younger. Details didn't seem to matter.

Then suddenly they hit problems. The money, especially from Canada, started drying up. They realized all the rents their tenants were paying were not set, standard rents but turnover rents: the more money the shops took, the more rent they paid. Before they were taken over, everything was fine: sales were high, rents were high. After they had been taken over, suddenly sales started crumbling and the rents started plummeting along with them. There was panic back in London. The chairman cancelled lunch at the Ritz. Whole-page corporate ads in the Lord Mayor's Show annual pro-gramme were dropped. But the half-page ads for the *Estates Times* went ahead.

'The first thing to do is look at the figures before you bought. Maybe they had been massaged.'

'OK. You go and look at the shopping centres first. See how they operate, see what we can learn,' the chief Executive decided instead.

I hate shopping. I'm the opposite of those shopaholics you meet on trips who insist on visiting the shops on the way from the airport to the hotel. 'Surely there's somebody else who could . . .'

Two days later I was in Belle Province, Quebec.

We all have problems trying to remember what little French, German or Serbo-Croat we don't know when we're in France, Germany or whatever they are calling the place where they used to speak Serbo-Croat. 'Er, bonjour, guten tag, dobradan,' is usually my first hesitant attempt, then when I realize my mistake it's a quick, 'Pardon, sorry, entschuldigen, scusi, oh what the hell?'

Most people suffer from jet-lag; on my first visit to Toronto and Montreal I suffered from language-lag. I couldn't remember which language I was supposed to be speaking. I went through the whole of my first meeting with the company's lawyers getting my torts and my tartes mixed up. I can still see the look on their faces as I explained that my masters in Angleterre had decided that in order to solve the problem they wanted to donner une tarte à quelqu'un. Which, of course, is not what I meant. At least, I don't think it was.

But even when you finally become language-acclimatized, you still don't know which language to speak – French, or whatever that other language is called. You also never know which language they are speaking: French, French-French, French-English, English, English-English, English-French, American, American-French ... and all in different accents: English, American, French, Serbo-Croat, Hungarian, Turkish, Bulgarian, Italian, Hong Kong Chinese, or whatever.

'Hi. Good morn—'

'Bonjour, monsieur, comment ça va?'

That was my first attempt at speaking Canadian.

It was also my first experience of the weather. In Montreal they say they have two seasons, 'l'hiver et juillet.'

It's the only place I've ever been where the hotel staff ring you up in the morning and ask what you are wearing.

'Well, I was thinking of the grey job,' I answered nervously the first time it happened to me.

'The one you've been wearing for the last three days?'

'Yes. Why?' This was going too far, even for a bowl of Vichyssoise.

'I wouldn't.'

'Well to hell with—'

'Because today it's extra cold.'

'So what would you suggest I wear? My all-white ensemble, or the black leather—'

'I'm trying to be of service, sir, monsieur.'

Go at the wrong time of year – I always go everywhere at the wrong time of year – and it's so cold the only thing the muggers are after in the miles and miles of overheated walkways, tunnels and shopping arcades that criss-cross the city underground are hats. Carry a hatbox, or worse still wear an expensive fur Davy Crockett hat, and you'll be mugged before you can say 80 percent of the world's fur market is controlled by Quebec.

'So how do I keep warm?' I asked my wardrobe Samaritan.

'Wear a cheap hat.'

That evening, to get my own back, I left my cheap snowshoes outside the room to be cleaned.

Some parts of the city can get up to eight feet of snow a year; in other parts of the province it can be as much as fifteen feet. They have frozen lakes the size of Ireland. Farms outside Toronto are the coldest farms on earth. In the north west, which is supposed to be littered with diamonds, winter temperatures can hit an unbelievable –40°C, sometimes even lower, if the really cold winds come beating in across the Arctic. Trucks and machines have to be kept running non-stop. Take a shovel out into the open and it will shatter if you put any weight on it.

Montreal is also the only place in the world, sorry, au monde, where they have language police, or tongue troops, wandering around making sure everyone eats, drinks, sleeps and even thinks in two languages. I mean en deux langues. Shortly before I arrived there on one trip, the language police had scored a major victory – against a packet of English jelly babies tucked away at the back of a shelf in some corner shop. They discovered the offending packet and sentenced it to death because the label was in English. Not English and – oops, I mean not French and English. As a result in Montreal I not only spend all my time battling against the elements but I am also scared out of my life in case I make a mistake, I mean faux pas. The crazy thing is that, entre nous, the French French are a tiny bit sniffy about Canadian French.

What am I saying? A tiny bit sniffy? They practically curl and die whenever they hear Canadian French.

'Ca, ca, ca, ce n'est pas français,' they splutter whenever they hear them.

'Laissez le bon temps roulez!' the Canadians say, slapping you on the back whenever you're trying to enjoy yourself in their glorious country.

Would Voltaire say, 'Laissez le bon temps roulez'? Would General de Gaulle? If the Académie Français heard what the Canadians were doing with their language they would have a massive heart attack collectif.

My first visit was to a nice Canadian shopping centre just outside Montreal. It was so cold I felt as though fifteen-metre-high oil rigs were drilling into my face and blasting in liquid ice. The first thing I wanted to do was try a Caribun, a lethal mix of red wine and white spirits which I had been told was the only way to ward off the cold. I was also worried whether, if I ever thawed out, I would understand what they were saying.

What was the first thing the manager – oops, I mean directeur, wanted to talk about? Not the weather, the state of the British economy or even Mrs Thatcher. 'My! That's a cute top,' he cried as we shook hands, perhaps a trifle longer than I'm used to shaking hands even in warm countries.

Cute top! I thought, hell, I mean, mon dieu. Who is this guy? It was just the perfectly boring jacket of the perfectly boring suit my wardrobe Samaritan had advised me to wear. 'What does he mean, cute?' I asked his secretary, an American-American who was sitting in on the meeting making notes in le dieu knows what language.

'It means he hates it,' she snarled, as if she had forgotten she was no longer living on the front line in New York.

I asked about turnover rentals, how they operated, the benefits for the developer . . .

'Okay, we'll progress the scenario,' he said.

Progress? What does he mean progress? What's he talking about, scenario?

'It means he ain't going to tell you nuttin,' snapped the secretary.

Afterwards she told me Canadians no longer believe in marriage. Instead, she said, they believe in mixed sexual partnerships. At least, in most cases. Her mixed sexual partner, she said, was Senegalese. I didn't ask how mixed.

Near Quebec City, I hit another problem. With its maze of narrow streets, its Victorian lamps, its mass of tiny restaurants, it was built to be the capital of a vast French North American empire stretching all the way to the Gulf of Mexico and west to the Rocky Mountains. But the perfidious British thwarted their plan.

The heart of the city, the only walled city on the continent north of Mexico, is vieux Québec, a single square kilometre which is virtually the Wailing Wall to all Québecois. 'Touch the wall and pray that we gain our freedom,' they say.

In 1985 UNESCO made it a world heritage site ranking it in importance alongside the pyramids and the Taj Mahal. The Québecois were convinced this was a great honour. Everybody else saw it as official confirmation of their irrelevance to the real world. For me, however, it meant English Canadians speaking Canadian French. In other words, Canadians who were eager to show that, having welcomed ex-Lebanese freedom fighters and American-Armenians into their midst, they were even prepared to make the ultimate sacrifice and welcome the French. Hence the need to sprinkle their conversation with French words in French accents.

'Gawsh. Jawly good. Oui. Seau, seau good of you to come.'

I was with the directeur of another shopping centre. The 'phone rang on his desk.

'Eau dear,' he said. 'Attendez un meaument.' He picked it up. 'Abso-louis-ment,' he drawled down the line. 'Abso-louis-ment.' He put the phone down. 'Are there any preservatifs dans les gateaux?' He leant across his desk at me. 'Je vous demande. Are there any preservatifs dans les gateaux?'

Wait a meaument, I thought. Aren't preservatifs . . .?

'Of course there are preservatifs dans les gateaux,' he

mumbled. 'No preservatifs dans les gateaux, ce n'est pas catholique.'

Now I am lost. Abso-louis-ment completely lost.

'Okay.' He swung round towards me. 'Now the fait is accompli, what next?'

You think that's bad, you should try understanding what they say in English. First, English which sounds like English, but isn't. At least I didn't think it was. Then English which doesn't sound anything like English at all. But is – I think.

I went into one shopping centre which looked like the snow capital of the world. It was alive to the sounds of ice skating, ice hockey, skiing, helicopter skiing, dog sledging. They were even demonstrating common or garden snowmobiles. What language they were speaking I couldn't tell you, even when the helicopter skiing was over.

I first met the big boss, I mean le grand chef, for coffee. A week in Canada and I was already ordering coffee like a Canadian. 'I'll have a decaff cappuccino medium,' I yelled.

The director yelled back that he was 'a half-caff' and promptly ordered 'A half caff, half decaff, cappuccino, medium, cold.'

To keep warm everyone around us was eating thick pea soup, meat pies, baked beans and warm maple syrup all smothered in an avalanche of thick cream.

In Quebec, he explained, you were not allowed to take alcohol outside in a bottle, so everybody carried walking sticks with hidden reservoirs inside, or chewed warm maple toffee curled around a large stick. On the wall of the restaurant, I noticed a poster: 'If someone you love is at death's door, our flowers will see them through,' it said. At least it was in English.

Later in his office he introduced me to his finance director. He was big in amateur dramatics.

'He always grabs Englishmen's parts,' the boss told me.

'To bay or not to bay, Zat ist de . . .' the finance director cruised through the door and waltzed towards me. He was wearing a shirt so fluorescent it would have lit up a thousand murky corners in a thousand French balance sheets. I grabbed a chair at the furthest end of the table, sat down and crossed my legs quickly.

'Zat is my best English part,' he purred.

'Sounds Danish to me,' I muttered.

'Danish! Zis ist not Danish,' he screamed. 'English. Zay haf no coolture. Pah.'

And that was the end of that meeting.

In other shopping centres I had fascinating discussions in I don't know what language with shopkeepers – oops, I mean client problem solvers as they insist on being called, about such challenging subjects as catering for the chronologically gifted and the physically challenged. I even got into discussion with a chemist, I mean a pharmacist, which I just did not understand, although he showed me massive computer printouts he had produced to analyse what he called the sheets-per-task ratios he had worked out for a particular range of products. It was only three days later, while I was suffering the after-effects of too many warm maple toffees on a stick that I realized what he had been going on about. I think.

In one shopping centre outside Toronto they were trying to think up a giant promotion to bring the punters in and push up those turnover rentals. Glendon, Alberta, they told me, had just come up with a great idea. Desperate to attract attention (if you've never heard of it, don't worry; that's why they want publicity), the mayor decided to create the world's biggest pyrogy. You've never heard of a pyrogy? Don't worry. This is the whole point of the story. A pyrogy is a giant kind of special dumpling they make in Glendon full of things like cheese and sauerkraut. The Mayor reckoned if he built not only the biggest pyrogy in the world but also, wait for it, the biggest electric pyrogy, everybody would come flocking. There would be annual pyrogy festivals. A pyrogy queen. A pyrogy carnival. Glendon would be on the map. He sold the idea to the town council. He also raised enough money from local businessmen to go ahead and build it. In the end it apparently looked like a giant white fibreglass leech sitting on the end of a fork, so you would realize it was meant to be eaten. Did they come flocking in to wherever it was to see it? What do you think?

'Hey, let's give Disney World a skip this year, Ma. There's some giant leech sitting on a fork out in the Canadian outback. Sounds more fun.'

'Sure, son. Nothing I like better than looking at a fibreglass pyro-whatever it is. Let's go.'

The whole thing was, of course, a disaster. But it was a disaster, according to the Mayor, not because it was a crazy idea – even in Canada, mayors never have crazy ideas – but because another town called Andrew actually got a grant from the provincial tourist board to build – are you ready? – the world's largest fibreglass duck.

'Gee, honey. Forget the pyro-thingy, let's go see the world's largest fibreglass duck instead.'

'Sure, Elmer. Sounds more fun.'

But my most memorable meeting came towards the end of my trip. I was somewhere on the outskirts of Toronto. I'd toured yet another shopping centre. I was in reception bang on time, but there was nobody there. After about ten minutes the receptionist, a Greek-Azerbijani, arrived. Another fifteen minutes and I was ushered into this super modern office about the size of your average domestic aircraft hangar, all chrome and leather chairs. Running the length of the room was an enormous oak boardroom table so long you could probably land a 737 on it providing you were quick.

The president directeur-general, I mean chief executive, vice-president administration and vice-president finance came in. The chief executive said he was schedule-independent. The vice-president finance looked so stressed I thought his eyeballs were going to start bleeding.

'He means he's late,' he said through his teeth.

I said I was thinking of committing schedule-cide, but they

didn't take any notice, so I asked about turnover rentals.

The chief executive leant across the table at me. 'I want to tell you, Peter,' he drawled, 'how here in Canada we believe that close members of caring families who have been de-accessed should be given a better home in an even more caring family environment.'

'Sure,' I said. 'Now about—'

'I just wanted to make that clear.'

I nodded as wisely as I could.

The vice-president administration now leant forward.

'Turnover rentals,' I said. 'I was wondering . . .'

Then he buried me, up to my neck, in . . . in . . . in . . . 'We believe in the synergistic multidisciplinary intrapersonal concept . . . We adhere to the cross-fertilization of entrepreneurial potentialities . . . We are of the opinion . . .'

I mean, I'm used to Americans and American gobbledygook. I've even fought my way through one of President Bush's speeches. But this . . .

The chief executive pushed his chair back and started wandering up and down the room, looking behind the pictures on the wall, picking the telephone up to check the dialling tone was still there. '. . . early stage market penetration . . .' the vice-president administration continued. The chief executive ambled across to the 'phone, called his secretary and asked her to go out and buy some dental floss for his daughter.

'Yes, dental floss,' he drawled. 'The stuff for your teeth.' His secretary was obviously as puzzled as I was trying not to look. 'Whaddyamean what flavour?' he barked. 'Any flavour.' He slammed the 'phone down.

'. . . strong sharp-end opposition . . .' I kept nodding as wisely as I could. 'Am I being coherent?' the vice-president administration suddenly stopped and looked at me.

'Affirmative,' I mumbled.

Now it was the turn of the vice-president finance.

'So as I understand it, turnover rentals should in a good year give you—'

He didn't wait for me to finish. He was off. '. . . Fiscal downturn . . . uplift of current liabilities . . . sub-optimal cost-profile . . .'

The chief executive got up again and went back to the 'phone. 'So what kinda dental floss is there?' An expression of intense interest swept across his face, far more than I'd noticed during our discussion. 'Hell. Make it strawberry.' He slumped back in his chair. 'Decisions,' he grunted.

'So in a good year, therefore, it's possible . . .' I began.

'Hell, I'd better call the kid and find out what flavour she wants.' He punched the numbers into the phone. 'Kids. They're more trouble than they're worth.'

'. . . mature configuration . . . disimproved revenue position . . . dividends would have to be realized . . . downsizing would be implemented . . . outplacement . . . right-sizing . . .'

'What in the name of . . .?' I was beginning to think, when the chief executive suddenly announced the meeting was over. I began to gather my blank notes together. 'Okay, Peter,' he drawled. 'If you could come with me.' I followed him down one long corridor and into another. At the end of it was his office.

'Okay,' he said slumping into a leather chair so big it probably took a herd of buffalo to make it. I stood the other side of his desk, just about in hearing range.

'Okay,' he chomped. 'These guys, what do you think of their make-up?'

Make-up! MAKE-UP! You mean all this time I'd been in a room with . . . Both of . . . And I hadn't . . .

'Yeah, their make-up. Whaddya think makes em tick?'

Any other country, I wouldn't worry about their problems. But for me Canada is different. I feel it's virtually my home country. At least that's what people keep telling me. Wherever I am, whether it's in Uruguay or Burkina Faso or even in Poland, people always think I'm Canadian. Especially in

Africa. All over Africa I'm always being taken, heaven help me, for a Canadian. I bet you a Toureg racing camel to a broken-down old moose, that within three minutes of landing in Togo or Mali or even Romania somebody is asking me if I'm Canadian.

Why, I can't imagine. I don't look Canadian. I don't jog. I don't drink beer. I don't leave my snowshoes outside my hotel room at night. Well, not every night. I don't even want to think about going to a hockey match. The only reason I can think of is, I suppose, that the places I go are more used to seeing globetrotting Canadians than stay-at-home Brits. Especially French Africa. Canadians are all over the place. Every road bridge I've come across boasts a plaque saying that it was built by the Canadians.

I'm not keen on being taken for a Canadian. I mean, would you like people to think you came from a country whose currency is based on loonies (on the back of their one-dollar coin is one of their famous native birds, a loon) and whose two most famous sons are what's-his-name, the inventor of the snowmobile, and Marshall McLuhan, who believed there was no point trying to go anywhere whether by ski, ice-skate or snowmobile because we're all living in a single global snow village anyway. Although how Quebec, with its lifelong obsession to be a mini-village within the greater global village, fitted into his thinking I don't know. As for the inventor of the snowmobile, he was another typical Canadian. First he strapped a Model T Ford motor on to the back of his sledge. Then after thirty-seven years he suddenly realized it wasn't going to work so he invented the snowmobile instead. Today there are snowmobile trails everywhere. All over the snow; all over the even more snow; and all over the my-god-does-this-stuff-go-on-for-ever snow.

Now be honest. I promise I won't tell anyone. Would you like people to think you come from a country like Canada?

Rio de Janeiro

Rio de Janeiro is the biggest 'don't' city in the world. It's even worse than Cairo. From the moment you happen to mention casually that maybe perhaps there might be the ever so slightest possibility that you might have to probably visit the place, you're buried in don'ts as high as the Sugar Loaf Mountain.

Everybody and everything in Rio is dangerous.

Don't put your briefcase in the overhead locker in the plane. They'll open it while you're asleep.

Don't use your credit cards. They'll charge you ten times as much. They'll make a second copy and keep it for themselves. They'll swop your card with a stolen card.

Don't take traveller's cheques. They never give you the right rate.

Don't carry a briefcase. They'll slash your knuckles to get it off you.

Don't wear a money belt. That's an open invitation.

Don't carry a camera, or a large bag.

Don't pick up any money you see in the streets or anywhere. It's a trick.

Don't change money on the street.

Don't go to McDonald's. They'll beg food from you while you're eating it.

Don't take cabs. They'll drive you all round town just to pump up the fare. If they drive you anywhere, of course.

Don't go to church and take communion. They spike the wine with rat poison.

Don't keep your wallet in your inside pocket. They'll lift it as fast as they'll sympathize with you for being British. If you do, put two rubber bands around it. That'll stop them.

And whatever you do don't drink too many caipirinha di cachacas and fall asleep on the beach.

One man, a Lufthansa pilot, woke up with stabbing pains in his midriff. Someone had stolen one of his kidneys. A Frenchwoman woke up and found she had lost an eye.

'An eye?'

'For a cornea transplant,' I was told quite sharply. 'You don't know anything, do you?'

If I had a sack of coffee for every time somebody told me not to go to Rio I could afford to buy my own personal armoured personnel carrier for my next visit.

'I wouldn't go if I were you.'

'Why?'

'It won't agree with you.'

'Why not?'

'Because . . .' And then it begins all over again.

A Northern Irish businessman told me it was like Belfast in the sunshine. 'And Sugar Loaf Mountain is just like our Cave Hill,' he added.

Gerry Loughran, who was famous for always sitting at the same table on the terrace of the St George Hotel in Beirut come shine, showers or bombs, told me it was like the Lebanon.

In theory, of course, they're right; Rio is not my kind of town. I don't like the sun. At least, I like it, but I don't go mad about it like some people. I know some guys who strip off practically stark naked as soon as the sun even thinks of breaking through the clouds. I was in India once with what I thought was your average, boring nine-to-five businessman. Which he was until the sun came up. After that, whether we were in meetings, visiting factories or trying out the local spices, you didn't have to worry about his credentials for the job, you could practically see them for yourself.

On the other hand, I'm not quite a fully paid-up member of the Enoch Powell School of Tropical Clothing. If the temperature does get into the nineties, I am prepared to undo the top button of my cardigan, unlike Enoch who, even with the mercury gushing out of the top of the thermometer, insists on wearing his waistcoat. 'Arabs wear lots of clothes,' he has been heard to grunt – in the most grammatical fashion, of course. 'Like them, I am indifferent to the heat.'

When I go to Rio I don't exactly pack a waistcoat, but I don't pack a short-sleeved shirt either. God help me, if I pack anything that even remotely suggests I might spend just one second even thinking about something other than business, EBH ('er back home) goes on and on about the fun I have travelling the world while she is stuck at home inside the same four walls, day after day, week after week, month after month. And go back home afterwards with even a speck of suntan, my life is not worth living – until the next trip.

I don't like beaches either, unless you call the Sahara the biggest beach in the world. As far as I am concerned, beaches give you nothing but wrinkles; keratosis and malignant melanomas. They also make you hot. I don't like music. And I definitely don't like anything that involves putting one foot in front of the other, let alone anything as extreme as the – what do they call it? – the Lambada.

But somehow, Rio – I hate myself for saying this – really is great fun. It's the air. It's the atmosphere. It's in the bars; in the food; in the drink; on the streets. Sugar Loaf Mountain at the entrance to the bay; that gigantic statue of Christ the Redeemer on Corcovado, 2,500 feet above the city; the mist rising over Copacabana; that marvellous avenue of palm trees in the Jardin Botanico. Palm trees! Can you imagine? In Brazil. Maybe it's because I thought they had all been chopped down. When I first saw them I thought I was in the wrong country. For me, especially as I'm using paper to say it, Rio, like Venice, has to be one of the most original cities in the world.

Sure, the statue of Christ the Redeemer, arms outstretched, looks as though he is urging the surrounding mountains to make one last heave and push the whole glorious, exciting thing into the sea. But I don't believe it. It's in a fabulous setting. Copacabana; Ipanema; the palm-fringed crescent of Conrado Beach (more trees) with its luxury hotels and apartments; they are all breathtaking. The baroque architecture of the old part of town; the baroque architecture of the new part of town; even the Theatre Colon – although I will admit nothing would persuade me to go into an English, let alone a Brazilian Colon. All around there are mountains – not in the distance, but at the bottom of the garden. From the top of an old cobbled one-way street which winds about a kilometre overlooking Rio, the view of Guanabara Bay is spectacular.

The Ciudade Maravilhosa, the Marvellous City, has also got to be one of the world's most beautiful cities. And since the US State Department warned off American tourists because of the dangers, some say it is even more beautiful.

As for finding Lufthansa pilots scattered over the beach with their livers hanging out, go anywhere within a hundred hospitals' radius of the Alps any day during the skiing season and you'll see exactly the same thing all over the snow. Go into any après ski party any night of the season and you'll see even worse things hanging out all over the place.

Funny thing, though; I've just started getting stabbing pains on my right side just below the rib. Maybe I should see someone about it.

No country in the world has had such a profound effect on my life as Brazil. Trouble is, it didn't do me any good. On the contrary, if it wasn't for Brazil I'm convinced I would today be a rocket scientist or a nuclear physicist. Probably even a winner of the Nobel Peace Prize. Or at worst, I'd have been something in the City, playing games with yield-curve swops, look-back options or even forward-rate agreements.

Instead I am what I am: a successful failure. The reasons: in those formative years when I should have been studying maths and algebra and all the other important subjects necessary for destroying the world, I had a Brazilian form master with a strong Brazilian accent and a stomach the size of Sugar Loaf Mountain. He would stand in front of the blackboard, one of those great big floor-to-ceiling roller affairs, in his long black cassock. He would scream at us like a demented parakeet. He would turn round to the board and write something that looked like an inscription from an Inca tomb. Then he would turn round to face us again. Trouble was, each time he turned round to face us his stomach wiped off all the Inca hieroglyphics he had just scribbled on the board. He would then stand facing us with an enormous smudge of white chalk across the front of his huge black cassock.

'Now boys. Vot is it huff I writ?'

He would throw something at me. 'Hrrschiddlestomb,' which I always assumed was me. 'Hrrskiddletom' – he never ever pronounced my name the same way twice in the whole five years he was supposed to be teaching us – 'Brrstitledome, vot is it huff I writ?'

He would swing back to the board, his great stomach taking a second swipe at the hieroglyphics. Now, of course, the board was perfectly clean, the hieroglyphics gone for ever. But his cassock was covered in even more chalk.

'Vot,' he would scream. 'Vot voy has this done? Vhere is my writing?'

Books, breviaries, bins – whoosh. Everything would go hurtling around the room. Some days it was like the second battle of Ypres but without the gas. We might not have learnt any maths but we certainly learnt how to survive under fire. We also, for the sake of our future as well as our survival, very quickly learnt how to think and speak his particular blend of Brazilian English. If we dared to pronounce the names properly we were slapped down, beaten with a ruler or had – whoosh – chalk, wastepaper bins or whatever thrown at us.

'This is not-a-da right. You know-a-da Inglesi better, hah?'

At first we would hesitate.

'Zoo. Owl long you speak-a-da Inglesi?' He would wave his stomach over us. 'Owl long? Vat hage haff you? Zwelf? Vorteen? Virteen? Vifteen?' Which gives you an idea of the standards of mathematics taught in Brazilian schools and probably the reason why their rate of inflation is completely out of control.

'Zwelve,' I remember mumbling once in reply.

'Zwelve,' he screamed, so loud I swear the statue of Christ nearly came tumbling down Sugar Loaf Mountain. 'Zwelf.' He drew his stomach to attention, or at least he tried to. 'Haf I been speakin dah Inglesi vor firsty-free years? Haf I?'

We all nodded weakly.

'Firsty-free years? Zoo.' He swung his stomach menacingly across the classroom. 'Spick I da Inglesi more hood has yoo? Si?'

'Si,' we all weakly surrendered. Brazilian logic had triumphed again.

The result was that for hours on end he made us write essays on *Vrightenlock* and *Detlour and De Hoary* by Grim Grin. In chapel we prayed to 'Our Vather, who hart in Heffin. Hawold be hss neem . . .' From time to time, when the dreaded subject of jobs came up, he would tell us to go the 'Korea vroom' on the fifth floor. Why on earth did we want to go to the Korea vroom? None of us was interested in Korea. We wanted a job. Korea was the last place anyone wanted to go. So, when the time finally came to break free and escape from our Brazilian jungle, nobody was ready. Nobody got a useful job; we all went into newspapers or marketing or, heaven help us, publishing.

English classes were not the worst problem. We might not

have had much practice speaking the Queen's English, but it didn't take us long to work out that *Vrightenlock* was really *Brighton Rock* and that Our Father who had sent us this man was not actually called Harold. The problem was maths; especially algebra. None of us had even heard of algebra until he started screaming it at us, so there was no way we could check what he was saying.

He would scrawl the figure 10 on the blackboard. 'Zat is nahn,' he would say, emphasizing the 'ahn' so it sounded like the death throes of a parakeet. He would then write x alongside it. 'Zat is a-nahn,' he would continue, again emphasizing the 'ahn' until it sounded like the poor bird had just died a horrible death. 'Voys, reveat haffer me.'

'Nahn,' we would repeat, parakeet fashion, until the classroom sounded like a rollcall at the bird house at London Zoo.

'Nahn,' he would say, walking up and down threatening us with his stomach.

'Nahn,' we bayed back at him.

'A-nahn' he would then shriek.

'A-nahn. A-nahn. Zat is a-nahn!'

His stomach would then swing towards me. 'Pie-nid-dlezum.'

'Nahn and a-nahn,' I would chirp back at him.

'Nahn and a-nahn,' the whole class repeated.

What none of us realized was that what was nahn and a-nahn to us was known and unknown to the rest of the world, so that in five years we barely passed beyond the x + x = y stage, and couldn't even think about working out 5a to the power of minus 7. The world of algebraic equations, co-ordinate geometry and, heaven help us, Venn diagrams was something we could never imagine. It was years afterwards on a trip to Athens that I realized that Pythagoras was not a Greek restaurant but the name of someone who had fallen off his hypotenuse.

The truth suddenly dawned on us one day when the headmaster, a painfully thin priest from somewhere like

Bolton, who seemed to spend his life playing imaginary pat-a-cake with himself, drifted into the classroom. (This man's fifteen minutes of fame came one year at the Headmasters' Conference. They were all asked what they were training their pupils for. 'For government,' said one. 'For Whitehall,' said another. 'For the army,' said yet another. The question was put to him. 'For death,' he said. Till the day he met his own death, I swear he never understood why he got his fifteen minutes.)

'Now Biddlecombe,' he said scribbling the simplest algebra over the blackboard. 'What is this?' He pointed to the blackboard in between playing pat-a-cake with the chalk.

'Hal-jee-bra,' I purred in my best Anglo-Brazilian accent. 'Hal-jee-bra.' I gave the word precisely the emphasis we'd been taught all those years.

He went white. He stopped in mid pat-a-cake. The chalk dropped on the floor. 'I beg your . . .' He stared at me. 'What did . . .?'

He swung back to the blackboard. He pointed at the letter x. 'And this?' He thumped the board with a long, long, thin, white index finger that looked as though he had inadvertently slammed it flat inside the pages of his breviary. 'What is this?'

'A-nahn,' I drawled triumphantly.

Well, that was it. All heaven broke loose. (It was a Catholic school, don't forget.) At one stage it looked as though I was going to be thrashed for insolence, kept in detention until the year 2013 and forced to work out algebraic equations until I reached infinity or the end of time, whichever came first. But when everybody else gave exactly the same answer, with exactly the same drawl and exactly the same intonation, we were merely sentenced to two weeks' detention for taking the St Michael out of our form master and made to fill page after page with meaningless co-ordinate geometry, thereby probably contributing to the destruction of the first swathe of Brazilian rainforest.

Our Brazilian master was never seen again. Some said he was sent back to the rainforests, where he probably provided sustenance for a couple of tribes of prehistoric Yanomami Indians for a couple of rainy seasons. Others said he went back to Brazil where he was responsible for teaching economics to all their political and economic leaders, which might be why today the country is in a mess, the currency is worthless, inflation is 20 percent a month and rising, government spending is out of control, there is a gaping US$20 billion hole in the budget, the streets are full of children who don't go to school, and when anybody asks what they are going to do about it nobody understands a word they say.

In his place we were given a tiny French priest who spoke impeccable English but knew less than we did about maths. Besides, it was too late. Brazil had claimed more innocent victims. I was never to understand the world of yield-curve swaps, look-back options and forward-rate agreements, let alone add up my expenses right first time.

Off and on over the next few years I kept stumbling across Brazil. Or rather, Brazil fruit and nut cases kept trampling all over me.

For a while I worked for an Englishman who'd just come back from Brazil. Actually he looked a bit like a Cadbury's fruit and nut. He was as thin as a bar of chocolate and about as dark. Every morning, in the days before even Old Spice was mentioned in male let alone mixed company, he would turn up at the office even in the depths of winter looking as if he'd just drifted in from Copacabana beach. His face was the colour of a pair of brown shoes I hadn't worn for three years. His hair was crinkly, greasy and jet Grecian-2000 black. His suits were that shimmering light electric blue. And this was in Wimbledon before McEnroe was born let alone heard of.

'Did I ever tell you about . . .?' he would begin as the office immediately emptied and the 'It's out of a bottle' debates would begin all over again by the coffee pot. We didn't have coffee machines in those days.

As it got colder and colder, he would turn up wearing lighter and lighter tropical suits and looking darker and darker, until when he sat down in the office you could not tell where the worn black mahogany panelling left off and he began.

The last time I saw him there was about four feet of snow on the ground, it was three degrees below freezing, and he arrived wearing leather pants, high-heeled cowboy boots, a luminous Hawaiian sports shirt open at the neck and displaying a silver cross on what looked like, I was told later by the office cleaner, a hairy, artificial, sunburnt doormat.

I never saw him after that. He probably either died of exposure or was arrested by the police, or both.

A few years later I was at a wine tasting. There was one elderly man in the group, a village cricket captain type with a blue blazer, Panama hat and moustache. When we started with the dry wines he kept shaking his head violently, shuddering and saying they were sour. The medium wines, he said, were too dry for him. It was only when we hit the Trockenbeerenauslesen, the Eisweins and the tiny sips of d'Yquem that he lit up. 'Beautiful wines,' he declared. 'But they're still too dry.'

I discovered later that he had been born and brought up in Brazil. He had practically been weaned on Lacrimae Cristi, grew up on Eiswein and hit middle age on d'Yquem. It was only when he came to England that he discovered the world of sour wines.

About vorteen, virteen or vifteen years later I was working for a big French worldwide trading group. The chairman kept threatening to invite me to meet him in Rio.

'You're kidding!' I would say.

'Kid. Why I kid? Is necessary,' he would always reply.

One year we were working on the company's annual report. Anybody who has ever lived through an annual report knows the only thing worse than an annual report is another annual report. But this time everything has been agreed: the paper; the colour; the typeface; the size of the staples; the charts; the tables; the photographs; the captions. And, I nearly forgot, the accounts themselves. Everything, that is, except the chairman's statement, which invariably takes more time and trouble then the rest of the report put together.

'Give me a draft, old chap. Look over it at the weekend. Give you the okay on Monday.' That's what they always say, but it never happens. Either they completely forget about it, or their wife gets her hands on it and wants it all changed. Especially the photographs. Hence, in annual report circles, the old rhyme:

> If the chairman proves refractory
> Include a picture of the factory.
> But only in the direst case
> Include a picture of the chairman's face.

In this case, the chairman wouldn't show it to his wife. Instead he kept saying he wanted me to come to Rio. 'Get a plane now. We agree it tomorrow.'

'What, all the way to . . .?'

Then the 'phone would go dead.

In the end we agreed everything in one of those tiny tourist hotels on the main square in Ostend.

'Sorry about Rio,' he kept grinning. He had four choux-choux down there, he told me. 'My femme goes and has a shave every now and then. It makes her happy. I have four choux-choux in Rio. It makes me happy.'

When I finally got there I could see why he kept grinning. Rio is not the only city I've been to which is built on a beach, but it's the only one where, wherever you are, everybody not only behaves but also dresses, or rather undresses, as if they were on the beach.

To give you the brief details, although nowhere near as brief as the Brazilians would. Never in my life have I seen so much naked flesh altogether at one time. From early morning. By bus, by taxi, in all shapes and sizes. Already dressed, or rather undressed, for the beach. Through clenched teeth, streams of perspiration and fogged up glasses I could just about see them streaking for Copacabana, Ipanema, Leblon, Botafogo in one thong after another. 'Merry crowds jostling and pitching and hustling/Small feet were pattering, rubber shoes a flapping/Little hands clapping and little tongues chattering.'

Having seen all the public parts of Rio, from the fountain in November 15 square, the oldest square in the city, to the Avenida Rio Branco with its offices and shops, there was no way I expected to see so many private parts as well. Rich or poor, it didn't seem to make any difference; it was as if they all wanted to outstrip each other. You couldn't tell who was filthy rich and who was just filthy. There was nothing but beach bums, everywhere.

The cariocas, the local name for Rio's inhabitants, have nothing to hide; they were so barefaced as to bare everything else as well. One or two old folk, with their sclerotic arteries pulsating away, looked as though the more they should hide the less they wanted to do so. And that's just the fellas I'm talking about. The Carmen Mirandas I daren't even think about until I take some more of those little white tablets. I'm at that age.

It was the string offensive to end all string offensives. I've never seen so little dental floss trying to cover so much space. And it wasn't even the thick dental floss. The only people not using it or, mad fools, keeping it for cleaning their teeth, were the security guards and porters lurking in the shadows, peering through iron bars, gazing vacantly through open windows, protecting everything that had been left behind. Most looked as though they would be rejected by even Group 4. But the élite, in square-shouldered suits and dark glasses, mostly working for Jewish companies, looked as though they had been packed off to Tel Aviv and trained by Mossad.

Most of the buildings they were guarding looked like Fort Knox. The houses were draped in iron railings. Apartment blocks were completely barricaded. Whole streets were blocked off and guarded by private security companies.

The crime rate is supposed to be so bad that nobody even wears the heavy duty key of the heavy duty safe in their hotel room any more, let alone a plastic St Christopher from last year's Christmas cracker.

Which I can't believe. My own view is that it's all been got up by the press. If Brazilians possess anything at all it is two bits of floss, or in many cases half a bit of floss, not even enough to clean one single tooth, two flip-flops and an ambition to renounce this minimum of worldly goods at the slightest opportunity.

The only violence I could imagine them suffering was from polyps attacking anything that moved – or rather, flopped. If there is a happy hunting ground for skin cancer it must be Copacabana, Ipanema, Leblon and Botafogo beaches.

Don't think I don't sympathize with them. At one stage, as I sat down completely drained and exhausted outside the heart clinic in the Rue Figuerida, just two deep breaths from Copacabana beach – a heart clinic on Copacabana beach! That's Brazilian town planning for you – to wipe the perspiration off my glasses for the umpteenth time, I seriously felt as though I was suffering from the effects of passive sunbathing. Polyps, I felt certain, were bursting out all over me.

How on earth does anyone even think of doing any work in this atmosphere? The answer, of course, is that they don't. Rio is an all-day siesta. Everything and everybody is relaxed.

Brazil is the fifth largest country in the world, the richest economy in South America and the ninth largest in the world. But business is down, way down. Nearly half the country's top three-hundred public companies are in the red.

The state oil company, Petrobas, is losing $10 million a day. The telephone service is falling from third world to fourth world levels. The most dangerous thing about walking through downtown Rio is not the police or their sworn enemies or the child gangs; it's businessmen getting so mad with the telephone not working for the vorteenth time that they hurl it through the window. There are more potholes in the roads than there is road. Enormous pits and caverns are all over the city, a reminder that the city went bust in the late 1980s and had to cancel its metro system. Government departments are often without electricity and water because they don't pay their bills.

Are they worried? Are they hell.

The world's biggest coffee producer since the 1760s, when a group of Capuchin monks began growing seeds smuggled in from what was French Guyana next door, they are now beginning to lose their grip. Their green gold is not so green any more. Guatemala, Antigua, Costa Rica, Kenya are all beginning to catch up. Even Brazil's bid to diversify away from coffee and into orange juice has hit problems.

Are they worried? They couldn't care a bean.

In other parts of South America, inflation is high. In Brazil, which obviously believes that the only thing that counts in life is size, it's stratospheric and still rising. Throughout the 1980s it careered along every year on triple figures. In 1992 it hit 1,149 percent. The last time I was there the cruzeiro was losing 1 percent of its value every 36 hours, 20 percent a month. If anyone had any assets, apart from their dental floss, they were revaluing them every twenty-four hours.

Were they worried? Were they hell.

Rich or poor, they're all millionaires. A Big Mac costs 200,000 cruzeiros. A hotel room overlooking Copacabana beach costs a mere one million cruzeiros. The cheapest new car? Well over one billion.

Buying anything in a shop takes hours, not because of the queues but because of all the noughts. The only way they can ring up the till is to divide the total into six or seven different items and ring in each one separately.

Get one of the little yellow Volkswagen taxis or fuscas, as they call them, which have one seat in the front for the driver and two in the back for passengers, and the driver spends more time winding the meter round and round to make sure it keeps pace with inflation than he does turning the wheel.

Nobody takes credit cards (apart from that little restaurant tucked away behind the Stock Exchange, but don't tell anyone). Companies that are still in business spend all their time checking no less than thirteen different price indices which are published daily, to make certain that if they have any time left to do any actual business they'll get back enough to more or less cover their costs. Quotes are invariably issued saying valid until 3.30 p.m. If invoices are not paid immediately they add 3,527 percent per day until it is. The aim is to get your money in as fast as possible and then make your real profits playing the money markets until you have no choice but to pay your poor hapless supplier. Like companies do all over the world – except that in Brazil you make big, big money playing the markets.

'Do people pay?'

'Of course. It's cheaper than waiting.'

'Honest?'

'How about that caipirinha di cachaca?'

Brazilian banks, as a result, are among the most efficient in the world. Money can be invested for a day at a time. Cheques are cleared within twenty-four hours or less. The Brazilian rich are also seriously rich. It is at the same time the richest, the most developed, and the poorest country on the continent. When it comes to technology they can stand alongside much of the developed world, but when it comes to hunger, poverty and disease they are amongst the poorest.

Brazil also boasts the world's biggest gap between rich and poor. The richest 20 percent of the population earn more than 26 times the poorest, an equality gap that does not exist even in Bangladesh or poor old Burkina Faso. Huddled in doorways, crowded into Rio Central railway station, asleep by the fountain in front of the pretty eighteenth-century Nostra Senhora da Candelaria church, scene of many society weddings, in Pope Pius X Square, dashing in and out of all the cafés where people sit drinking their *cafezinho*, tiny thimble-size cups of strong, sweet, black coffee so thick you can stand a spoon in it, and on practically every street corner running errands for the *bicheiros*, the gangs behind Rio's illegal *jogo do bicho* gambling racket, you see them: broken-down old men, gnarled old women, young boys, girls, but mostly children.

At night the lucky ones go back to their *favelas*, or shanties, which tumble down the mountain slopes surrounding Rio. But there are *favelas* and *favelas*. Some as almost as bad as the worst slums you'll find anywhere. There are no permanent buildings. The shacks are made of wood, scrap, sheets of corrugated iron, anything. There is no heating or lighting, apart from oil lamps, and no sewage system. Everywhere there is that fetid smell. Some families are so desperate, I was told, they boil the ink out of newspapers before eating the pulp.

Other *favelas*, high on the hills overlooking Rio, tucked away in tiny alleyways, are as luxurious as anything in avenue Foch in Paris. They have heating, lighting, running water, telephones, television and exquisite furniture.

Rich or poor, there's only two subjects Brazilians are interested in. The other is the latest soap. Mention the weather and you get the glass eye. Mention Reginaldo and his obsession with Yasmin and you're in. Talk about Pedra, *sobre* Pedra, and you're a friend for life. Say that *Doce do Amor* is the greatest thing since sliced coffee beans and the deal is yours, whatever the price.

I've never known a country so totally hooked on soaps. Okay, so you expect the girl at reception, the tea – oops, I mean coffee lady and probably most secretaries to be interested. But your rough, tough, hard-bitten, worldly-wise sophisticated businessman as well? Soaps are more important to Brazilians than the real world, especially as the off-screen antics of the stars are often more exciting than the on-screen antics. The star of one soap, *Body and Soul*, was actually murdered by her on-screen lover. The affair, which involved allegations of Satanism, seven days of masses and threats of

107

mob lynchings, practically eclipsed the ousting of one president and the installation of another.

'What's the idea of splitting Brazil in two? You keep Rio but get rid of everything to the north?' I asked someone.

'That Yasmin,' he purred across the table. 'Did you see those . . .?'

'I read somewhere that people are complaining that the richer, more populous south is subsidizing the poorer, larger north. Without them . . .'

'And when she said to him . . .'

'. . . you'd be a richer country . . .'

'. . . the look in her . . .'

'Nearly 90 percent literacy. Over 8 percent of households would have telephones. Life expectancy of over seventy-two years . . .'

'Oh mama mia,' he broke down sobbing and thumping the table for all he was worth. A crumbling economy, soaring inflation, worthless currency, corruption everywhere; that he could live with. But Yasmin on the telly, it was too much for him. He couldn't take any more.

So now I've got a problem: what do I do the next time I go to Rio? Do I do an Enoch Powell, dress up to the eyeballs and hang on like grim death to my wallet, briefcase, money belt and camera, never let my credit cards or traveller's cheques out of my sight, go nowhere near a cab, McDonald's or any churches, and definitely on no account change money let alone pick it up in the street?

Or do I stick a note on my stomach saying, 'You've already got my liver' and reach for the dental floss?

Buenos Aires

I don't care whether you are one of the world's top 10-goal aficionados, the other friend of Prince Charles, or a fan of Jilly Cooper, to me Buenos Aires is just like home: it's cold, it's damp, and whenever I'm there it's always raining. It's not even warm rain. It's like living in a shower with one of those newfangled all-in-one French taps jammed on freezing. By the end of a week of non-stop rain not only are you praying for webbed feet but you can sing and dance better than Gene Kelly. To say they get rain in Buenos Aires is like saying the Atlantic is a pond. R.S. Thomas says somewhere that rain is really the 'tumbling of water out of the sky'. In Buenos Aires, I tell you, it tumbles. They have monsoons for breakfast.

Okay, I admit it looks like Paris and sounds like Spain or Italy, but damn it, in spite of all that healthy-looking gloss and brilliantine it still actually feels like London. On a Monday night. In a recession.

The first thing that struck me about Buenos Aires, apart from the rain and the fact that everyone keeps looking at themselves in the mirror, was its size. I mean, I know Argentina is the eighth largest country in the world. On the map it looks as if it is slipping down the edge of South America like a long slimy finger pointing at something over the top of Rio Galagos. Which was pretty much the way the economy was then going as well. But that was just for a brief period of, say, fifty to sixty years, when it was racked by political turmoil

109

and almost continually soaring inflation, and auditioning for a role in an Andrew Lloyd Webber musical in order to pay off its debts.

Today they are through the worst of it. The Andrew Lloyd Webber role came off. They are now playing everywhere that *Cats* and *Phantom* and that Sunset thing are not playing. And the money is rolling in. As a result, they are now one of the good boys of South America. Inflation, having soared to 4,924 percent in 1989, has fallen steadily to 1,344 percent in 1990, 84 percent in 1991, to an unbelievably reasonable – for them – 12 percent in 1993 for consumer prices and an even more amazing 3 percent for wholesale prices. The reason: privatization. Every year the state-owned sector was costing US$8 billion in subsidies alone. Now subsidies are on their way out. The peso, their fourth currency in twenty years, is now linked one-to-one with the US dollar.

In the pre-Andrew Lloyd Webber days, Juan Domingo Peron used to rain down scorn on America and everything American. Today America, everyone agrees, is 'the greatest country in the world, like it or not'. To be friends with the Americans is practically their sole objective. They were the only South American country to send troops and warships to Kuwait. They sent troops to help the United Nations in Croatia. The president, Carlos Menem, even used to lose regularly at tennis to George Bush, which shows what lengths they will go to. The basket case is now the wealthiest country in South America. Which, if nothing else, goes to prove how much money you can make being in an Andrew Lloyd Webber musical.

All those years I was crying for Argentina, I used to imagine that Buenos Aires was like, say, Lisbon or Madrid. Maybe just big enough for a decent tango. No way; it's enormous. Bigger than London, bigger than Tokyo, not quite as big as Seoul. Most of it, of course, is sprawl, although it is genuine up-and-down Argentinian sprawl. Many flats and office blocks look like cheap imitations of the worst 1950s London County

Council tower block architecture, if that's the right word. Some office blocks have literally been stuck straight on to the end of other office blocks, or in one case, a church.

The parts that are not sprawl, however, are spectacular and very French. There are huge squares like the Plaza de Mayo where in the bad old days when it obviously didn't rain, on the balcony of the Casa Roseda, the Pink House, Evita what's-her-name used to make all those passionate speeches. The Avenida Belgrano is always very elegant. With its big houses and huge apartments it reminds me of Quay Branly beside the Seine, the kind of arrondissement where you bump into French Presidents on their way home at three in the morning when it's raining fleurs-de-lis.

Inside, out of the rain, I imagine, are the beautiful people who spend their lives pouting and preening in front of mirrors and trying not to spend too much time accidentally catching glimpse of themselves in the windows. And that's just the men.

During the day, I like Recoleta with its tree-lined streets, elegant mansions and fabulous restaurants. During the night, or rather early morning, Corrientes, the street that never sleeps, looks Spanish or Italian but sounds definitely Buenos Aires, with los tangos being belted out of every doorway the way Andrew Lloyd Webber's original girlfriend used to belt out her speeches on the balcony. There are two theories about the patent leather hairstyles, perpetual broad grins and impossibly tight pants the snazzas wear. One is that the tango was originally born – if that's the right word – in the brothels of Buenos Aires, so what do you expect? The other is that it used to rain non-stop even in those days. By the time the snazzas had run from the taxi to the door of the brothel, stopping only three times to admire themselves in shop windows, their pants had shrunk. Hence the silly grin. To me this means two things: first, Argentine brothels must have been the most inefficient in the world if all the snazzas could then do to amuse themselves was to dance with other snazzas, and second, the snazzas only started dancing with women because the other snazzas stopped going to the brothels because they got fed up dancing with other snazzas. Maybe there's a moral there. Whatever the social and economic significance of the tango, when the bars and clubs in Corrientes start blasting it out you can practically hear the hand-clapping and foot-stamping all the way to Rio Galagos.

Drive around the Plaza Dorego, on the other hand, or stroll around La Buca, the working-class district, with all its multi-coloured shops and houses and noisy cantinas, and not only is it much quieter, it is also more Spanish. Wander along the Avenida de Mayo and drop into the Café Toroni, the oldest café in the city, and you are in Italy; the old-fashioned Italy of musty old rooms, leather armchairs and high ceilings that you still occasionally find hidden away in cathedrals, abbeys and the Travellers' Club in Pall Mall. One corner of the café is definitely Spain and Italy. Well, to be precise, it's the Opus Dei Spanish/Italian world of medieval loyalties, Machiavellian honesty and P2 accountability. Two old Italians are sipping their cappuccinos and muttering away in *cocoliche*, the original Spanish as spoken by the early Italian settlers and founder members.

One of the dons gives me his card. 'Give me a call,' he says. 'We must talk.' Old habits die hard.

The Avenida 9 de Julio, the main street which runs through the centre of the city, is about twice as wide and three times as long as the Champs Elysées, with about five times as many cafés, bars and restaurants. Like the Champs Elysées it is also packed with traffic. Not Argentine traffic. But Paris traffic. Giant forty-ton trucks race three abreast down the middle of the boulevard, I mean avenida, refusing to pull across let alone let anyone else overtake. There are roadworks and road ups and downs and diversions everywhere. There are also long delays and traffic jams for no reason at all.

The cafés and bars seemed to be crowded with playboy-gauchos as slippery as iguanas, with names like Pepe and

Ernesto and Guillermo who, when they are not playing polo or acting out Jilly Cooper's fantasies, are busy trying not to look at themselves in the mirror, or trying to look like Englishmen. From some reason Burberry sports jackets, Marks & Spencer blazers and grey flannel slacks seem to be the in thing, old chap. All of them are sipping coffee and nibbling medialunas – Argentine croissants – and poring over the small ads looking for flats which, after polo and before the tango, seems to be their second largest national obsession.

With so many bars and restaurants to choose from, I once asked a portenos, a local Buenos Aires resident, how you can tell the good ones.

'Bullocks.'

'I beg your pardon,' I mumbled.

'Bullocks. Dirty great big ones. Outside the best restaurants. You can't . . .'

'Excuse me, but are we talking about . . .'

'. . . miss them.'

'. . . the same thing?'

In Paris they are a little more discreet. Perhaps a restrained menu here, maybe the name of the chef there – in small letters, of course, There might even be the oh-so-subdued reference to a Michelin star or three or four. In Buenos Aires if you want to know what they are serving in a restaurant, it is actually standing there outside. In the rain. Life-size. On four legs. Staring you in the eye, daring you to come in and sink your teeth into all his darling little sons and daughters, who have all been slaughtered because you won't eat tofu salad and soya bean roulade.

Stroll along almost any street in the centre of town and it's like judging day at the Smithfield Show organized by Madame Tussauds. One evening, just off the Avenida Carlos Pellegrini, I counted so many cattle I felt like the Marlboro Man at the start of the annual trek north. On the corner was an enormous lifesize Hereford bull, just glaring at me. In the rain. Across the road were two more, one black, the other white, standing either side of the entrance. In the rain. Looking me straight in the eye. Instead of checking the menu, I found I was checking the cattle. Too much fat on that one. This one's a bit thin in the rump, could do with a bit more feeding up.

When we kept cattle ourselves we used to buy them in as three- or four-day-old calves and bring them on until they were around eighteen months or two years. I always remember one little calf, whom I called Ryan's Daughter. (At the time John Whitaker was winning all the show-jumping competitions on Ryan's Son, who always threw in a couple of high kicks whenever he won a competition, and it seemed silly not to correct the balance.) When she was tiny I taught her to eat out of my hand, which is unusual for a calf. When she was in the pen with the others or out in the field she would run up to me as soon as she saw me or when I called out to her. I would give her a pat, stroke her and make a big fuss of her. She would jump up and down with delight. Which was fine, until she started getting bigger and bigger and bigger. In the end, it was practically dangerous. I would go out into the fields. Somehow she would spot me. Then there would be half a ton of black beef thundering towards me like a centurion tank. As if that wasn't risky enough, she would insist on a pat and a stroke. Which again was all right until she started leaping up and down with pleasure. Not being a trained matador, it was an interesting experience. Many's the time I wondered which of us was going to survive to tell the tale. Eventually, like all the others, she had to go back to market to be sold on before meeting her final destiny. I never had any qualms about it. But seeing the actual fully-grown, stuffed animals standing there outside a restaurant, looking at you with their big, sad, trusting eyes, was a bit too much.

For a second, I could appreciate how lobsters must feel swimming around in those tanks in restaurants dreading they are the next in line or, I suppose, on the line. I was in a restaurant once in New England when Ma, Pa and the kids came in. You should have heard the screams when Pa chose the lobster he wanted from the tank and had it killed – oops, I mean prepared, on the table in front of him.

Faced with all those lifesize relatives of poor old Ryan's Daughter, I did what any soppy, soft-hearted animal lover would do. I averted my eyes and hurried past. Into the restaurant.

Inside I quickly realized they were not worth even the slightest pang of conscience. In Paris the restaurants are charming, elegant, inviting. Some are even frivolous and frothy, especially after a couple of bottles of champagne. But then, after a couple of bottles of champagne even Algiers would appear frivolous. Depending on the champagne, that is. In Buenos Aires the restaurants are about as exciting as a dripping raincoat. They're functional; they're dedicated to maintaining the country's reputation as the world's leading producer of beef. Go to virtually any restaurant in Paris and you feel as though you are indulging yourself. Go to a restaurant in Buenos Aires and you feel you are there solely to contribute to the country's beef production statistics.

'Señor?'

'I'll have a . . .'

'Señor.'

'Rare to medium.'

'Señor.'

'With . . .'

'All included, señor.'

On the way out, I swear the big black Friesian at the door took my name, breed and herd number to send to Ryan's Daughter's descendants.

Buenos Aires hotels are in a class of their own. The worst class in the school. They're not like your typical bland international hotel. They're not like hotels in France, Egypt or even in Turkey. No way do the staff want to make your life easier or more comfortable. In fact, they actually hate people –

especially visitors. No way do the bar staff want to serve you They hate alcohol and all its works and pomps. No way are the restaurant staff going to give you anything to eat. They're all anorexics and think everybody else should be as well.

My room was big and drab, like an old-fashioned railway hotel after it has been modernized by British Rail. None of the doors or cupboards – not wardrobes – would close because they had so many layers of thick cream paint on them. There were no coathangers. But, fair's fair, there was hardly any light either so I didn't notice that the rail at the top of the cupboard was also missing. The bathroom not only had those rare antique toothbrush-holder tiles and heavy silver radiators, which of course didn't work, but an antique hand waterpump for filling the bath and flushing the toilet. It was like a Blackpool hotel before the war. The Boer War.

So it's my fault, for always wanting to stay in local hotels rather than the international chains which are the same wherever you are. But Buenos Aires is one city that has almost made me change my mind. All the hotels I've stayed in there look as though they were built to honour the first-ever visit of Queen Victoria to Argentina. But when Albert told her what his cousins were saying about the weather even her sense of duty deserted her and she cancelled the trip.

One morning I managed to pump enough water to have a halfway decent bath. To pump up enough for a shower was too much to contemplate. The problem then was getting rid of the water. I pulled the plug. Nothing happened. I dressed. By the time I was ready to go down for breakfast the water had just begun to trickle out. I left the room, waited eight-and-a-half minutes for the lift operator to wind himself up to me on the fourth floor, went down and had a typically English breakfast: cold, stodgy, outrageously expensive.

It was raining, surprise, surprise. I asked reception if they could get me a taxi. The manager was wearing a Burberry sports jacket and standing under one of those old English hunting prints.

'No, sir, we cannot get taxi. It's raining.'

'Thank you,' I smiled. 'Have a nice day.'

No reply.

On my first visit, I arrive at the airport and go up to one of the girls at the official tourist assistance desk.

'Excuse me, could you . . .?'

A shrug. That's all. She didn't even look up. I could have been at home.

Taxi drivers never, ever get out of their cosy heated cabs to help with your luggage. They won't even swing across the road to drop you outside your hotel or the office you're visiting. You have to stand in the pouring rain waiting for a gap in the traffic before you splash your way across six lanes to the other side. Pure British.

Then, looking and feeling like a drowned English rat, you're met by a short, sharp Versace frock and ushered into the presence of a jazzy Burberry suit with a Hermes tie and a suntan as black as the best Schneider riding boots.

'Just like home, is it?' he neighs. 'So pleased.'

I once got a cab just off Carlos Pelligrini. Like most big cities, Buenos Aires has two airports, one for international flights, one for domestic. Nothing complicated. But I learnt a long time ago that everything is complicated. I told the driver I was going to Montevideo, next door in Uruguay.

'Which airport?' I asked him.

'Yes.'

'International (Esceza) or domestic (Aeroparque)?'

'Yes.'

'I'm going to Montevideo, Uruguay.'

'Yes.'

'That's international. Okay?'

'Okay.'

We drove for nearly an hour in the pouring rain, through flooded streets to the international airport (Esceza) and, you've guessed it, for some reason I cannot understand international flights to Uruguay go from domestic (Aeroparque).

In case you think it's me, I once saw another Englishman asking the way to the American Express office which, as everybody knows, is in the Plaza San Martin.

'American Express,' he was saying. 'You must know it.'

'No.'

'Express Americano.'

'No.'

Then, chugging round and round in circles, he was screaming, 'Yankee Choo-Choo. Yes?'

I go to change my airline ticket.

'We open at nine. You wait a minute. Yes?'

Was that a German accent?

'Yes, of course,' I say meekly. I walk up and down in front of the desk where everybody is sitting waiting for the magic hour. I smile broadly at each of them. I look at my watch. I think of taking it off, shaking it and putting it to my ear. But the German accent is looking right through me so I give in. Then, on the dot of nine, 'Good morning, sir. We are now open. Can I help you?'

I clamber over the security fencing to get to the counter. Nobody says a word about it. Obviously that's meant to be removed at 9.05.

I once stayed in a typical modern Victorian hotel just off Carlos Pellegrini. One morning I had spent so much time getting soaked fighting to get taxis, desperately trying to persuade them to take me where I wanted to go and then finding everywhere was closed when I got there, that I decided to spend the afternoon trying not to get soaked by running in and out of the secondhand bookshops along the Avenida de Mayo. Now you know and I know that I probably wasn't going to buy three volumes of *The Mystical Doctrine of St John of the Cross* in Spanish, but as soon as I even dared think of looking at the cover of a book, the old soldier assistants would hustle along, push me out of the way and, though the books were all standing to attention, start straightening them up again. For which I was duly grateful. It enabled

118

me to formulate the second Biddlecombe law of book titles: British and American book titles run top to bottom of the spine; everybody else's books run bottom to top. Who says a rainy day is a wasted day in Buenos Aires?

Some people say the Argentinians are like that because they genuinely admire the English. In spite of Mrs Thatcher and you-know-what, they look up to us and for some crazy reason want to be like us. Ignoring people, treating them like dirt, providing little or no service, is their way of being British, and you must admit they have a point. On the other hoof, it could be because, like the English, Argentinians are much happier dealing with horses than with human beings. And nobody is happier or better at dealing with horses, especially in the super, smooth, deluxe world of high-goal polo. Not for nothing are they known in snobby English polo circles as 'hired assassins'. In fact, in spite of some recent interruptions in play, many seriously snobby English English, as opposed to English Argentinian people who all seem to be called Tarquin or Julian, still can't make up their minds between supporting Mrs Thatcher or the legendary Argentinian players like the Heguys, Pieres and Gracidas families. Me? I think I'd prefer to support the Heguys, Pieres and Gracidas.

Only twice in my life, however, have I come close to playing polo. No way am I a Guillermo, an Ernesto or even an Adolfo, let alone, heaven help me, a Tarquin or a Julian. But I can see myself strapped in all the leathers, hurtling across Cowdray Park, Palm Beach Polo Club or even Galen Weston's Place, at 40 mph, a big stick in one hand, three or four other ponies bearing down on me, sticks flailing everywhere, hoofs thundering towards the goal. The Brigadier would be wondering whether he could persuade me to join Henryk de Kwiatkowski's 22-goal US team; Omega waiting to sign me up for a sponsorship deal, and Jilly Cooper desperately trying to get my telephone number – for research purposes, of course.

The nearest I've come to it, however, was quick lesson standing on a kitchen chair in Windsor Great Park one

Saturday morning trying to practise the swing. For some reason I can't remember, I was with a less-than-pukka group of Americans. While I was swinging the club, or trying to, as the chair kept getting in the way, and dreaming of another night sipping champagne in Annabel's with all the other 10-goal aficionados, our instructor was trying to explain the rules.

'We have four players, all on horseback. The aim is to score a goal.'

'You mean . . .?' drawled what sounded like a New York accent.

'No, the pony doesn't have to kick the ball,' our instructor continued in his best, clipped, Guards Polo Club accent. 'You have to hit the ball into the other net.' A pause. 'While on the pony.'

My chair moved and hit the club again. How it kept moving and ruining my perfect swing I do not know.

'Now, number one is your scorer. He is supposed to hang around the other team's goal so that he can score the goals. Number two is the tackler; he is supposed to get the ball off the other team. Number three is then supposed to collect the ball and hit it down to number one to score. Understood?'

'What does number four do?' said another American accent, straight out of Kojak.

'Number four usually owns the team, pays the bills, picks up the tab for the champagne and has first choice—'

'We don't wish to know that,' drawled, from the back of beyond, a very liberated female voice which sounded Southern discomforted.

Hey. I did it. The chair stood still. Guards Polo Club, here I – damn. It moved again.

'Each chukka lasts seven minutes. There are between four and six chukkas per match. Between each chukka . . .'

'That's when you get to meet the—' began the New York accent.

'We don't all share your . . .' said the great liberator.

Wow. That was a good swing. So was that. And so was—

'So why do they dress up like ice hockey players?' said the Kojak voice.

'It's a tough sport. The ponies can be going at 30 to 40 mph. The ball is probably being whacked backwards and forwards at over 100 mph.'

And another. And another. Gee if I can control a kitchen chair like this, what can I do with a – damn. It moved again.

'So how do you rate a good player?' asked the liberator.

'Beginners start at minus two. The best are ten.'

'You mean, we do all this and we don't get to kill anything?' said the New York accent.

After that, I can't quite remember what happened except that my handicap must have plummeted immediately to minus $63\frac{1}{4}$.

The other time I came close to playing polo was in Accra, Ghana. I was staying at the big, luxury Lonrho guesthouse on the edge of town. The captain of the local polo club, Mohammed, was a regular visitor. He was the biggest bicycle importer in the country, but I never worked out the connection with Lonrho. One evening while we were in training for some pretty serious drinking after winning the Gold Cup, he asked if I would like to play a couple of chukkas with their local team. I jumped at the idea. But nothing came of it. My theory is that Guillermo, Ernesto and Adolfo got on to him. They were scared of the competition.

Once more into the monsoon, dear raincoat. Once more.

I've known guys who can make cabs materialize out of thin air. Me, I'm running up and down the street for weeks on end, darting from one side to the other; I'm leaping around the corner and back again just in case one is trying to slip by unnoticed. These guys come out, languidly raise their hand, and there it is, right in front of them. They open the door, collapse inside and they're off. I'm still running up and

121

down like a demon possessed. Especially when it's raining.

Today was obviously going to be another one of those days. An old lady who looks as though she could be Eva Peron's grandmother with articular windgalls, if not an acute case of the bog spavins, is hobbling up and down the centre of Avenida Pte Roque Saenz Peria for ten minutes, three streams of traffic hurtling past on either side, looking for a taxi. Nobody takes any notice. Then suddenly a taxi pulls up outside the bank opposite her. A high-goal polo player invented by Jilly Cooper grabs the door and leaps in with the greasy smoothness of a gallon of brilliantine. He is obviously off to Tigre Delta, the swish end of town where I'm told they practise by shooting goals through Henry Moore statues. Eva Peron's grandmother throws herself in front of the on-coming traffic. But in vain. The polo player has scored another easy goal. If that's the way they treat Eva Peron's grandmother, what hope have I got?

I decide to walk to Plaza San Martin. I walk up towards the Obelisk in Avenida 9 de Julio. The whole street is flooded. A bus hurtles by. I am drenched from head to dripping toe. Obviously his brother is the one who drives the 159 from Streatham Hill to Oxford Circus.

I splash my way across Esmeralda. The paving stones sink beneath my feet. I see a taxi turning the corner at Suipacha. It's already taken. I hop, skip and jump along the pavement. The next street is closed. They've been digging the road up now for three months. I have to go to the next turning. That means an extra twelve minutes. Already I'm soaked. What's triple pneumonia on top of double pneumonia? A taxi shoots past and draws up in front of another bank. I leap for it. Another polo player, obviously wavering on a 10-goal handi-cap, emerges from the dry office opposite and leaps imme-diately inside. Obviously going to one of those courses on corruption run by Buenos Aires University. What hope have I? London taxi drivers don't take any notice when I am jumped; why should an Argentinian driver be any different? I turn right into Carlos Pellegrini. By now it's raining cats, dogs and a couple of polo ponies.

Suddenly I think of Tony Curtis in *Some Like it Hot*. 'Is water polo dangerous?' somebody asks him. 'I should say so,' he drawls. 'Why, the last time I played, I had three ponies drown right under me.'

Three? This rain is enough to drown three whole teams of high-grade polo ponies. Multi-coloured buses flood by. Cars swish by. Every taxi ever built zooms past. I stumble across Tucuman. By now everything is wringing: my raincoat, my suit, my shoes. I swim into Avenida Cordoba. The whole avenida is full of demented Argentinian polo ponies. Some are pawing the ground, others are cantering up and down, swinging round on a one-peso bit, neighing and whinnying like mad and cantering back again. They all have briefcases; they are all dripping with sweat and flaring their nostrils. They all want a cab. I take my place, like any newcomer, at the edge of the herd. Suddenly down the street comes the yellow roof of a cab. The herd becomes electric, like a group of stallions scenting a mare on heat. One of the oldest stallions gallops across four lanes of fast-moving traffic into the middle of the road. He must be at least a Gran Oficial del Order de Libertador San Martin or I'm a drowned rat. He rears up on his hind legs, his arms flailing wildly. The yellow roof becomes a taxi. His arms flail even wilder. There's a red light in the window – it's for hire. He's practically six inches off the ground. The taxi flashes its lights and begins to pull up. The old stallion drops his arms, bends down to pick up his briefcase. Suddenly, from the other side of the street, one of the young bloods rockets across four lanes of traffic and, just as the taxi is about to stop, swings open the offside door, shoots inside – and the taxi hits 70 kph before the old stallion has put hand on briefcase.

Now all hell breaks loose. The old stallion stands in the middle of the road, roaring and bellowing. He knows he has fought his last fight. From now on he's just an ex-Gran Oficial

123

del Order del Libertador San Martin. The herd must find a new Gran Oficial. All that's left for him is the clubby world of leather armchairs and cigar smoke. All along the pavement, every soaking, dripping body turns on every other soaking, dripping body. The fight for the next cab is on. If that's the way their Gran Oficials are treated, what hope is there for the rest of us? What hope for me? I've only done it on a kitchen chair.

The rain is still coming down in straight lines. If we can't get a cab now what's it going to be like in five minutes, ten minutes, an hour, when even more people are looking for cabs? And more nerves are frayed. And more tempers are— Quick! There's a— No. False alarm. It just looked like a cab. All the same, fifty-three people tried to get inside it. Is that . . .? Another false alarm. There's one! Hell. No red light. It's already taken. The herd settles down to wait. Some paw the ground; others gallop up and down the edge; a few old warhorses stand to attention, sniffing the air, hoping to detect a cab before the others. Still the rain keeps coming. Still the four lanes this way and four lanes that way keep ploughing on with not a—

Quick. There's one. A yellow roof. Is it a taxi? It's a taxi. There's a red light in the window. It's— Everybody is on their toes. This is the one. Probably the last one in the world. The old warhorses band together and move across, literally across, the road. They're weaving and dodging between the traffic, flapping their hands. The young stallions are cantering along the pavement. The yellow roof is getting nearer. Two-and-a-half blocks away. Still nobody has jumped it. Two blocks away. Its light is still on. Cars and trucks are swerving all over the street to avoid the old warhorses splashing down on it at 37.3 kph.

The stallions are now into a gallop. Pedestrians are being knocked sideways, umbrellas are rolling loose on the pavement, two old ladies are screaming. I'm hobbling along behind, eager for the action, hoping against hope if I wave my passport the driver will never have heard of Mrs Thatcher and you-know-what and have pity on the under-handicapped. One-and-a-half blocks away. Still it's free. Three old war-horses look as though they are going to have to fight to the—

Then it happens. A swift young thoroughbred is out of the bank building opposite, straight through the traffic into the taxi before it even stops. It swerves violently to the right. It's gone. The warhorses ... I can't stand it any more. I collapse into the nearest bar. I've had it with Buenos Aires. The rain. Taxis.

'When do you close?' I can remember asking the barman after my zwelf glass of Scheider.

'We are open always,' he says.

When I am thrown out three hours later, it is still raining. The Avenidas are now full of empty taxis. I walk back to the hotel in the pouring rain just to spite them.

It took ages getting through to the old don's number. First I couldn't get a line. Then I could get a line but no ring. Then finally it rang. And rang. And rang. And rang. And rang. I thought, it'd be quicker to—

The 'phone answered. A girl mumbled something.

'Scusi. Is that ...?'

'Moment.'

Then on came Nat King Cole, who for ten minutes, while I waited for the girl to come back, told me again and again that I was 'unforgettable'. Eventually, just as old Nat was beginning to sound a trifle insincere, she was there.

'Scusi, is—'

She was gone again. Just one more Unforgettable, I was thinking, just one more, and—

'Si, si. No problem. You come here. Si.'

He wanted to meet. His address was Avenida Eva Peron. Could I come across?

'Si. No problem.'

I haven't been brainwashed by Andrew Lloyd Webber, unlike the rest of the world, but I must admit I thought Avenida Eva Peron must be somewhere in the middle of Buenos Aires. Somewhere near that balcony. Not on your life. It's way out in the polo sticks, in the middle of nowhere, on the way to a town called Moron. Which says something about either Eva Peron or Andrew Lloyd Webber.

It was raining again. After a thousand battles, hundreds of fights to the death and seven hours running up and down every street in Buenos Aires getting soaked to the skin, I finally got a cab.

'Avenida Eva Peron,' I muttered casually as I poured myself into what was already a fish tank at the back of the cab.

The driver gave me that look that said he'd never heard of Andrew Lloyd Webber either,

'Avenida Eva Peron,' I mumbled, in my best Spanish accent.

He crunched the cab into gear and headed off – towards another taxi to ask if they had heard of Andrew Lloyd Webber's friend. And then towards another. And another. And another. Nobody had heard of Avenida Eva Peron.

In the end I started jumping out of the cab myself in the still pouring rain – Buenos Aires taxi drivers, like London taxi drivers, never leave their taxis – and asking everybody who was still out swimming in the streets. Eventually I hit lucky. An old lady thought she knew where it was. The driver clapped his hands, stroked his moustache and we were off. Not towards the centre of the city, but in the opposite direction. Towards Patagonia for all I knew.

'Hey!' I shouted. 'Avenida—'

'Avenida Eva Peron,' the driver shouted back, jabbing his finger vaguely in the direction we were hurtling.

The big stores and shops and offices quickly gave way to the drab, miserable suburbs you find anywhere. It could have been any one of a dozen countries. There were squat, square blocks of flats stuck on to other squat square blocks. Everywhere was becoming unkempt, scruffy, dirty. Bus shelters were collapsing all over the pavement. Awnings were falling, twisted, from upstairs windows. Cars were dying by the side of the road. Patches of grass and heaps of rubbish were piled up everywhere. Nothing looked as though it had seen so much as the outside of a tin of paint since Eva first clambered onto that balcony. There was graffiti everywhere. Not even this rain could wash it off.

Now we swung off the road, swept down a slope and landed in the middle of an enormous lake virtually covering the road. The engine spluttered, a burst of steam shot out from the bonnet. Then the engine just died – like that; no warning. In the middle of this enormous lake. In the middle of nowhere. In the still pouring rain.

Deliberately staring me in the face, laughing at me, was a poster saying Unidad e Accion.

Was I going to get out, put on my diving suit and push? No way. Should I start screaming obscenities at the cab driver for this and everything that happened during the Falklands War? Oops. I didn't say that. Didn't even think it. I just sat there. Smiling.

The driver turned the ignition key. Nothing. And again. Nothing. And again. Less than nothing. Keep on doing that, I thought, and even I with my limited knowledge of cars know that you'll kill the battery if you haven't drowned it already. And another turn of the key. Nothing. Another turn. If this guy continues we're ... A slight cough. Could there still be life in the ...? Another turn. Another cough. Groups of people appeared from nowhere and stood around the edge of the lake. Typical, I thought. Waiting to claim the salvage. Another cough. Another turn of the ... Steam from the ... Another – and – cough – the engine miraculously was turning. It was running. It was— We were saved. Even with a flat battery, we were moving. We were swimming ... making waves. We were out of the lake. Water was pouring out of the car, but we were on dry land again. Or at least, compared to where we had been. And we were moving. How it happened I don't know. I honestly thought I was there for ever. But we were on our way again.

We coughed, spluttered, swam the rest of the way. Avenida Eva Peron, as isolated as the old lady herself towards the end of her reign of terror, was in the middle of nowhere. The office was another straight-up-and-straight-down building in a non-descript avenida that would make a Korean street market seem the centre of the world. All the drains were blocked. Water was everywhere. But only up to my ankles, not my neck. It felt, I swear, as if in Buenos Aires it even rains inside the buildings. I was absolutely soaked to the skin. Again.

What's more, as you've guessed, the old don wasn't there. It was pure Spanish/Italian/Argentine.

That's it, I decided, I've had enough. Back to the hotel. Except we can't get back to the hotel. Now they have dug the road up. I climb out near the Obelisk on Avenida 9 de Julio. It is still raining. I take a short cut back to the hotel. More roads have been dug up. There's mud everywhere. The water is flowing into great gaping trenches and cascading out the other side in a sea of mud. I splash through the mud.

Inside the hotel, I discover the faxes I left to be sent have not been sent. The lift is not working; the flooding is affecting the electricity. I climb five flights of stairs. Inside the room nothing has been made up. The bath is close to overflowing with everybody else's bath water in Argentina. I throw the suitcase on the bed. Wet or dry I'm throwing everything that moves into it. With the exception of the brilliantine and the mirror. The Argentines need them more than I do.

I put on my raincoat, grab my umbrella, look again at the bath. It is now overflowing. Water is pumping into it from the plughole.

Okay Buenos Aires, you've beaten me. I've had enough. If it's like this here, I might as well be at home.

Santiago

I'm sorry, but I'm afraid I just can't take Chile seriously. For me, it's torture. There's something about it that makes me, well, nervous.

It's a funny shape. It's long: it has over 5,000 miles of coast stretching all the way from deserts in the north to the frozen waste of Tierra del Fuego in the south. It's thin. Some people say it looks as if Brazil and Argentina are trying to push it into the Pacific. Other people, I don't know why, say it's like a long, thin, highly polished jackboot. Most important, it's too long to fit on to Chilean television. For weather reports, they have to cut it up into three chunks. Which, when we live in an age dominated by the media, could be dangerous.

Santiago is virtually mountain-locked, way up in the Andes – a crazy place to put a city, especially with all that coastline. Flying in is a bit like flying over Southern California. There is nothing but scrub-covered mountains. Then rows and rows of neat, pleasant little houses, with swimming pools, and Mercedes and Range Rovers parked outside.

The airport, however, is typical South America; hot and slow. There are more dogs lying around in the sun than there are passengers. The place seems empty. Maybe that's why Chile is known as the Great Britain of South America.

Once you've landed, you've got a thirty-kilometre drive into town, on the other side of a mountain. You're driving along. You can't see the tops of the mountains. All the houses have satellite dishes and seem to be called Bellavista. Everything is parched and burnt. The occasional horse is tethered to the occasional tree. A Mercedes overtakes us, wheels wobbling dangerously. This is not the Chile I imagined. Then you turn a corner and there's nothing but vineyards. Argentina might produce more – it's the world's fourth largest producer – but Chile, I reckon, makes the best wine in South America. Especially red wine. The best for my money is Antigua Reserva, made from Cabernet Sauvignon, by the Cousino Maccal.

Past the vineyards, past a couple of factories, then into Santiago, which again is nothing like South America. Everything is pleasant, clean, up-to-date. There's none of the usual hustle and bustle: no traffic jams, no blaring of horns; nobody selling things in the street, no beggars; no loudspeakers belting out non-stop sambas; no shacks or shanty towns; nobody living or dying on the street. Everybody is smart, polite, well-dressed. Mobile phones are running around all over the place. Offices are pleasant. Shops are crowded.

I finish my meetings and wander round the government buildings. I watch the soldiers outside the president's office. In the Playa de Armes, the main square, people are sitting around in the sunshine. Nobody is wearing a sombrero.

Sometimes, they say, even though he is no longer president, General Pinochet suddenly decides to review his troops. From nowhere the Playa is smothered with his special forces. Everyone else then dashes for cover, a safe house or the airport. He comes out in full-dress military uniform dripping with so many coloured stripes he looks as though he is suffering from medal fatigue. He walks up and down, gives them a big salute and disappears again. Within seconds everything is back to normal.

Maybe I'm going crazy; maybe I've been drinking too many pisco sours, some killer Chilean cocktail, but suddenly I find myself wandering around talking to myself, asking myself questions and giving myself answers.

So what's wrong?

I don't know. It's not what I expected. It's nothing like Buenos Aires or Rio.

You mean, it doesn't have that carnival atmosphere?

No way.

What about the people? Are they friendly?

They seem okay. Very relaxed, very pleasant. Maybe a bit reserved. They're pretty unusual, though. They seem to like the English. There's a big English church in Santiago. Whenever they want to raise money, it seems funny, but they go to London rather than Frankfurt.

So it's pretty relaxed?

Except when the special forces are on the street.

You mean, the government is jumpy?

No, it's not the government. It's Pinochet. Seems he's a law unto himself.

How come?

Well, he was president. He seized power back in 1973. He said he wanted to save Chile from the Communists.

Did he?

It depends who you talk to. Half the world says he was talking nonsense, there was no real threat from the Communists, he just wanted to get rid of them. And he did. Over 1,000 people just disappeared between 1973 and 1990 when he gave up. The other half says that, whatever the reason, he handed the country back to the civilians and he handed it back in far better shape. He was the first to introduce free-market economic policies in South America. Chile is in much better shape than before. Trouble is, he insisted on remaining head of the army.

So, he just likes playing soldiers. What about the city? Big? Small? Old? New?

It's an open, bright, modern city, a bit like a mini-Boston in the sunshine. There are nice leafy suburbs, big mansions, lots of exclusive condominiums. In Parque Arauco, the rich end of town, there are shopping centres as luxurious as any you'll see in California. Wealthy Chileans – or are they Californians? – drift in and out. They stop, they look, they buy. They seem to do that in every shop they go to. A live jazz band is playing in the background. La Victoria, the poor end of town, is dusty streets, modern houses. More basic than the poverty you see in some countries.

Everything is very neat, clean, pleasant. You see nuns with long blue headdresses saying their prayers in the open air. Everybody is relaxed, wandering around, sitting down, chatting in the sunshine. But no sombreros. There are lots of fountains, statues of men on horseback, flowerbeds. Oh yes, I nearly forgot; all over the place you see Banco O'Higgins, which to me is hilarious. I mean, you're in the middle of nowhere. You're in the foothills of the Andes. You turn a corner. There staring at you is Banco O'Higgins. It's crazy. Then gradually all over the place you see O'Higgins on everything else as well. There are ironmongers called Ferreteria O'Higgins. There is even a street called Libertador O'Higgins. It's crazy.

Cafés? Restaurants? Bars?

Sure, there are a million restaurants. French, Italian, Spanish, Mexican.

Any Indonesian restaurants?

No. Funny that. I didn't come across any.

Probably because they were scared in case anyone ordered a nasi Goreng.

I beg your pardon?

A nasi goreng.

I thought that's what you said.

Go to the opera?

I don't know about that; but last time I was there, Madonna was in town. Everybody, but everybody went to see her. I was told there were lots of white faces in the audience.

You mean, because of all that leather gear, the boots . . .?

What do you think?

So what are they like as businessmen?

Thanks, I suppose, to Pinochet, Chile's managers are red hot. Having licked their own country into shape they are now in demand all over South America. In retailing, they are setting up hi-tech supermarkets complete with bar-code scanners all over Argentina. In power, Chilean companies now provide most of Buenos Aires with electricity. In oil, they are exploiting the deposits on the Argentine side of the Magellan Straits. In gas, they have set up a US$1 billion joint venture with Argentina which will give them 8 cubic metres of gas a day.

'How come you're so good?' I asked one top manager in his office at the back of the Playa de Armes.

'We know the scene. We've been doing it longer than anybody else.'

Mrs Thatcher's favourite think tank, the Adam Smith Institute, goes on and on about the way to privatize state enterprise. I wondered how the Chileans do it.

'Simple,' he grinned. 'So many state payrolls are over-inflated with cousins and aunts and uncles of the boss. The first thing we do is get every employee to get their own wages in person. You'd be amazed how many don't turn up.'

So what's the problem? What makes you so nervous?

All right then, if you want me to spell it out. I thought it would be more, you know, G-E-R-M-

You mean German. You mean you thought it would be some kind of Wagnerian monstrosity designed by Levi Riefenstahl in between stringing together yet another documentary on the 1936 Olympics. All heroic works of architecture, statues of strapping young men. The Meistersingers playing non-stop at the local opera house; Straus in the hotel lobbies; military muzak in the lifts, and *Coriolanus* playing at the local theatre.

Well . . .

And lots of old men, all five-foot nothing in their shiny shoes, trying not to click their heels when they meet; sitting around in Lederhosen and crewcuts and Charlie Chaplin moustaches, discussing once again in big Gothic letters their triumphs in battle to their sixteen-stone babes who keep patting their giant, slavering Dobermann pinschers and lilting, 'Jonny, wenn du Geburtstag Hast', a bit like Weimar Berlin in the sunshine? And hotel lobbies full of big burly men in dark glasses, carrying violin cases with Entebbe stickers all over them?

Well, yes.

Instead, it is actually verging on the pleasant, and you're disappointed?

Not exactly disappointed. I mean, I'm not prejudiced, honest. I'm as fairminded as the next cynical, twisted sceptic. I am more than prepared to accept everything at face value, take people at their word. But somehow, I admit, I thought it would be different. I mean, all those stories you read. I mean, I was in Frankfurt once, going to a meeting at Eschborn. I was walking along that main street near the Haubtbahnhof, past a travel agent's. In the window was a sign advertising family holidays in Chile. 'Make this year the year for that family reunion,' it said. 'Visit Chile.'

You're making it up.

It's true, honest. I was also told Chile is the only country in the world which men suddenly decide to go to on holiday by themselves and then send for their wives and families later. And I thought it was going to be full of toothless old Rottweilers held together between a truss and an abdominal support going on about being retired Volkswagen salesmen, and Hitler's only mistake being not to control inflation, cut interest rates or boost the economy. Instead all the Germans I met kept on about having their bowels sluiced out by colonic irrigation.

Not military enough for you?

Well, the whole place was crammed with policemen leaning against brick walls in the sunshine. The people, I imagined, would be quiet, reserved, hesitant, going about their business looking neither to left nor to right, keeping their heads down. Oh, yes, and I thought the trains would run on time.

And it's nothing like that at all?

No, nothing. Except once I saw an old man near Station Alameda who was complaining he was not getting his rightful pension. He said he kept writing to Berlin, but they never answered his letters.

So what was he?

Something in a Schutzmannschaft unit or something. I think it's something to do with transport. I asked him, but he said he couldn't remember all those years back. Oh yes, I did have a slight turn one evening in Pio Nono. We'd been eating hamburguesa al vinto tinto and knocking back the old pisco sours. I asked if they took credit cards. The waiter, all stainless steel glasses, said yes, which one? I said Mastercard. I swear he almost clicked his heels.

Not good for you, you know, all that eating and drinking. Especially hamburgers. Bad for the heart. How many times have I told you to—

I know, I know. But I don't care what you say, I reckon Santiago must be one of the healthiest places on earth. After all, how often do you read about all those broken-down, clapped-out old guys dying of cancer? They drag themselves halfway across the world to Santiago, then, hey presto, within weeks they're 9,000 feet up clambering all over the Andes.

You're joking.

No way. Some German magazine said a group of Germans with all the gear were out climbing the Andes. Who did they meet on top, strolling around with his walking stick but what's-his-name? I mean, mein Gott, it makes you think. I was in the hotel lobby one day, and the guy in reception was on the phone having this crazy conversation.

'You speak English?' he said. Silence. Then he said, 'You speak Spanish? You speak French? You only speak German, okay.' Then he went on, 'Sir, the maid has to come into your room. She has to clean your room. I know she did it last Wednesday. But I'm sorry, sir, it is necessary. It's our regulations. Yes, sir. Thank you, sir.'

You mean, ex-Communists from East Germany and other parts of Eastern Europe wanting to settle in a staunchly anti-Communist country?

Sure. But maybe this climate is not as miraculous as all that. I mean the last time I was in Santiago I had this twinge in my back. Could hardly walk. Didn't seem to do me any good.

Maybe you haven't got millions stashed away in Stasi bank accounts in Liechtenstein, and friends in high places.

Maybe. But I'll tell you one thing I noticed; Santiago might cure their problems, but somehow it seems to make them forget things.

You mean it has some kind of side effect?

Maybe. It's funny, but nobody I met who suddenly had to go there for health reasons could remember anything more than, say, ten or fifteen years ago.

Strange that.

What?

What you were saying.

I've forgotten.

It is a problem, though, what to do with all these old ... boys. I mean if it was the States they'd probably destroy the tapes, go back to New York and carry on as lawyers or join some Washington think-tank. They can hardly do that can they?

Listen, I must tell you. I met a group of old boys in a bar in Parc Arauco one night. They all had typical Chilean names like Schneider and Steinhausep. They looked as though they were members of the Richard III fan club. One of them, who made Albert Speer look a softy, seemed to be their leader. His Engelchen was about sixteen stone, wearing a man's suit, highly polished shoes and what looked like a Marlene Dietrich wig. She looked as though she slept with a lock of Heinrich Himmler's hair under her pillow. We were talking about how Germany had big problems trying to integrate the old East Germany into the old West Germany.

'They are trying to integrate West and East, ja,' said the

Albert Speer look-alike. 'Zo what they doing ist lower standards of West to meet standard of East. Ja.'

I thought about it.

'Ja,' he barked.

'Ja,' I replied immediately, on the perfectly democratic principle that at that particular moment there were more of them than there were of me.

'Inflation is high, very high, ja, in Germany.'

'Ja.'

'It is so high, they have special signs by road announcing inflation. Ja.'

'Ja.' I nodded, although it was two days before I realized that the signs he was referring to were not some mysterious inflation signs I had failed to spot in years of driving through Germany but the electronically controlled speed limit signs that go up and down according to the traffic flow.

Another old boy then butted in and kept referring to 78s. I thought he meant the records we used to buy years ago. Again it was days before I realized that 78s was his code for people who were actually seventy-eight that year and had not for some reason been outside their door since 1947.

So in that case, my alter ego persisted, it is, you know, efficient?

No, not at all. I mean, I thought of all places it would be, well, security conscious. But for example, the airport's a piece of cake. It couldn't have been more relaxed. On the way in they were casual: no checks, no x-ray machines. The exact opposite of, say Pittsburgh where they give you a going over before they even let you into the airport. Six 747s can land at the same time, and you've all got to queue at a single x-ray machine for them to check everything: hand luggage and duty free as well as suitcases. It takes ages. On the way out they were so laid back they practically did backward somersaults. For the first time ever my luggage was actually checked in and despatched before I got anywhere near the check-in desk. A porter just grabbed it out of my hand, marched to the top of the queue, grabbed a bunch of tickets, weighed it all and threw it on the conveyor belt. Before I could say, 'Excuse me, sir. Regulations insist that I ask if you have packed this . . .' it was gone. When I finally got to the desk, nobody asked if I had any baggage, let alone where I wanted it to go. Security at Rio Gallegos on the desolate southernmost tip of Argentina at five o'clock in the morning was a million times stricter. Yet somehow, miraculously, my bag turned up at my next port of call unharmed, first out of the chute, with all the correct labels on.

What about the body search?

Well, there are body searches and body searches that bring tears to your eyes. I know one American who, when he goes through any security check, immediately throws his hands in the air for the body search. Then when the security man's hands are barely halfway up his trouser leg he begins rolling his eyes and screaming, 'Further! Further!' Invariably the guards scream their hearts out and disappear up their own x-ray machine leaving him free to wander in with his portable advanced gas-controlled nuclear reactor.

Was it like that in Santiago?

No.

So you've got no complaints.

No.

So, did you make any good contacts?

Sure, I told you, I met all those old guys. They asked if I'd like to go to their reunion dinner on April 30th.

Why April 30th?

I don't know. They said it was someone's birthday.

You going?

Sure. I mean, I want to do the Reich – oops, I mean right thing.

Natürlich.

138

Singapore

Okay, now pay attention at the back. Everybody say after me:

I must love my country.

I must be polite.

I must not chew gum.

I must not pick the fruit off the trees.

I must pay to drive into town.

I must turn up on time for weddings.

I must not eat too much at buffet lunches.

I must not throw litter away.

I must not have long hair – especially if I'm going to appear on television.

Oops, I nearly forgot: I must flush the lavatory.

Happy? Not embarrassed? Fine. Then you'll feel at home in Singapore. Some people think it's a bit OTT, the ultimate Nanny island/city/state. Don't do this. Don't do that. Mind how you cross the road. Don't talk to strangers. Mind your Ps and Qs. And wipe that grin off your face.

There are signs everywhere. In restaurants you expect to see signs saying, Don't talk with your mouth full. In shops: A fool and his money are soon parted. In people's homes: The devil finds work for idle hands. In fact, there probably are. It's just that they are all in Chinese and I can't read Chinese.

A German I know calls it Verbotenland. 'Everything is Verboten-this, Verboten-that and most definitely Verboten-the-other,' he says.

Verbotenland or not, Singapore is a huge success. If countries could be given a stock exchange rating Singapore would be the fund manager's favourite. BZW would be throwing circulars at it. Every pension fund manager would be chasing it. Even the *Guardian* would be writing it up.

Me, I think it's the biggest Raffles prize of all time. But don't tell their ministry of information or they will set their psychological defence unit on me. Again. And it wasn't because I forgot to flush the lavatory either.

I'll never forget the first time I went to Singapore. The day before, I had been locked in meaningful conversation with the most inefficient, ineffectual, irritable ditherer in the world. Say good morning to him at 10.20, when he boasted he arrived bright and early in the office, and at 4.55, when he left after a long hard day, he would still be trying to make up his mind whether it was or not. In other words, if you don't quite understand what I'm saying, he was the company chairman, your typical dynamic son of the founder of a typical family company north of Watford.

Turnover was down. Profits were beginning to slide. Dividends were static. Their share price was languishing. The City was saying they had lost their way, there was no management, they had begun to drift. If they didn't do something and fast they were a sitting target.

'What do they mean, lost our way, no management, beginning to drift?' he kept asking me after I finally got in to see him, practically three-and-a-half hours after the time he had insisted we had the meeting. He had been unavoidably detained, his secretary had whispered to me, discussing the flower arrangements for his mother's birthday party at the end of the year. Which was unusual. Usually we discussed the flower arrangements for his mother's birthday party during the meeting, or other important subjects such as what he should wear for the local hospital's charity cricket match; why he hadn't been invited to appear yet on *Any Questions*; and whether he stood any chance of making a hit you-know-where after the trade association's annual dinner at the Savoy next year.

The City's criticisms were obviously beginning to bite.

Grabbing the chair nearest the chocolate biscuits left on the boardroom table, I threw myself straight at it. 'The first thing we must do,' I began, 'is look specifically at the City's criticisms, see if they are true, and if so take steps to correct them. Next, we must look at the good points within the company; look at our successes and begin to put across our strengths.'

'You mean create a dynamic, go-ahead, efficient image of the company?' he gasped as he staggered in his long-since-fashionable Herbie Frogg suit from the table to his desk.

'Well, you can only do that if the company really is dyna—' I began.

'I like it,' he said as he slumped into his leather-backed swivel chair looking as if he had had an overdose of radiation treatment. 'That's what we want. A dynamic, efficient image.' He paused to get his breath back.

'Okay,' I said. 'Let me look at some—'

'No,' he gasped. 'I don't want you to do anything. I just want you to think about it. I'll think about it as well,' he panted. 'Don't want to rush into anything too hasty, do we?'

'No, of course not,' I said. 'Especially if we're going to create a decisive image.'

'Exactly,' he puffed. He got up and stumbled around his office which looked down on the main railway station. He picked up files, flicked through them, put them down again.

'Exactly.' He took a book off a shelf, ruffled through the pages and put it back.

'Exactly,' I muttered in a decisive demonstration of solidarity.

'In any case,' he gasped as he returned to his desk and picked up his latest executive toy, 'I'd like to discuss with ... with ...'

'Exactly,' I said.

The following day I was in Singapore or Singa-Pura, Lion City. At first I couldn't believe it. Sing-a-poor it definitely was not. It was a dream. It's like landing in the middle of an enormous golf course. There is grass everywhere – not your ordinary grass but that bright vivid green grass that you only see in advertisements for tennis courts and golf courses.

I don't normally go bananas over airports. There are one or two more important things in my life. But Changi is not your ordinary airport. It's more a cross between a first-class hotel and a theatre or concert hall. All my life I've spent turning up in dirty, squalid airports; negotiating my way through customs; wasting years queuing and queuing yet again just for the forms to change my money; then outside fighting for a halfway decent taxi and slowly chugging my way into town.

Changi is a revelation. It must be one of the best airports in the world. In fact, it's almost worth going to Singapore just to see it. I was through customs and immigration in four-and-a-half minutes! Can you imagine how much of my life I have spent queuing at customs and immigrations throughout the world, and here I'm through quicker than it takes to order a Chinese take-away by phone anywhere in the world. Except China. Fifteen minutes after landing, you've actually got your luggage! Three minutes and you're in a cab. On some trips it's taken me fifteen days just to find my luggage and another fifteen before it has arrived. On top of that it's got a hundred shops, twenty restaurants and special seating for ten times the people who are constantly queuing at Heathrow. There's even a grand piano on a stage in the lounge with a black-tie-and-tails pianist serenading the world-weary traveller.

One day I swear I'm going to transit in Changi and spend my summer holidays there. Except. Except. Changi Airport for all its smooth, quiet, unhurried luxury and efficiency is littered with Verboten signs: Do not congest this exit; Seats reserved for elderly and families with young children; Blue seats for smokers.

You can hardly put your boarding pass, let alone your passport, on the seat (not blue) next to you without a squad of smiling (they're always smiling) litter control executives surrounding you, demanding, 'Something to throw away?'

But I can forgive them all that. If it's a temple to efficiency, they have no qualms about letting in the moneylenders. Any airport that gloriously calls its foreign exchange desks 'money changers' and puts signs up all over proclaiming their presence does not deserve my litter, at least until the day they drive them out.

Outside the airport, the palm trees are standing to attention, not slouching like their poor African cousins. The banyan trees are in neat lines, all their tendrils hanging straight down to the earth. The creepers growing over the bridges look as though they are following precisely Regulation 617b (para a): Creepers, the growing of, over bridges. Hell, they even cut the grass verges on the side of the road. Which is obviously why its supporters call it Garden City.

The more restrained, however, call it Paradise. The climate is fantastic. Well maybe it's a touch too warm and a touch too humid and, okay, it does tend to rain a lot between October and January. And I mean rain. Sometimes as much as a day. And often every other day, for weeks on end. Everything, as a result, is super clean and neat and tidy: the hotels, the apartment blocks, offices, factories, even the rubbish dumps at the back of factories. Most of them are cleaner and a darned sight tidier than the inside of many British factories. The

Ministry of Education; the Mobil petrol stations; the Grace Assembly of God; even the car wash on Alexandra Road – there's not a grease mark, a speck of dust or even a blade of grass out of place.

Singapore is probably the cleanest, some say most antiseptic, place on earth. Bacteria, if they ever dreamt of making an appearance, would stand no chance of getting a visa. Cockroaches would never get through customs. A speck of dust – not allowed. Unless, of course, it's been agreed and confirmed in advance, in triplicate, and the form filed in the correct alphabetical sequence. So conscious are they of the need for everything to be neat and tidy and in its place that when it isn't, the first thing they do is tell you why. All the parks have big patches of long grass, so they put a sign up telling you why they haven't cut the grass. It's a designated Long Grass Area. It's for the birds. Can you imagine that in England? In England if we did that, we'd have to put up signs saying why we cut the grass.

If – perish the thought – an escalator has the courage to be out of action they get it fixed: but now; not tomorrow, let alone in three weeks' time like British Rail or the London Underground. What's more they immediately explain the situation with signs saying, 'This escalator is temporarily a stairway'.

If you even think of dropping the tiniest piece of paper in the street in Singapore you can be sent to gaol. Actually drop something and the worse thing imaginable will happen to you: you'll be condemned to work for companies north of Watford, where they are convinced they do everything properly and more efficiently than anywhere else.

'But these are just charts and graphs. Every company has charts and graphs. I want something more exciting.'

'But if you're making a presentation to the City you've got to include charts and graphs. How can you show—?'

'Look, this is a young, dynamic, exciting company.' The chairman levered himself up from his leather chair and hobbled over to the window which looked out on the back of the railway station. His Herbie Frogg suit was even baggier than usual. His face was puffed up as if he'd been going to Elvis Presley's doctor and had been hitting the cortizone too long. 'We've got to be different,' he said panting for breath.

'The City wants to see the figures. Charts are the only real way—'

'There's got to be another way.' He gulped for breath. 'We've achieved a great deal over the last thirty years.' Another gulp. 'We're a big success story, you know.'

Success story? Singapore is *the* success story! In the thirty years it has taken him to grow his father's operation from £5 million to £50 million, Lee Kuan Yew, or LKY as he is known familiarly, has turned a dirty patch of land the shape of a lozenge and practically balancing on the equator into the biggest success story in Asia.

To the north, across a tiny strip of water, the Johore Straits, is Malaysia. To the south is Java, the most developed of Indonesia's 13,000 islands. East is Borneo. West is Sumatra, one of the most undeveloped of Indonesia's 13,000 islands. If you can see it from Singapore, travel snobs will tell you, it's going to rain. If you can't it's raining already. Old South East Asia hands simply tell you to forget about the weather and have another drink.

Some say LKY just hit lucky. If any patch of dirt east of Watford had 2.8 million polite, hardworking, well behaved, punctual, educated, efficient, honest, Confucious-oriented people, nearly 80 percent of them Chinese, even our illustrious, decisive Herbie Frogg of a chairman couldn't fail to make it a success. Others say LKY was simply a dictator, admittedly a benevolent one, who was surrounded not by yes men but by yes, sir men.

An old Dutch trader I know delights in saying that Singapore belonged to the Malayans, was developed by the British, conquered by the Japanese and is now run by the Chinese. An American banker calls it a teenage Hong Kong. 'It's bright, alert, smart, clean, interested in keeping fit. But wait,' he pauses, 'until they discover sex and drugs. Then you'll see what it's really like.'

Nevertheless LKY actually did it, and today Singapore is a highly developed, post-industrial urban miracle with probably the highest standard of living in Asia.

The Central Provident Fund, their savings account, is worth S$50 billion. The Foreign Exchange Reserves top US$40bn. Voluntary savings make up 47 percent of GDP, about the highest savings rate in the world. They are currently investing nearly S$3.5 billion a year in its industry. Overall the economy is growing at around 5.6 percent a year. Now that's success.

Some say LKY did it, but at a price, the price being Singapore's famous neverending list of dos and don'ts:

No trespassing

No dumping

No parking

Pedestrians use crossing

Death to drug traffickers

Don't drink and drive

There are rules and regulations about everything, everywhere. There's probably even a rule or at least a regulation setting out how many rules and regulations there should be.

Drugs: not only are you absolutely forbidden under pain of everything Sir Thomas Stamford Raffles held dear even to think of bringing drugs into Singapore, you're not even allowed to bring in any cigarettes duty free. And everywhere there are fully armed soldiers lounging as casually as any soldier can, tapping their rifles up and down on the floor to

---

remind you. Just in case it should have slipped your mind. You have been warned.

Tax forms: you must send in your tax forms bang on time – no reminders – or you face a minimum S$1,000 fine. You have been warned.

Cars: you've got a car, you can go wherever you like. But not in Singapore. Throughout the city there are restricted zones. If you've got a permit, you can drive in. If you haven't, you can't. So back up and let somebody else in who's got a permit. You have been warned.

Taxis: not only does good old LKY insist that only one passenger sits next to the taxi driver but he also tells you what type of person he should be. Minimum height: 195 KN/m^2. And if, heaven forbid, the taxi should exceed the statutory 50 kph speed limit, a special alarm sounds inside the car telling the driver he's broken the law and probably automatically adding a black mark to his record for life. You have been warned.

Chewing gum: forbidden. Unconditionally. FORBIDDEN. Singapore is the cleanest place in the world when it comes to chewing gum. There's no gum on the trains. No gum on the buses. And, goodness me, no gum on the streets. In fact, it's almost as clean as the pavement outside the Wrigley building in Chicago. You have been warned.

The second quarter growth figures: leak them to the press and you're up on a secrets charge before you can say, 'But they're only government statistics.' You have been warned.

Hang your washing out of the window? Never in a million years. LKY would have apoplexy. Raffles would turn in his grave. The whole fabric of Singapore society would probably be rent asunder. Have you been warned.

Some people maintain good old LKY is a benevolent dictator; he just wants to be obeyed. My own theory is that all those years ago he had to somehow jump-start the economy. Other presidents and prime ministers have done it by building enormous prestigious empty hotels and office blocks. LKY decided to hand out enormous government contracts to the sign-writing, printing and poster industry. This created jobs, stimulated the economy at just the right pace and helped build a calm, efficient, stable society.

Love him or hate him – if such a thing is allowed – you can't argue with his success. Since the early 1950s his People's Action Party has dominated the country. At one stage it controlled every seat in parliament. Today, safe and secure with all that money in the bank, the last thing they feel is safe and secure. They feel vulnerable. They are being repeatedly urged to forget the good old reliable Kiasu mentality that has made them the success they are and go mad and take risks.

In one way, it's the last thing they should do. They are good at what they are doing. They are organizers, fixers, arrangers. Other people put up the money, build the plants and factories. They make them Sing-a-rich. On the other hand their very success makes them take risks. They can't leave the money piling up forever in the bank. They've got to make it work.

The great fixer himself also realizes that not even Singapore can stand still. They've got to get out there, spend their money, invest in where the action is and bring even more money home. That way they ensure they keep what they've got. They also stop somebody else from getting their hands on it.

If our dithery old chairman north of Watford had been able to achieve a fraction of their success over the same period, he would not now be getting even more grey hairs about whether or not to use charts and graphs to illustrate what little success he had managed to achieve since the company was handed to him on a silver plate by his father.

Come my next visit to Singapore I checked into my hotel. No problems. They had my reservation – with the correct spelling. The porter took me to my room. It was all ready and made up. I put my briefcase down – and the 'phone rang.

148

'I've been thinking. If we really are a dynamic, go-ahead, efficient company, can't we make a film or something? That would be different.'

'Sure. But you said you didn't want to spend more than £10,000 on a three-month programme: research, preparation of material, checking with all concerned, preparing the presentation, producing the charts and graphs, holding a meeting to announce the preliminary figures, arranging presentations to selected brokers . . .'

'You mean there's no leeway at all in those figures?'

'No, I'm sorry. I'm already . . .'

'Well, see what you can do.'

'If you want, I'll see if we can maybe use slides in a film format. We could try that.'

'I'll think about it.'

Singapore is a planner's dream. If it isn't planned, it won't happen. It's a hi-tech, state-of-the-art tribute to blueprints, long-term concepts, integrated studies and everything else we don't believe in in this country.

I mean, my goodness, they believe in such revolutionary mind-boggling concepts as building office complexes, and at the same time providing transport facilities to take people there and back again. They believe in making hotels, entertainment and cultural facilities easily accessible. They even, wonder of wonders, believe in putting recreational facilities in areas where people want to take their recreation. But if Singapore is really heaven on earth where the mobile phones are multiplying faster than the people, it got there not just because of its emphasis on planning, but also because it seems to have the German efficiency, the Swiss attention to detail, the Japanese emphasis on quality and the age-old American obsession with marketing and service. In other words, the traditional Confucian software of Asia: order, consensus and the family.

As if that's not enough, Singapore also leads the world not only in technology, but in the infrastructure that supports it. And it is planning (planning, again) to stay that way. It is determined to have a hi-tech optical-fibre national grid, able to carry fast two-way television, telephone and data transmissions, by the mid-1990s, at least ten years ahead of the Japanese and probably a million years ahead of we Brits who developed the damned concept in the first place.

Already it has a nationwide electronic data interchange network which cuts days off processing the paperwork involved in the simplest import/export deal. You want to get your import/export documents approved? Anywhere else in the world you need a stamp from this government department, a signature from that, two signatures from the other one, not to mention a stamp, signature and two bits of paper from the Chamber of Commerce. Oops, I nearly forgot, and a crumpled US$50 bill in a used envelope for the man with the big home overlooking the bungalow belonging to the Minister of Justice.

Not in Singapore. You send an electronic document to the relevant government office; within half an hour it's back, agreed, approved, ready to go.

'I've been speaking to the brokers. I went down there yesterday to see them. They said a film was too expensive.'

I had another call from Britain's answer to the hi-tech revolution sweeping South East Asia. 'Yes, that's what I—' I began.

'They said we should use slides but somehow animate them so it looks like a film but isn't. Can you do that?'

'Yes. I said last—'

'That would save money, wouldn't it?'

'Sure, it's cheaper than a film. But you're still going to have to spend—'

'But isn't there a cheaper way?'

'Sure. We can just have flip charts. That's the cheapest possible way of . . .'

'I'll think about it. It's just that if we really are a dynamic, go-ahead, efficient company we must make certain we get that message across.'

Already Singapore is a hub for international business, a crossroads between East and West, the gateway to Asia with the highest standard of living in the region.

Are they satisfied? Not on your life. The planners say they cannot stand still. The rest of Asia is racing to catch up. The only way Singapore can stay ahead of the pack is to be better than the rest of them. Hence their Concept Plan to provide facilities for an increased population of four million; to improve their quality of life continually and to develop and expand their role as the hi-tech business and commercial centre of South East Asia.

Already they boast the world's best airport, the largest port, an excellent transport infrastructure and superb telecommunications. Now, on a whole stretch of reclaimed land around Marina Bay, they are planning (that p-word, again) to extend the downtown area to build a multi-billion dollar super hi-tech twenty-first-century add-on to their super hi-tech twentieth-century city complete with super hi-tech hotels, state-of-the-art shops, technology-based towers, covered galleries, air-conditioned walkways, rooftop swimming pools, tennis courts, squash courts and helicopter pads, research-oriented restaurants and super modern bars and cafés.

Towering over everything will be spectacular super hi-tech fifty-storey twin office towers. There'll be steel, concrete and glass everywhere, but there will also be plenty of trees, grass and foliage. There'll be wide open spaces, parks and special facilities for jogging as well as flying kites.

To ensure it's a twenty-four-hour city – another revolutionary concept – they are building 6,000 housing units in four- to twenty-storey apartment blocks scattered throughout the development. It's already in the computer. So are traffic flows, transport routes, cycle tracks, continuous walkways and helicopter flights. They have even calculated the height of the seedlings they will need to ensure the trees are mature when the first residents move in.

'It will be a business centre of excellence,' the Urban Redevelopment Authority's chief of Conservation and Urban Planning, Mrs Koh-Lim Wen Gin, told me. There was no doubt in her voice. It has been planned.

'The bank's had a good idea. I saw them yesterday for dinner. They said lots of companies are now using flip charts.'

I'd just got back from the Urban Redevelopment Authority and the white-hot hope of British technology was on the phone. Again.

'Well, it is the cheapest possible—' I began.

'Which would mean we wouldn't have to spend so much money, and we could still get across the fact that we are a dynamic go-ahead . . .'

'Sure.'

'But we would still need some text.'

'Well, why don't we print the charts up as a spiral-bound folder and put the text opposite?'

'That's a bit cheap, isn't it? We mustn't look cheap. We are a dynamic, modern, efficient company, you know.'

In 1960 Singapore was assembling black-and-white television sets by hand. Today there are 250 electronics companies producing over £13 billion worth of components, sub-assemblies, and what are known outside technology-illiterate circles as sophisticated front-end products. They also produce half the world's total output of computer disk drives. Some Singapore-based electronic companies are now selling to other Singaporean and Malaysian companies more computer chips and other technical bits than they are to the whole of the UK, France or even Germany.

During one visit I was at the Raffles Country Club with a group of expats. Working in Singapore, I guessed, must be a dream: no worries, no headaches. Everything happens when it should, everything arrives when it should. They agreed. Except for one thing – mould. Singapore is so close to the equator and so humid you can hardly leave a knife and fork on the table without it being instantly covered in mould.

In most parts of the world, when expats gather together they discuss the latest rumours about the president; have they heard about the Central Bank drawing up new regulations; and wasn't that gunfire they heard in the hills last night?

In Singapore, they talk about mould.

'Maid turned the dehumidifier off for the weekend. Came back, all my video tapes covered in the stuff.'

'Same thing happened to me. Affected the playing head in the VCR. Ruined everything.'

'That's nothing. The wife left the car window open. You should've seen the mess.'

Less important than the problems of mould are such questions as whether to pull the factory down and put up a super modern one in its place and whether there'll be any work force there if you do.

On my first trip to Singapore I visited a big US electronics company. It was a brand new plant. They had just moved in. Three years later they were thinking of pulling it down and building an even better one.

'But you've only just moved in,' I began.

'I know,' the big boss said, 'but the government are offering us enormous incentives to do so.'

In the UK, our dynamic chairman, when he wasn't making the flower arrangements for his mother's birthday party, spent his time consulting his brokers and banks about whether he could afford another can of paint for the reception area at head office. In the end, of course, his mind was made up – by his wife. No. Instead he bought her another fur coat.

In Singapore, they tear down whole office blocks, factories, even blocks of flats to ensure they always have the latest technology in the latest and most modern environment.

'But what happens if the tenants don't want their block of flats pulled down?' I asked.

'The government gives them a vote. If a third say it comes down, down it comes.'

They think of everything these Singaporeans.

The other problem was staff, which I must admit surprised me. Singapore is practically 80 percent Chinese, around 15 percent Malay and the rest Indian. The Chinese are not Chinese Chinese but Malay Chinese. Many of them fled Malaysia, or the States of Malay as it was, over forty years ago when the Communists started causing trouble, and have been trying to make up their collective mind ever since whether to go back. In the old days, back in the 1980s, if they joined a company they were there for life. Not any more.

'Charlie Wong. I haven't seen him. Is he travelling?'

'Gone to join Motorola.'

'What about Hun?'

'With IBM.'

So great is the turnover that one company has been forced to bring their long service awards down from ten to five and now three years. What's more, with only twenty-six employees, they are having presentation ceremonies every week.

Part of the reason is the enormous demand for trained people, part is the gradual breaking up of traditional Eastern concepts, and part is good old Singapore dollars. Everybody wants more of them. Especially the Chinese.

'But don't they ever do anything wrong?' I asked.

'Sure,' an American said. He pointed out of the window. 'Over there on the other side of the lake is one of the army tank training ranges. Somebody obviously made a mistake the other day and took a shot at the golf course. It created an enormous crater.'

'Did you complain?'

'No,' he laughed. 'We all agreed that for the first time in our lives we could now all get a hole in one. We didn't say a word.'

I got back to the hotel, there was a fax waiting: 'Urgent. Don't take any action until we speak. Still considering proposal.'

I called. Our hi-tech human dynamo was out. I spoke to his secretary.

'He said he thought he had arranged to play golf with the bank manager, but he wasn't certain,' she said. 'He still went, just in case.'

Sometime gone midnight the phone rang. 'You don't mind me ringing you do you. It's just that this is important and I want to get on with it. I don't like hanging around.'

'No. Sure.'

'Look, I was driving back from my nephew's barmitzvah on Saturday and I was discussing this with my wife and she had a good idea. She said we should make up our charts, copy them, bind them into a little book—'

'And add the text opposite.'

'—and add the— How do you know? Have you been talking to . . .?'

'No. It's just that I—'

'It's a good idea, don't you think?'

'Sure.'

'Proves you should listen to the wife sometimes, doesn't it?'

Zzzzzz.

Okay, so I still like Raffles Hotel even though it has been restored to its former Victorian glory. Not just because the famous Long Bar is the only place in Singapore where you can throw peanuts on the floor without being arrested. Somerset Maugham said it stood for 'all the fables of the exotic East'. To me it looks and feels as though it was built, as Scott Fitzgerald said, for great emotional moments. Like throwing peanuts on the floor without being arrested.

The more telephone calls I received from our great leader north of Watford, the more time I found I was spending in the Long Bar.

'It should be called the Long Wait Bar,' an American told me. 'Order spring rolls and by the time you get them they're out of date.'

Many people go on about the way the hotel has been modernized, especially after they've had four or five Singapore Slings. 'Just look at what they've done to the poor old lady,' an old colonel type was practically weeping into his gin and bitters one evening I was there. A merchant banker says it's lost its character altogether and now stays at the super modern Mandarin which he says is more traditional.

Doing anything to Raffles was a gamble. But something had to be done. There's a limit to how traditional you can be and survive. Even the Galle Face in Colombo, which is another Raffles, is having to say goodbye to its oldest residents, the cockroaches, and modernize. For me, it worked: the modern, revamped Raffles is still the same old Raffles, with the same old atmosphere.

Three drinks and I can see old Raffles, probably the last civil servant to come up with a good idea, wandering around the Long Bar picking up the peanut shells. There he was, Lieutenant-Governor of Ben Coolen, stuck on the south-west coast of Sumatra. Across the water he could see this dirty patch of ground. China was slowly opening up. The spice trade was expanding; you can see the advantage of a British trading post on the way there and on the way back.

What does he do? He doesn't write a memo. Instead, clever boy our Thomas Stamford Bingley Raffles, he does his lobbying. He gets Warren Hastings, then Governor-General of India, on his side. Then he gets Temenggong and the elder son of the Lage Sultan of Johore on board as well. Then, on February 6, 1819, he does the deed: he establishes a trading post for an annual fee of 5,000 Spanish dollars to the Sultan and 3,000 to Temenggong. Singapore is born. By 1860 it was doing over £10 million worth of trade a year. By the end of the nineteenth century it was one of the most important parts of the British Empire.

What did Raffles get out of it? Precious little. But then, poor man, he was a British civil servant and not an Italian one.

Two more drinks, and there is Joseph Conrad crossing the bar looking at everyone under his Western eyes; Somerset Maugham is into his Cakes and Ale and Richard Hannay keeps on about the thirty-nine steps he had to walk from the door till he found an empty seat.

Three more and I'm wandering around the old Arab quarter, Arab Street, Baghdad Street, Muscat Street and Bussorah Street, huddled alongside the huge gold-domed Sultan's Mosque. Here you see Malays, Javanese, Buginese, Boyanese and Arabs looking for their prayer mats, buying their holy books and stocking up on everything the thoroughly modern Muslim pilgrim needs for his trip to Mecca.

At one stall in Baghdad Street run by Muslim Indians I treated myself to a ginger drink and a slice of cake, and met a German businessman looking for a cultural experience. He told me about the old Bugis Street, famous throughout the South China Seas for its scruffy shops, even seedier bars, and pondans, the transvestites in their pink lipstick, great diamanté earrings and huge beehive hairdos. The new Bugis Street, he says, is as exciting as a 'Jeffrey Archer novel'.

The new Singapore had banned all homegrown transvestites; the only way they could find any for the new Bugis Street was to import them from Malaysia.

Chinatown, between South Bridge Road and new Bridge Road, is another mass of tiny narrow streets. Like all

Chinatowns it is dripping with birdcages, whether for pleasure or for lunch I've never found out, as well as the usual chunks of bark, lumps of horn, reptile skins and about 1,000 different types of fungus and seeds of every description.

Up and down Serangoon Road, Jalan Besar Canal and Syed Alwi Road, Little India is full of saris, sandals, beads and bangles. I like going there late at night. The mosque is still lit. People are busy catching up on their prayers. There are stalls selling everything you can imagine.

Quick, there's Joseph Conrad. No. A trick of the light.

I get back to the hotel. The 'phone rings. It's you-know-who again.

'I've got it,' he screams. 'We promote ourselves as' – he pauses for effect – 'boring! Boring! Boring! The most boring company quoted on the London Stock Exchange. What do you think?'

I grasp for the right word.

'We then have a competition among analysts to nominate the most boring thing about us. Then we have an award ceremony. Then we ... Hullo. Are you still there? Hullo. Hullo ...'

Seoul

Maybe I've been lucky. But I don't think I've been anywhere in the world as drab and as dreary and as depressing as Seoul. If anywhere, as poor old Gerard Manley Hopkins said, is 'seared with trade; bleared, smeared with toil; And wears man's smudge and shares man's smell' it is Seoul. Dammit, South Korea is the only country in the world where champagne is not champagne but the name of a fertilizer.

From the moment you get off the plane you're slap bang up against it. There are no gentle avenues of trees, no sweeping lawns, no impressive driveways, triumphal arches or welcoming choirs of local singles giving you a quick alloa and a non-marital rum punch. Instead, staring you in the face, right opposite Kimpo International Airport is the Raja Furniture Store.

Seoul is business. Seoul means business. Business is what you're here for. Business is what it is all about. Seoul, as a result, is the biggest city in the world. It's also one of the most densely populated. It sprawls all over the place. And it's still sprawling all over the place, and probably will continue to do so while there's business to be done.

The centre should be impressive; it should be as packed with fabulous buildings as the millions of printed circuit boards they produce are packed with components. No way. Every office block, warehouse and factory looks as though it was designed by rejects from the London County Council

Ration Book School of Architecture, Class of 1947, motto: Austerity rules.

The occasional hotel relieves the gloom. But inside they are all virtually the same: drab, functional, designed to a budget and furnished under budget. Jacques Attali would have a heart attack if he ever had to change planes in Seoul, let alone spend the weekend there.

The Nam San Tower, admittedly, breaks up the monotony. Home of one of South Korea's biggest conglomerates, one of the mighty chaebols which control more than half the country's GNP, it should be bright and sparkling. But it isn't. The so-called fashionable Apkujung-Dong area with its Gucci, Godiva and Givenchy stores, its trendy cafés and occasional Porsche, looks as though it was designed in Eastern Europe and swopped in some barter deal for a couple of dozen microchips. Even the 'Orange Tribes', the South Korean yuppies who are supposed to blow over US$6,000 a month on fashionable this and thats as well as the occasional others, in a country where the annual average income is only about US$6,500, look as though they came in on an economy package from Oxfam.

Namdaemon market, near the southern gate of the old city, where you can buy genuine jewellery, furs, clothes, sauce-pans, eelskin wallets and Ralph Lauren shirts at half the price of anywhere else, lacks the authentic buzz and excitement you find in any other flea market east of the Gare du Nord.

Itaewon, especially just past the fire station, should sparkle. It is full of bars and clubs and restaurants. There are Indian restaurants, a Moghul Pakistani restaurant. Towards Man-namdong there is even an old German restaurant complete with Schwartzwalder Kirschtorte just like Mutter used to make, but it still somehow doesn't sizzle.

Regular visitors tell me the only way to put any life and soul into Seoul is to fill yourself full of soju, which is practically raw alcohol, fill your wallet full of won and be prepared to karaoke all night. For my money the only part of Seoul I've

160

ever discovered that looks as though it knows how to enjoy itself is Market Street. But then it's serious enjoyment, not your frivolous enjoyment. And it's Eastern, not Western, enjoyment.

All along the street in winter, late at night, and probably in the middle of summer as well, you see hoards of Mongol tribesmen, squads of Tartars with big beards, lonely Tibetans and every other Eastern face under the Oriental sun selling everything you can imagine and many things it is safer not to try to imagine, huddling around open fires gently simmering dog stew and dreaming of computer-controlled electronic overcoats with their own built-in heating system. If they weren't Mongols or whatever and if they weren't in South Korea, they would probably be dreaming of the South of France and summer drinks like summer girls: long, cool and half full of gin.

I plodded along Market Street one evening from the Hamilton Hotel. In ten minutes I reckoned I saw as many different peoples as if I had spent ten years tramping the Old Silk Route. Outside the Viva department store were a group of retired Afghan freedom fighters. Further along I came across Azerbijanis selling fresh fruit, a Chinese family from Turkestan selling dried fruit and a group of Muslims from Iran selling seafood and something that looked suspiciously like the roots of a tree that had died of Dutch elm disease. An old Korean woman, who looked as old as the stars, was selling typical Korean dishes like roast chestnuts, baked sweet potatoes and dog. But don't worry, not your ordinary dog. The Koreans will only eat dog if it has been beaten for two hours non-stop to tenderize it before ... before they kill it. After all they're not savages, you know. For them a dog is not for Christmas. They can make it last until at least January 3.

You think eating dog is bad. I was told that along Market Street some Vietnamese stallholders do a roaring trade in armadillos and cobras, which they kill, clean and cook while you wait. I was also told – perish the thought – there was a

Filippino who made a fortune selling fertilized duck eggs, with the duckling inside ready to be hatched.

I decided on a coffee instead. It was only when I finished it that the wizened old Vietnamese witch sloshing it out into broken cups told me the best coffee in the world came from her home town, Dalat. It was made from coffee beans vomited up by weasels.

Drab, dreary and depressing it may be, but Seoul certainly gives you food for thought. Pass the smelling salts, Mr Kim. I'm about to throw up.

Except, except, except – excuse me but that damn coffee keeps repeating on me – the South Koreans can't see anything to complain about. Some people say it's because they're a bunch of sensitive, civilized, animal-loving gourmets. My theory is that they all drive so fast they haven't actually seen what's going on around them.

From the airport to the centre of town; from nice, peaceful, residential Kangnam to Yoido with its 150 skyscrapers and still counting; or even from outside the 1988 Olympic stadium along the river to Hyundai's head office; as soon as they even think of climbing behind a wheel – Nigel Mansell move over – it's another twenty-four hour Indy.

In Singapore a little bell tinkles inside the taxis if, horror of horrors, the driver goes over the speed limit. In Seoul, if Big Ben was bonging its head off inside their taxis the drivers wouldn't take any notice. Moscow is the only place that's worse. Not because they drive even faster – they don't. Or because they are more reckless – they are not. But because they have no road signs and, worse still, no road markings. Nobody knows which side of the road they should be on, or if they do know they can't find it because there are no markings. The reason the South Koreans drive the way they do, I'm convinced is because they make 27.5 million cars a year and have to sell 90 percent of them as replacements every six months.

A German engineer I met on another Siberian evening

drinking that, that, that coffee in Market Street, told me that if you get stuck behind a truck along one of the eight-lane highways that criss-cross the city you could easily see another floor go up on a factory before you moved off again. 'This I guarantee,' he said.

Don't listen to him. It's not true. They're weasel words. The coffee had obviously begun to affect his brain. The South Koreans drive cars just about as fast as they build them. The trouble is the roads are built not for fast cars but for ox-carts. Good old General Yi Song-gye, later known to his enemies as King Taejo, set down Korean road regulations over 600 years ago on the basis of ox-carts. Small roads were one ox-cart wide. Medium-sized roads had to be two and major roads seven ox-carts wide.

Once, Ayrton Senna's Korean killing-cousin drove me at 40, then 60, then 80 mph, then finally at 143.497 mph along a seven ox-cart wall of death, all the way from Kangnam to the centre of town, swinging round corners too narrow for a single ox-cart, hitting the curves, swerving around buses, trucks and the occasional sensible, boring drivers doing a mere 103 mph. Trouble was, the whole time we were side-by-side with a car driven by Nigel Mansell's killing-cousin. My serene, contented, placid Buddhist driver, Mr Kim, had his claws gripped tight on the wheel. His tongue was hanging out. He was panting wildly. Saliva was dripping everywhere. His eyes were staring ahead like a weasel straining to cough up its coffee beans. We screeched. We skidded. We braked. At one time I swear I could smell either the tyres burning or more likely my soul burning, hopefully in Purgatory. I felt as though I had formed some wild suicide pact with the Mr Kim in the car alongside us, and that together we were hurtling towards or own kith and kim.

Quick – watch it – there's the – Through my half-open eyes, instead of seeing gorgeous palaces, solemn temples, even the great globe itself, all I could see was a slight continuous black/grey blur. Quick, there's the Nam, San – No it wasn't, it was the

– No, it's the Imperial – Quick, There's the – Damn, missed it.

Then in a second the other car was gone. We were now hurtling faster and faster along the ox-cart wall of death. On both sides of the Han River I got the vague impression that there were nothing but huge flyovers criss-crossing the city and probably each other as well. It's as if it's a huge symbol of the enormous network of trade that the South Koreans have built up in just twenty years. Some road junctions I swear, were as wide as the South China Sea and definitely far more dangerous to cross.

In Moscow they're just as crazy, except there, because they try to make things simpler by removing the road markings, everybody drives blind, making their own individual bourgeois highway code as they go along. Thanks to this far-sighted policy, Ewan Marwick, who ran the Glasgow Chamber of Commerce – he also knew how to tell any number of wicked stories to visiting delegations – was killed in a smash on his way to Moscow airport.

In Seoul they have road markings, but they travel so fast they can't possibly see them. An old American Korea hand who looked as though he'd been left behind when Hawkeye and Hot Lips shipped out in '53, told me that it's their culture. They are used to doing everything in packs. If one travels at 143.495 kph they all travel at 143.495 kph.

'The Korean for we or our is uri,' he said. 'Everybody says uri this and uri that. They can't help it. They never say I or me or mine. You understand?'

'We do,' we said.

The taxi screeched to a halt. I tumbled out. I felt like kissing the ground, except it would probably taste of burning rubber.

Outside Seoul, whether it's in the suburbs, in the new towns which look as though they are built to look immediately old, or on the massive new factory estates, or rather empires, being built around the city, it's the same story.

Kwangmyong, on the outskirts of Seoul, if Seoul has any outskirts, is like the derelict industrial areas you find nowadays all over the United States: empty containers rot away by the side of the street; pallet boards are piled everywhere; there are bundles of steel reinforcing rods, wooden scaffolding posts and huge rolls of piping scattered all over the place. In one street there were steel girders all over the road; another was piled high with bricks, tyres, empty water tanks. Behind all this I managed to spot the occasional tiny block of flats with its traditional pagoda roof, although I couldn't swear anyone was actually living there.

Asan City, on the west coast about 100 kilometres south of Seoul, is full of giant, gaunt tower blocks of flats with the street numbers painted ten-storeys high on the side so that, presumably, the most shortsighted of postmen can't deliver their mail to the block next door.

Shihung is home for hunched, derelict greenhouses, a million drums, and the only cemetery I've ever seen for broken-down, exhausted cranes, obviously worn out by a life of toil and drudgery. Hopkins would have written an ode to it.

Sunvan looks like one continuous building site with factory after factory piled on top of each other.

Wongok Park, as opposed to Wongok Dong (everybody gets them confused) is full of back alleys, a thousand tiny shops and Pepsi Cola signs on every bus stop.

But the size and sprawl of Seoul has not daunted the South Koreans. While the rest of the world agonizes about urban sprawl, the degradation of the environment and the waste of natural and human resources, the South Koreans have taken a bold new line on town planning.

'We have decided there will be four new industrial cities: one for metal companies, one for chemical companies, one for electronic companies and one for engineering companies. All companies in these industries will go to these cities. We have spoken.' That was how an official in the Ministry of Industrial Affairs – another Mr Kim – put it to me.

'But what happens if they don't want to go?' I wondered.

'They will want to go.' He smiled that administrator's smile.

'But say, for example . . .'

'If other companies go, they will want to go. If they are in the same sector they will want to be together. They are in the same family. They buy and sell from each other. They will have no alternative.'

'Sure, in theory . . .'

'And the first companies, the important companies, we encourage . . .'

'By offering them incentives . . .?'

'By telling them they are breaking planning regulations at their existing premises and in order to comply they must pay . . .' He smiled that administrator's smile.

One of the four new industrial parks, Sihung City, looks like a cross between a building site and a Russian gulag and about as heartwarming as the VAT man at Christmas. Criss-crossing the whole area as far as I could see were massive, fourteen-ox-cart highways. I was lucky it wasn't snowing. On a cold day temperatures are as low as −20°C, which is obviously one reason for high productivity. Instead it was quite warm: −5°. In the two seconds it took me to get double pneumonia racing from the car to the unfinished but fully operational new factory I was visiting, I could see nothing but mud, ice and the foundations of the factories that would very quickly line all those highways.

What's more, the South Koreans are planning to set up a special industrial zone at Asan City for foreign investors. Some say this is a sign of the positive attitude the government is taking to attract foreign investors. Others, of course, say it is a sign of a negative attitude, because although they want their money they don't want them poaching the best people from Korean companies, and the best way to stop that is to pen them all up together where they can't cause trouble. Clever guys, these Mr Kims.

Some people call them the Irish of Asia, just as they call the Dutch the Jews of Europe. Why, I don't understand. The South

Koreans are nothing like the Irish. They're nothing like the Chinese either. They don't seem to be concerned about art, culture or whatever. They're nose to the grindstone, let's get on and get this done, don't let's waste time on any silly nonsense like art or culture. Others say they are like the Americans; only interested in getting the order. Once they've got the order they ring the bell and start chasing the next contract. Judging by the factories and plants they've obviously been throwing up overnight for the last twenty years, I'd say that was probably true.

'Quick, we've got the order. Build an extension.'

'I'll get in the architects. Maybe Norman Foster could . . .'

'Forget the architects, just build an extension.'

Maybe I'm wrong. It has to happen one day. Maybe there's a whole world of fun and games and goings on in Seoul that I've yet to come across. Maybe there are cloud-capp'd towers and gorgeous palaces. Maybe the whole place is littered with solemn temples. But I've never seen them. Maybe the South Koreans are the biggest laugh since Genghis Khan. Maybe they're the most artistic nation since Michelangelo. Maybe they're more cultured than Melvyn Bragg. But I doubt it.

All I know is, they are invariably young, clean-cut, well-groomed, smart, dark-suited and clean-shirted. Or if they are not, they look it. The first South Koreans I ever came across were disciples of the Rev. Sung Myung Moon of the Holy Spirit Association for the Unification of World Christians. In other words, Moonies. They were all young, clean, smart, crewcut – and American. In any hotel in the world, if there's a conference on called The World Something for the Improvement of Value and the Betterment of Statistically Significant Potential, attended by lots of clean shirts and smart suits, you can bet its the Moonies.

The first time I arrived in Seoul I had quite a turn. I thought I'd run into either a Moonie convention or the end of the world. After all, the South Koreans seem to have a monopoly on preparations for the end of the world. The hotel was full of smart young Mr Moonies and smart young lady Moonies, hovering all over the place. In the background were old Mr Moonies and old lady Moonies. But it was neither a Moonie convention nor the end of the world. It was something designed to create far more misery – the local marriage market. Sunday is Sunday all over the world, but for the Koreans, *sun* means 'arranged meeting'. Even though South Korea's clever electronics engineers have come up with the world's first electronic matchmaking machine, the traditional approach still holds sway.

Into the coffee shop dressed in all their finery came one family after another. Moon-Sook sits at one table. If she's graduated from Seoul's prestigious Ehwa Women's University she sits there quiet, demure, sweet, charming as if she's never heard of the damn place let alone graduated with honours in politics, economics and philosophy. Mustn't scare the poor lad away. Everybody else huddles around a table close by. Then in comes the other family. The boy joins the girl. Not as bad as the last one, he probably thinks. At least she hasn't got a hare lip. Probably as good as I'll get. Hell, what's the difference? They'll all go bananas whenever I get home smelling of booze. The rest of the family huddle around another table close by. Has she stopped fiddling with her orange juice? Has he stopped smoking? Are they at least talking? Everybody is trying desperately to look as though they are trying desperately not to look desperate. If you see what I mean.

Joong-mae, or arranged marriages, I gather, still account for 60, maybe 70 percent of all marriages. To the Koreans all this yon-ae or love-stuff is so much Foo-ling-yoo. It's the formal things that count: money, family background, good character, the right home, money, family background.

It's the same in business. Seniority, status, family connections still count. People still defer to the elderly. There is respect for the older man. As a result, you can't cold-call a Korean company, you must have an introduction. Without a proper introduction not even the doorman will talk to you. When in Korea one does as the Mr Kims do. Finger the designer gear. Wear a boring business suit and a boring business tie. And when you finally get through the door, you don't just flick your business card across the table. 'Hey, Kim baby! So where's yours?' You have to present it.

You hold your card in your right hand. You slowly extend your right hand with the card in it. As you do so, you gently support the elbow of your right arm with your left hand. Then, if you can do two things at once, you bow gently. Not from the neck. From the waist. So you thought Japan was difficult.

Then, as in Japan, you study his damned card. Don't just stuff it in your address book and forget it. The Koreans are sensitive little flowers, who can be easily upset if you don't treat their business card like Holy Writ.

With these delicate formalities out of the way, you're now in the jungle. These friendly little Mr Kims are killers when it comes to negotiation. Not so tough as the Chinese; not so inscrutable as the Japanese; but still pretty tough and inscrutable. As far as I can discover there is only one good thing about negotiating with the South Koreans. You don't have to go through the rigmarole of trying to remember everybody's name. They're all called Mr Kim. It's fantastic. Well, something has to be fantastic in Seoul.

At Samsung Electronics, the biggest electronics company and one of the world's largest producers of memory chips, I met Mr Kim. At Korean Electric Power and at Korea Heavy Industries and Construction I also met Mr Kim. And at Goldstar, Daewoo Electronics, Hyundai Electronics and even at Doo Ray Metal Industries which manufactures aluminium wheels I also met Mr Kim. But whether I was at Samsung, Korea Electric, Doo Ray, or even Mee Fah, So Lah or Tee Doh, the procedure was always the same.

'Good morning. I am Mr Kim.'

'Good morning, Mr Kim.'

'And this is Mr Kim, our sales manager.'

'Good morning, Mr Kim.'

'And this is Mr Kim, our finance manager.'

'Good morning, Mr Kim.'

'But I'm sorry, Mr Kim, Mr Kim said that Mr Kim would give me the figures and I know that if Mr Kim knew that Mr Kim had said Mr Kim would give me the figures then Mr Kim would do everything Mr Kim said Mr Kim would do to make certain Mr Kim would give them to me.'

'Yes. I talk to Mr Kim about it.'

Some say that's being inscrutable. No way. They're just baffled because they don't know who the hell you're talking about. But they're never going to admit it, especially to someone not called Mr Kim.

Korean is one language I do not speak and I can't for the life of me understand how anybody else can speak it either. I spent twenty years of my life one morning listening to a discussion between a finance man and some mysterious government figure. I swear all they kept saying was, 'Yeyeah.'

'Yeyeah shim shong-Haradimsong.'

'Finchongdeyah.'

'Yeyeah. Yeyeah. Koodmeera.'

'Yeyeah. Yeyeah.'

How can you talk like that and have a GDP of around US$300 billion and be the fourteenth largest economy in the world, between the Netherlands and Australia? It's not right, is it?

It's difficult to remember that forty years ago all this was nothing. The whole country was devastated by war and napalm, and suffering from the after-effects of Hawkeye and Yossarian. Seoul is still well within range of North Korea's heavy military and only thirty-five miles from the 38th parallel, the mines and tank traps of the demilitarized zone protecting the world's largest surviving and most successful hardline Communist dictatorship. North Korea's economy is one tenth the size of South Korea's. Its factories are crumbling, its people going hungry. But it's still operating the biggest nuclear weapons programme in Asia. At Panmunjon, talks are still going on in the same wooden huts to try to settle peacefully the first battle the United Nations tried to settle with force. There are still 40,000 US troops stationed here. Britain only ended its military commitment in 1993. Sirens used to scream over Seoul at night whenever the military thought they might be in danger of being liberated by their brothers in the North and shown the error of their ways. But no more.

'We don't think of North Korea any more,' the manager of a big American bank in Seoul told me. 'We think about Japan instead. North Korea is another world. It's history. My kids don't even know where it is.'

Can you blame them? They have more important things to worry about. South Korea is one of the great economic success stories of all time. From practically nowhere when Hawkeye was packing his bags, GNP per capita hit US$3,000 in 1987 and doubled again in five years. Economic growth is always around 8–9 percent a year. And it is still industrializing like mad. In the next fifteen years they're building no less than eighty-five new power stations to provide the energy they forecast they will require. That's about the time it takes us not to build a single nuclear power station.

But even that, it seems, is not enough. Singapore, Hong Kong and Taiwan are still doing better and still pulling further ahead. Thailand, Indonesia and the Philippines are catching up, thanks to their even cheaper labour, even lower production costs and even fiercer determination to succeed.

Unless they do something, the once mighty South Korea, still the seventh largest economic power in Asia, fears it will be relegated alongside Guam, Macau and New Caledonia. Believe me, all the Mr Kims were worried stiff. Even the taxi drivers and barmen were worried. They have been living off the fruits of their success, paying themselves too much money, cutting down the hours they work, while the rest of South East Asia has been working longer and harder for much less. As a result, productivity is too low, their hi-tech is

171

slipping and they are too expensive. Besides, they have been adjusting from the days when they were run by military General Kims and a handful of giant state corporations to rule by political Mr Kims in a more relaxed, free enterprise society. Businessmen have been cutting back. Civil servants have voted for a wage freeze. The new civilian president has decided to give up golf. He has turned all the former presidential homes built by the military into museums; removed the ornate chairs used by ministers; removed the practice golf range from the Blue House presidential mansion.

Will they succeed? Of course they will. Have you ever known a Mr Kim to fail?

I hate bringing this up. Actually I hate bringing anything up, but Seoul is the one place that makes me think again about my vocation in life.

In South America I've eaten my way through every meat you can think of from chicken's hearts to one-eyed Irish warthogs. In Africa I've had everything from bananas to gombi, a spinach-like vegetable which, when cooked properly, looks like green slime. The only way to eat it is to swirl it round and round the bowl, or better still conch shell, so fast that it doesn't stick to the sides, and shoot it straight down your throat. Then pray like hell you haven't run out of liver salts. I've also had my unfair share of sheep's eyes that look like delicate little balls of fluff lovingly extracted from a cat's throat. And when you eat them. YaaaaAAAAHZONK. It still brings water to my own eyes.

In Algeria I was once about to pounce on yet another camel couscous when a colleague leant across the table and mumbled something about what's worse than finding a maggot on your plate. I looked down. There was half a maggot in the middle of the plate. In Manchester years ago I was lucky to escape with my life when I was attacked by a secondhand salmonella sandwich which practically followed me out of the bar and into the train. In Osaka I once had a meal which made me yearn for a fortune cookie telling me the party was nearly over.

And don't ask me which restaurant saw me swallowing whole packets of Imodium for weeks after I'd had their oysters, bacon and beer mustard sauce, otherwise New Zealand won't let me back in, though that might not be a bad idea from my stomach's point of view. I don't care what anyone says, I am still convinced it was the accumulation of cardboard packaging that finally dried me up. As a result my arteries are probably as gunged up as the next patient's in the queue for a triple-heart-bypass job.

Seoul, however, is where I almost learnt to give up food altogether and eat hamburgers for the rest of my life. Not veggie burgers. I've still got some principles left. But the real, old-fashioned hamburgers they serve in the States. With maple syrup on top.

It's not that the restaurants in Seoul are not attractive. They are, especially if you favour the Great Hall of the People style of architecture. It's not that the staff are not friendly. They are. As soon as I go into any Korean restaurant, whether in Seoul or in a tiny bar in Fooling Yoo, for some reason the staff obviously think I'm European and insist on telling me that their sister is in London and thinks it is slow after Seoul; that their brother is in Paris and thinks it is too quiet after all the clubs in Market Street, and that the only place they want to go is Frankfurt because that's where all the money is.

And it's not that the food does not look attractive, because it does. If anybody can make dried-up fish skins and lumps of gristle look good, the Koreans can. At first I used to think it was all in the presentation, in spite of the tiny paraffin heaters, which always go out before the food is heated, in order to conserve vital supplies of energy in the economic struggle against Thailand for the number one economic spot in South East Asia.

173

Then I thought it was the ingredients. Indians say they can never get a good curry in India, not because they don't know how to cook it but because they can't get decent ingredients. In New York, Paris, or even Bradford you can get the best possible ingredients. Therefore in New York, Paris or Bradford you get the best possible Indian food. Maybe the same thing applied to South Korea. But a stroll through the back streets of Shinhung soon changed my mind. The Koreans have the best of everything: the best dogs; the best monkeys. Then I realized. It's not that I don't like Korean food, or that I'm allergic to it. It's just that Korean food is allergic to me.

All over the world I usually turn up late for restaurants. First because I believe in earning my daily bread before I go out celebrating. Second because I find, apart from in the UK where everybody is always racing to catch the last bus home, everybody else eats late. I long ago discovered it also means that you get larger portions and, if you're lucky, a drink afterwards with the chef.

In Tokyo, however, turning up late once meant that I missed the start of a typical ah-so Japanese meal.

'You missed start of typical Japanese meal,' the waiter said as he ushered me past a table of twenty Samurai warriors and their empty plates.

'Why? What was it?' I asked.

'They just eat live monkey,' he said. 'We chop head off at table. They all cheer. You come next time. Yes.'

'No,' I said and ordered a large snake.

In Seoul I eat early and I eat everything I can get my hands on – before going out to dinner. Pacific gold roasted salted macademias. Maestrani Krachnuss. The inevitable packet of Toblerone. I empty the mini-bar. The two chocolates left on my pillow by the housekeeper because she's got a crush on me. All the packets of Blue Diamond mixed nuts I've been given on planes the previous month which I've been saving for emergencies. Many's the time I've even been tempted to wrench a couple of leaves off the plants in the room, but I find that after two hours in Seoul I'm already hallucinating about them and it would be like eating a friend.

I remember my first Korean meal. I arrived in Seoul late one evening. We drove along the wall of death at a reasonable 97.63 kph. I got to the Hotel Shilla which is so big it's practically got its own time zone, as well as its own climate. On one trip the air-conditioning was so cold that I began thinking of saving my colleagues any further problems and going for a walk outside.

I got my bags out of the taxi and went in. Two-and-a-half miles later I was at the reception desk. The Shilla must be the only hotel in the world where the reception area is bigger than a conference room for 10,000 people. I resisted the blandishments of Monsieur Kim to indulge myself in a glass of Beaujolais Nouveau – it was Beaujolais Nouveau day plus one – which was being served in their La Continental French restaurant. I turned down the offer from Signor Kim of a traditional Italian meal of lentil soup with stuffed pig's trotter followed by angel-hair pasta with vodka at their La Fontana Italian restaurant. I even gave up the chance of having Master Kim build me my very own gingerbread house in the Shilla bakery. I wanted to try Korean food.

I unpacked and headed for the Korean Restaurant Sorabol. The hotel was crowded; or at least I could hear faint echoes coming from across the vast empty wastes. The restaurant was empty. Crazy, I thought. Coming all this way and all people want to do is eat Italian or French and drink Beaujolais Nouveau.

Three waiters made for me as soon as I stepped through the rice-paper door.

'Good evening, sir. You from England, my sister is . . .'

'Nice table in the corner, sir. Are you French? Do you know brother? He is . . .'

'Here's the menu, sir. Of course, I want to go to . . .'

I chose the spicy angler-fish soup with hot beansprouts and pepper sauce. Next I went for bulgogi, thinly sliced grilled

beef marinated in a mysterious 3,000-year-old Korean season-
ing. I couldn't taste a thing. I tried kimchi, cabbage marinated
in vinegar, brine, chilli and garlic which tasted like, well,
cabbage marinated in vinegar, brine, chilli and garlic. Okay, I
thought, I'll go for the big time. I ordered a plate of kalbi beef
ribs. Nothing. I couldn't taste a thing.

I tried a bottle of wine. Maybe my tastebuds needed
something to get them going. I asked the brother of the sister
in England for the wine list.

'Try Korean wine. Velly good.'

'Korean wine? I didn't know you made wine in Korea.' I was
impressed. Normally . . .

'. . . We bring in Riesling from Germany. But we make it here
in Korea. It is Korean wine. Yes. My sister. She says in
London . . .'

Even the German Korean Reisling was tasteless.

I asked for more pepper sauce. It didn't make any difference. None of the staff seemed to notice, they were too busy
going on about their sisters and brothers and how they
wanted to go to Frankfurt.

Next I tried something that looked like frozen cat's vomit.
Nothing. Maybe it's me, I thought. My tastebuds have gone.
After all these years of bombarding them, they've finally
given up.

I asked for more pepper sauce. Nothing. Couldn't taste a
thing. They were deliberately giving me all the foods that were
allergic to me.

Normally I don't eat sweets. They're bad for me. But this
time I needed to taste something. I ordered something that
looked like a Victorian jockstrap smeared in Pedigree Chum.
I didn't feel as though I'd eaten anything. But the smell came
at me in straight lines.

By now I was pretty desperate. For all the satisfaction I was
getting I might as well have spent the evening curled up with
a book on post-modernism and the rediscovery of value.

There were no distractions either. None of the excitement

you get in restaurants in other countries. In Africa, people wander in all the time selling newspapers, government secrets, drugs. In France they wander in selling newspapers, flowers – there are no government secrets in France; they're all printed every week in *Le Canard Enchaîné* – and drugs. I was once in a restaurant in Pittsburgh when halfway through my prime rib this guy came in with a little girl.

'Excuse me, sir,' he said, coming up to my table. 'I'm having problems with my car. It's run out of gas. My wife's got my credit cards. I wonder if . . .'

Everybody around me leapt to their feet. 'Okay, Buddy. Out OUT. OUTTAHERE.'

It was a four-star scam. 'They're trying everything.' 'Fancy coming into a restaurant.' 'Why did they let him in? I'm goin' to call the CEO.' Half the restaurant returned to their prime ribs. The other half made for their mobile phones.

'Sorry, sir,' the head waiter rushed around trying to put out the fire. 'He said his friend was in here. He wanted to see him.'

In this strange Korean restaurant, however, there was nothing but food. I ordered some more hot pepper sauce. Two hours later I began the trek back across the great open plains of the reception area to the lift. Back in my room my first instinct was to raid the mini-bar for microchips or even macrochips. Instead I leant against it for half an hour trying to feel full by association.

Suddenly I started hallucinating about huge slabs of beef-dripping on brown paper sandwiches. I was wandering round the Galway Oyster Festival eating buckets of horse stew with brown bread and Guinness. I'd have given anything for cassoulet swamped in goose fat; or a mique, a gigantic dumpling stuffed with pig's liver, an everyday speciality of the Dordogne; or a BLT, a bacon, lettuce and tomato sandwich on East Croydon Station. Dammit, I'd even have gone for one of those super hi-tech, protein-rich Japanese burgers, made out of raw sewage, soy bean and additives. That's how desperate I was.

The result is that whenever I'm in South Korea I can't concentrate. I'm wishing I was somewhere else. I've got a meeting with a Mr Kim. I'm wishing I was in Paris. I'm visiting factories. I'm counting the days until my next visit to Sihung City. We have dinner in town. I can't help it, I'm dreaming I'm in New York.

I'm not saying Korean food is one of the world's great gastronomic secrets nobody has let me in on. It's just that I'm frightened to go there too often in case there is nothing left of me to come back.

Kuala Lumpur

Now I know I'm not exactly a Virgin Soldier, but I admit that for years I was in the dark about Malaysia. Ever since I discovered it was the substitute for South Pacific in the film – come on, you didn't think the South Pacific really looked like that did you? – I have thought of Kuala Lumpur as a substitute city: a substitute to Singapore if you wanted a stop-over where, in the privacy of your hotel room, you could chew gum and read the latest government estimates of their GDP without fear of being arrested; a substitute banking and business centre to Hong Kong if you were Chinese; or a substitute holiday spot to Bangkok if you were a Japanese salaryman snatching your first long three-day holiday away with your fellow salarymen and family for five years.

Malaysia, I knew, was one of the fastest growing countries in the world. I also knew that when growth slowed from their usual 8–9 percent a year to a mere 6 percent they were all practically falling on their mata keris, their unique, wavy double-edged daggers with the serrated edge to increase the pain. Apart from that my only information came from an old guide book, *To Siam and Malaya in the Duke of Sutherland's Yacht*, I discovered in a hotel in Troon while everybody else had gone out to play golf in a force nine gale.

When I finally got to Kuala Lumpur, Malaysia got its own back on me. Zap. The lights went out. I was back in the dark again.

Kuala Lumpur, or KL as we old South East Asia hands say, has grown so far and so fast that power supplies cannot keep pace. You're wandering around with your head buried in your phrasebook trying to find out what the hell kesihatan kecema-san kuarantin means. Zap. You're not only lost, you're well and truly in the dark as well.

Start munching your way through a sambal kepah, a Penang speciality of mussels in a spicy chilli sauce, or even Hameed's famous fish head curry in the central market. Zap. You can't tell your sambal from your fish head. But whatever it is, it's spicy as hell.

One evening I was perhaps wining more than I was dining and zap, the lights went out, just as I was going into the tandas, or toilet. But I was okay. I remembered where everything was.

Everybody complains about it, not least those who can't remember where everything is and create all kinds of prob-lems that would be a capital offence in Singapore. Offices complain: the lights go out, PCs, photocopiers and fax machines grind to a halt, telephones go on the blink, lifts come to a standstill, air-conditioners cut out. Shops complain. Not only do they lose business, they lose everything off the shelves as well. When the lights are on Malaysia is a strict Muslim country, but when the lights go out, shopkeepers have quickly discovered, they are not as strict as they should be. On top of that there are all those flowing robes, some as wide as a garden marquee, and there's not a shopkeeper in the country prepared to risk his life stopping the wrong one, even though in some cases they might be trailing three electric cables behind them. Banks complain, because security locks jam which take days to unjam.

'So what do you do?' I asked one bank manager.

'We don't bother, now,' he said. 'We leave all the safes and doors and locks open.'

'You mean anybody can walk in and take what they want?'

'Sure,' he grinned. 'It's better than being trapped in there ourselves for days on end.'

Factories complain. Production comes to a standstill. And when you're chasing 9 percent growth a year that's the last thing you want, especially if you're trying to persuade foreign investors to put their ringgits where your electricity isn't. Petrol stations complain. During one blackout I stumbled into a petrol station in the centre of town. They were still in business. They had an exercise bicycle connected to a car battery powering the pumps.

Drivers complain, although how they can tell the jams are caused by the traffic lights not working and not by the sheer volume of traffic, I do not know. I do know that the jams are no way near as bad as in, say, Bangkok or Taiwan or Jakarta. They only seem worse because the place is full of one-gear cars. Malaysian drivers seem content to stay in line. Nobody, not even the taxis, sorry teksis, tries to swing out and overtake. The bad news, therefore, is that everywhere is further away than it would be anywhere else in the world. To get a 9 a.m. flight, for example, you have to leave around 5.30 a.m. or you'll never get through the traffic. KL is not for late risers. The good news is that at least you know you're going to get there – not something you're certain about elsewhere in South East Asia.

My own feeling is that there wouldn't be half as many jams if the lights didn't keep going out. I'm sure people prefer sitting in their cars, where they can at least turn the light on and use their mobile phones, to banging their heads against the office wall because the power has failed.

I'm also convinced that if the lights didn't keep going out we would never have had *The Clockwork Orange*. If everything had been alright I'm sure that Anthony Burgess, that Malayan education officer and expert on everything under the sun, would have called it *The Electronic Orange*, and we'd still be happy wandering around council housing estates late at night and talking to strange young men.

If life is one power cut after another, why don't they install generators?

'We did,' everybody tells you, with that tone in their voice. 'The problem is we didn't expect so many power cuts, so the generators can't cope.'

With the lights on and the air-conditioning at full blast – sometimes I have to wear an overcoat – Malaysia Inc., no thanks to Mrs Thatcher Ltd, is the fastest growing economy in South East Asia.

Mention Mrs Thatcher's name in most parts of the world and everyone from expats who went native in 1927 to young students and government ministers, will grit their teeth, slap the top of the bar and go on about the Iron Lady. Once, in Bamako in Mali, I was at a government reception when I was pointed out by a minister as the only Englishman present. 'La Dame de fer,' he bellowed across the room at me. 'Vive la Dame de fer.' Everybody applauded and drank a toast to the Iron Lady. 'And now,' he boomed at me, 'you please for me to pass the clap on to zee Madame Thatcher, yes?'

In Kuala Lumpur, nobody mentions her name in any context. In fact there was a time when English businessmen were desperately trying to look Norwegian, Dutch, Canadian, or, heaven help them, like New Zealanders, which shows you how desperate they were, in order not to be thought to have the slightest connection with Mrs What's-her-name.

The reason: in 1983 Mrs Thatcher insisted that overseas students at British universities had to pay their way. Fees were practically trebled at a stroke. Everyone went bananas. But the Malaysians went more bananas than anyone else. They begged, they pleaded, they did everything they could to make her change her mind. Which, as we all know, was impossible. So the Malaysians retaliated. They pulled all their students out of British universities and sent them elsewhere.

The wily old Prime Minister, Dr Mahathir Mohammed, then announced – not that they were going to stop trading with the UK, that would have been too crude – the launch of a Buy

British Last campaign. In future all British tenders would be last on the list for consideration, with the result that a British car or box of chocolates, even a British box of matches, is about as common in Malaysia today as an Anglophile govern-ment minister, civil servant or businessman. What was once, thanks to the Virgin Soldiers and General Gerald Templar's campaign against our political enemies, virtually a British preserve is today a happy hunting ground for our commercial enemies.

'Such a pity,' a Chinese banker told me with practised inscrutability as we wandered down the road on the outskirts of the city from the Chinese temple to the Japan club for lunch. 'Such a pity.' As we turned to go in, he swung round quickly and pointed in the direction of the Golden Triangle, the super-luxury, ultra-modern heart of the new Kuala Lum-pur with its eighty-five-storey office blocks, which makes Canary Wharf look birdseed.

'Quick. There.'

I swung round.

'I'm sorry,' he said. 'I thought I spotted a Range Rover.'

Other people see it differently. 'Mrs Thatcher did them the best favour she could by getting them to throw the British out,' a French businessman told me. 'Made them stand on their own feet. Made them what they are today.'

With or without Mrs Thatcher's help, by the year 2000 they are determined to reach fully developed country status. And I'm sure they will, with or without French help, even though they keep on about their economic crisis. Economic crisis! An economic crisis for the Malaysians is when growth slips back from a not bad 9 percent to what is considered a disastrous 7.6 percent.

'We must correct the bottle-necks and move back on the faster track,' a leading member of the Federation of Malaysia Manufacturers told me. If only we had those problems.

For years Malaysia was the world's leading rubber producer. In the early 1970s, rubber, tin and petroleum made up over 90 percent of their exports. Then they decided to industrialize like mad. Partly because of prices; rubber prices had been doing what rubber cannot do – falling like lead. Partly because they didn't want to be solely dependent on one major crop. In the old days when grown men and maharajahs could do what they liked, everybody wanted rubber. Today five large tyre companies are responsible for over 50 percent of the world market. It was too risky to be dependent on rubber. Partly because they wanted to build up their other industries. Rubber was labour-intensive. It was better for all those people to be churning out microchips than wandering around tapping trees.

Malaysia, as a result, has slipped behind Thailand and Indonesia, the big two currently responsible for more than 70 percent of world rubber output. Trees are being either left or chopped down. The old open multi-storey rubber-drying houses are standing empty. Land near towns is being sold for redevelopment. Plantations are being turned over to palm oil, or into more golf courses and the old tappers retrained as golf professionals.

Today, manufacturing is the backbone of the economy, and growing by as much as 10 percent per year. There are almost as many factories in Malaysia as there once were rubber trees. Manufactured goods account for 70 percent of their exports. They send television sets to Japan, cars to Britain and palm oil and tropical timber to the world's supermarkets.

Here, however, they are convinced they are facing another crisis. The Americans have started campaigning against the use of tropical oils, and palm oil products. The Australians are going around slapping labels on all Malaysian timber coming into the country saying whether it is a product of 'sustainable forest management' or not. Now the Malays are tearing their hair out in case they wake up one morning and find an environmentalist chained to every tree.

'How do we know what is sustainable timber management?' rapidly balding Malays keep asking you.

'Forget it,' I always say. 'It's the temperate timber lobby. They're behind it. They're trying to steal your market.'

It's not true but it somehow seems to cheer them up a bit. The only things, apparently, that go to their heads are getting a new wig and the state of the stock market.

A Malaysian I met once in Brussels told me he was big in wigs. They were big business in South East Asia, especially Malaysia. For men. Most men had this thing about going bald. They would do anything they could to keep their hair on. If that wasn't possible they would go for a hair transplant, stage-by-stage, so that nobody would notice the difference. Not for the Malaysians the instant brillo pad, not there one day and there the next.

Stage one for them is a scalp pad to cover the bald patch, nothing more. It has to fit perfectly and match the colours of the scalp. Most scalp pads are so good they even stay on in the shower. 'They are so good even your wife will not know you've got one,' he told me. Not, of course, that I'm interested in wigs.

'Stage two begins the fight back, with one, two, maybe a handful of strands of hair being attached to the pad. This way nobody should notice any difference. Stage three and maybe up to stage 257 continue the process; always just a few strands more so as not to arouse suspicion.

'But surely somebody is bound to notice?' I said.

'Only if you compare one holiday picture with another. If you do it slowly, a strand at a time, nobody notices. If they do you just say your hair must have started growing back.'

He wanted to buy a British wig company, revamp it and use it to sell wigs and wig-making services all over the world.

The Malaysian stock market, one of the biggest and most dynamic in the region, is, surprisingly, twice the size of the Singapore exchange in capitalization terms. But just as it out-Singapored Singapore and switched a lot of foreign investment its way because everything was half the price, so Vietnam, Cambodia, even China, are now trying to out-

Malaysia Malaysia. They may not be as modern but they are at least half as cheap again, and if they have lights, they don't keep going out.

Some Malays see foreign investors deserting them overnight.

'Not at all,' I kept telling them, 'you don't have any problems. If it's going to happen it'll take time. You'll be able to adjust your policies.'

'But we do have problems,' a slightly balding government economist protested. 'Look, I'll show you.' He opened his desk drawer and spread a mass of figures in front of me. 'Now look.'

I looked at the top of his head to see if I could spot the join. Zap. The lights went out.

In many ways, Kuala Lumpur is Singapore's younger brother. It is certainly as impressive as Singapore, maybe more so. It seems to be built to US proportions, have a French flair, Japanese money and Chinese efficiency. It's the only city I know where you can start the day with a traditional Malay teh tarik, Malay tea poured from pot to cup at arm's length to cool it; go to a Protestant church and listen to a sermon in Tamil; have Kentucky fried chicken for lunch; spend the afternoon watching the Chinese play cricket and end up with an Indian meal for dinner.

Thirty years ago it was all hot, steaming, 100-million-year-old impenetrable jungle, low-rise buildings and cheap bungalows. The tallest building was the tower of the Sultan Abdul Samad building in Merdeka Square, just thirty-nine metres high. Today, even though half the country is still hot, steaming, 100-million-year-old impenetrable jungle, KL is full of gleaming, striking, graceful buildings. I'm no expert on architecture but they all seem to be slightly Islamic, slightly Malay and heavy with symbolism. Take the offices of the Malaysian Pilgrims Fund on Jalan Tun Razale (jalan means street) near the corner with Jalan Ampang. At first glance it simply looks like an hourglass, but look again and it's a lamp lighting the way to Mecca. There is no formal entrance, just an open courtyard. In the corner is a mosque.

The fifty-storey Menara Maybank, for a long time the tallest building in the city, looks a bit like a kris, the traditional double-edged Malay sword. Locals call it the Dagger. 'When will you be back in the Dagger?' they ask me whenever I'm in town. In other parts of the world, especially those parts where people believe the quickest way to a man's heart is through his back with a dagger, it's the other way round. Certain people keep asking me, 'When will the dagger be in your back?'

The gleaming, new, blue National Library on Jalan Tun Razak looks like the tengkolok, the traditional Malay folded beret. Why the tengkolok? Because the tengkolok protects your head. Inside your head are your brains. Under the tengkolok of the library are books. Books represent a country's brains, right? Right. And I worked all that out without looking in a book either.

'The buildings are so high in Kuala Lumpur', one banker told me, 'that we can actually look down on the weather.'

'If you throw salt out of a window in Kuala Lumpur, they say that Singapore is rocked by tropical rainstorms,' added another, obviously proud Malay businessman, who either had no worries or an exceptionally good wigmaker.

But whatever the height or the symbolism, they seem to go up before your eyes. The buildings, that is, not the wigs. Their new tengkolok library, which looks far too hi-tech to even think of containing anything as old-tech as books, went up in about eighteen months. The British Library has taken over eighteen years and it's still not finished.

Wigs can take easily eighteen months, maybe two years, maybe longer. 'Don't forget, we've got to pretend it's your real hair growing back slowly, of its own accord. It doesn't happen overnight.'

The second time I met my Malaysian expert on wigs – no,

I didn't buy one! – he had quit his full-time job as finance director of a major international electronics group and was trying to raise money to take over various wig- or hat-replacement companies, as he now called them, and put together a big group.

'I didn't realize there was so much money in wigs,' I remember telling him.

He practically collapsed. There were four different types of hair, he said. European, Asiatic, French refined or curly, and African–American. Most hair today came out of China. Most women sold their hair for money; some even grew it especially for wigmakers. It was sterilized, graded and processed in Hong Kong, where they had just developed a technique for making Asian hair look like European hair. Then what happens? When it gets to Europe, women want all the kinks and curls put back in again.

But it's well worth all the aggro. Bundles of hair can be imported from Hong Kong for literally pennies. Made up into even a tiny hairpiece, wigmakers can charge £200, maybe £300. A full wig costs thousands. Which, I thought, was enough to make anyone lose their hair in the first place.

One of his first clients, he told me, was a typical fat, balding, middle-aged English businessman, interested only in his job and his golf. But his wife had dragged him along to the clinic for a wig. He had only agreed for the sake of peace and quiet. They had made him a series of hair replacements, slowly, slowly extending the hair across his scalp. It had cost him thousands.

'Was the wife happy with the result?' I asked.

'Not at all,' he said. 'Once he got a new head of hair, he went out and got himself a new car, a new set of clothes – and a new wife.'

And if the Malaysians can't build their buildings much faster than they build their wigs, they just go out, find what they want, dismantle it, bring it home and rebuild it.

Antara Steel Mills wanted a 250,000-ton rolling mill. They

went to Sweden, bought the old Forsbacka plant, dismantled it and shipped it back. Then they wanted a smelt shop. They went to Sidegus in Spain, bought theirs and shipped it back. I dread to think what they'll do if they ever need a big statue symbolizing their liberty.

Roads are built almost as fast as the speed of the traffic. A 600-mile highway from Singapore in the south to the Thai border in the north is scheduled to take around four years to build. To widen less than three miles of the M1 near Luton is taking three years – and three years to plan. Golf courses, which stretch nearly all the way to the Thai border where, of course, they are interested in other things, are completed in an afternoon.

They are even building their first totally modern, fully landscaped, all-mod cons cemetery, or memorial park as we say in Forest Lawn speak, on the Kuala Lumpur–Seremban highway. Like their hotels it is coming complete with Islamic arches, exquisite pavilions, lakes and, oops, I nearly forgot, a columbarium which – Forest Lawn speak again – is where all the you-know-whats are stored. It will also have single and standard double plots as well as garden plots, family plots and special family plots which, I was assured, I could buy on either a pre-need basis or on an immediate need basis, which I thought could be a little bit rushed. I said I would think about it.

With all this activity, money is pouring into Kuala Lumpur so fast they haven't got time to count it between the power cuts. I went to a reception in the Putra World Trade Centre which covers about half of Kuala Lumpur and towers a thousand storeys high. It was for millionaires, only millionaires, from mainland China.

'You mean China has that many millionaires in Malaysia?' I asked the organizers.

'Sure. Millions.'

'You mean millionaires in Chinese currency?'

'And in US dollars. There must be more than a million. Some

of them, especially those in Shenzhen, are double, treble millionaires. Lots of them live in Kuala Lumpur.'

'Not bad,' I heard one Malay saying to another as they left. 'You had a couple of trillionaires, a few billionaires and some poor millionaires.'

'Next time we'll try and get some rich people,' the other grinned.

One of the millionaires, I was told, had just built an enormous sumptuous house in KL right next door to the waterworks.

'You mean right next to it?' I said. 'But surely with all his money . . .?'

'You're forgetting,' he interrupted. 'For the Chinese, water means good luck. It's the best site in the country. Everybody is now trying to build houses alongside waterworks.'

One reason Malaysia is so successful is that it is the only country in the world where it is a crime to hang around. Seriously. Hang around the shops too long, or take your time crossing the road, and you will be surrounded by policemen who have been doing nothing but hang around waiting to spot anyone hanging around. Some very busy Malay politicians call it 'a phenomenon of such proportions that it can no longer be ignored', and set up committee after committee so they can sit around all day talking about it.

Some say the solution is not to ban hangers-around from shopping centres, but to establish special sections where they can hang around watching educational films about the merits of running around. Others take a stricter view: round them up and send them out to work, they demand. A handful of extremists go further still: turn down the air-conditioning, they say, then nobody will want to hang around anywhere. What's more, it will save on electricity, so maybe there won't be so many power cuts. All I know is I didn't dare go in a single shop the whole time I was in Malaysia. I was scared in case I walked too slowly and got picked up by the police. Can you imagine the shame? Being caught out shopping, of all things.

Other people say the reason for their success is quite simply the Chinese. Wherever you have Chinese, you have success. Drop just one Chinaman on a desert island and before you can say Robinson Crusoe it'll be choc-a-bloc with factories, traffic jams and half a dozen banks overflowing with cash.

It's not just their emphasis on management training and education. I've never been anywhere in the world where there are so many walking-up-and-down management seminars, conferences and round tables taking place. They have to be walking-up-and-down, or delegates would get arrested for hanging around chatting, swopping business cards and trying to get away early because of the traffic.

Elsewhere in the world, if government ministers and businessmen are not in their offices it's because they are 'travelling' or they've been summonsed by the president or they have some mysterious meeting with a certain person in town and will be back 'aprés quelques minutes, monsieur.'

In Kuala Lumpur they're not in their offices because they are at seminars on Islamic management techniques or headaches and industry, presumably created by implementing Islamic management techniques. Sometimes I think there are more seminars than there are government ministers and businessmen to attend them. I was in Kuala Lumpur once when all hell broke lose because a minister turned up at an important key-note seminar only to discover he was the only one there. Everybody else had apparently heard there was a better seminar taking place elsewhere in town and gone off to that without telling him. The organizers practically held another seminar to apologize to him.

The main reason KL is such a success, I reckon, is those damn power cuts. Because everybody knows there is going to be another power cut, everybody rushes around like mad trying to get everything finished before it strikes. That's why there are traffic jams all the time: in the morning, during the day, in the evening, during the week and at weekends. There are traffic jams as people rush off to the mosques. There are traffic jams to the racetrack as well. To prove my point, the government recently decided to move the racetrack out of the city centre and in its place build two eighty-five storey office blocks – the biggest twin peaks in the world – two slightly smaller twin peaks, yet another luxury hotel, a six-storey shopping centre for people not to hang around in, and a park, in order to create even more traffic to make people work faster still.

If you can actually get to a travel agent through the traffic, Kuala Lumpur is the only place in the world where you can see the seats on the airline computer being taken while you are trying to make up your mind whether to sit by the window or by the—

'Please to hurry, the seats are being taken.'

'Is it smoking or—'

'Quick. There's only—'

'It's not by the emergency—?'

'Sir, please to decide. Now there is only—'

'Okay, I'll take the window. No—'

'Please sir, you are too late. All seats now taken. Next flight tomorrow.'

Next time, I'd learnt my lesson. I skidded into the travel agent. 'Okay, quick,' I shouted. 'Seven o'clock flight.'

'Yes please, sir.'

'Window.'

'Yes please, sir.'

'No smoking.'

'Yes, please—'

Zap. Another power cut. The computer went dead. It took me three days to get out of the country. Not because they were inefficient, but because they were too efficient.

The threat of power cuts, I'm convinced, is also responsible for their bad spelling. Why spell taxi, teksi, alcohol, alkohol or gin stinger, gin stengah? It's either because they are in such a hurry to finish their letters and reports before the next power cut that they scribble out the first thing that comes into their heads and don't have time to check it, or because the power cuts have blown the memory on the word processors and they have gone electronically dyslexic. I mean, why is sandwic not sandwich; kopi not coffee, and teh not tea?

Some people say East meets West in Singapore and Malaysia. Knonsensey. Malaysia is still East. Squeezed between the gleaming new buildings and the skyscrapers you can still see tiny old clapboard houses. Inside you get the impression families are living the life they would have lived before Raffles was thought of. The streets are a shade scruffier. There are flecks of dust on the pavements. The open-air bars and restaurants are a shade noisier. But maybe not for much longer.

Chow Kit, along Jalan Tnanku Abdul Rahman, used to be the rough, tough, gangster area of town. A bit like the old transvestite area of Singapore with the pondans with their pink lipstick, beehive hairdos and great dangling earrings. Today all the Malay and Chinese traders, medicine men and genuine sellers of everything from fake designer jeans to fake Rolex watches are gone. So are the pondans. It's like Singapore – clean, safe, boring. The Ministry of Domestic Trade and Consumer Affairs (Enforcement Division), the Federal Territory Religious Department (Enforcement Division), and the Immigration Department (Enforcement Division), not to mention the police and customs and excise have had their way.

For years there seemed to be constant battles between the old-time shopkeepers, stallholders and tramps and the obviously Singapore-trained administrators. One day they would be there, the next they would be gone. Two days later they would start creeping back. Then the Indonesians started moving in, which is when, the Malays and Chinese say, things started getting worse. Even violent. Today the old shops are still there. The occasional sheet of corrugated iron blocks up the odd doorway. Instead there are coloured patterned pavements, overhead shelters.

The nine hereditary Malaysian maharajahs have, however,

proved more difficult to shift. At present they are above the law; immune from prosecution. Until recently they were even, can you imagine, protected by law from criticism by the press.

Most, no doubt, like all royals, are well behaved, sober, responsible citizens who love their wives and children, give to charity, talk to their plants and send their polo ponies Christmas cards. The joker in the pack is Sultan Mahmood Iskandar of Johor (not Jahore, which is in India). He is obviously under the impression that kings are supposed to behave as kings. As heir to the sultanate he was taken to court for what was described as sadistic brutality. Four years later he killed a smuggler, or rather an alleged smuggler. When it was his turn to be king, from 1984 to 1989, he killed his golf caddy. After he stepped aside he went for his hockey coach.

The result is that the whole system will probably go the way of Chow Kit. At present the maharajahs' legal immunities are slowly being abolished. Other privileges are likely to be whittled away. In theory they are not allowed to dabble in politics, go into business or use their position or influence for financial gain. In practice, they do all three; some just to survive, others for the fun of it. While I was there on one trip there was a row over whether the fiercely religious Sultan of Kelantun, the big, sprawling north-western state, should be allowed to import a fiercely non-religious Lamborghini tax-free. The fact that he not only owns great tracts of industrial development land in the region, has his own private army – paid for out of central government funds – and is one of the biggest landowners next door in Singapore, seemed irrelevant.

Nobody is going to come to their aid. Arguing for the freedom to live like a king, have lavish parties, sell rainforests for financial gain, build air-conditioned stables for your 200 polo ponies and go around forgetting to repay multi-million-dollar bank loans and kill golf caddies is not exactly the most come-hither political platform. Although I might make an exception for the air-conditioned stables.

The Sultan of Pahang, on the other hand, actually goes around admitting he can make mistakes. What's more – shock, horror! – he wants people to point them out to him. Although what will happen to anyone who takes him at his word we don't know.

At the same time, Malaysia is becoming more and more Muslim. Not so much strict Muslim as Church of England Muslim, if you know what I mean. They seem to accept the general drift of what Mohammed had to say but in their own slightly reserved, slightly restrained way.

The Iranians, the Algerians, maybe even the Egyptians are like the Charismatics: everything is done at boiling point. But, though room service in Malaysian hotels will provide prayer mats any time, the Malaysians are – I trust they won't tear their hair out – much more English about their religion. Sure, they have their strict rules, but they don't enforce them as rigorously as the others. They have their mosques, but their mosques are like their railway stations and the railway stations (nobody mention St Pancras) are a bit like their mosques.

Some women wear veils, but only the too-dong, the short veil that covers the hair, not the full-length black bell-tents that cover everything but the eyes. Some tried, but the prime minister, himself a Muslim, very cleverly came up with an answer that virtually banned it and caused only the slightest raised eyebrow, if you were quick enough to spot it under the too-dong.

'People dealing with civil servants and other officials should see the face of the person they are dealing with,' he said. 'How can they, if their face is hidden by a veil?'

Brilliant. The problem, and the veils, disappeared before you could say consumer protection.

Like the Church of England again, they don't seem to have the hang-ups other religions have about who can or can't be a member. A hard-drinking, cynical, bitter, twisted Fleet Street journalist I've known for years went to Kuala Lumpur over twenty years ago. He wanted to marry a Muslim girl, so he went native, as they say, and joined the ranks.

'How difficult was it?' I asked him as we strolled into an old haunt downtown.

'There are strict rules,' he grunted in that embarrassed way we all adopt when talking about religion. 'There are lessons and classes. You have to attend them every week for over a year.'

'So that's what you did?' I said as we got to the bar.

'No,' he grinned. 'I got a plane to Sarawak, chatted up a government minister I've known for years, got him to sign my certificate there and then. Don't really believe in it, of course. Did it for the wife.'

The barman came up to us.

'Two large Scotches.'

'Not for me, old chap,' he butted in. 'Don't drink any more.'

'To please the wife?'

'To please the wife.'

I ordered two Cokes instead. But we never got them. Zap. The lights went out.

Jakarta

It was slightly unnerving. I arrived at Jakarta's airport with its Pizza Hut roofs. We sailed through the formalities with McDonald's efficiency. The sun was shining. It was around 90°F. It had been a good flight, except that the company wasn't so hot. I was sitting next to an Australian bank clerk who kept telling me he was taking a 'sickie' to do all the islands. This prevented me from seeing all the 13,000 islands that make up Indonesia, the land under the rainbow, and all that's left of the huge prehistoric land bridge that at one time would have enabled Asians to flood into freedom-loving, All-Kevs-are-equal, sickie Australia 600 miles to the south without the fuss and bother of applying for a visa.

To me Indonesia is the stuff of legends and adventures – Conrad adventures, not Jeffrey Archer adventures: South China Sea, Java Sea, Flores Sea, Sumba Sea, Banda Sea, Molucca Sea, Celebes Sea, Timor Sea; islands that are still in the Stone Age; tribes that go around naked; people who solemnly greet you with a courteous, 'I honour your faeces'; the spice trade.

The spice trade began in Indonesia. Well, 1,500 miles to the east, to be precise, on the archipelago of Banda, which some people say is home to one of the best hotels in the world, the Maulana, even though it has no hot water and only serves fish and rice. In the seventeenth century, under the Dutch, Banda was the world's sole supplier of top quality nutmeg, vital for preserving meat in the good old days when meat was healthy and vegetarians were a disease.

Today, however, for most people Indonesia is a two-week bridge between dreams and reality: a real live tropical paradise, with unspoilt beaches and a simple, uncomplicated lifestyle. Except that unspoilt single rooms cost anything up to US $1,200 a night, two-bedroom simple suites up to $1,450 a night, and uncomplicated three-bedroom villas anything over $2,000 a night. For that pittance you can mix with unspoilt, single, uncomplicated Balinese gardeners, waitresses, beach boys and wood carvers swopping drinks at US $25 a shot and munching jadefish baked in ginger for anything up to $100 depending on how unspoilt and uncomplicated the five-star hotel or restaurant is.

Scott Fitzgerald called the Plage de la Garoupe on Cap d'Antibes a 'bright tan prayer rug of a beach'. From 5,000 feet, Indonesia's beaches looked like expensive, bejewelled, magic carpets. But not for me. I had a string of meetings already lined up. It was going to be tough.

Through customs; no problems. In the arrivals hall there was the usual motley collection of chauffeurs, couriers, excited secretaries and mistresses huddled around the entrance. In the distance, sprawled all over the benches, were one or two wives and mothers who had obviously fallen asleep in their eagerness to see their loved ones again.

Then it happened. A tiny, thick-set man in a sweaty white suit with a blue baseball cap came straight up to me. He was the perfect shape for a Sumo wrestler except that he was ten stone too light and about five feet too short. On his forehead he had that hard patch of skin, the mark of a devout Muslim, which comes with banging your head on the floor during prayers.

'I want you to be hospital here,' he smiled. We shook hands. East of Canary Wharf I shake hands with anybody and everybody. He looked as though he'd been left out in the sun too long and had started sizzling. His teeth resembled Stonehenge on a foggy day.

'I vice you. I vice you everything.' He waved at one of the drivers to take my suitcase. 'First we go to hotel,' he grinned.

Don't ask why, but I followed him and the driver to the car park. I climbed in the back of the car, which had lace curtains on the seats. He climbed in alongside the driver.

He turned round, the hard patch on his forehead glistening in the sun. 'With me you will be very hospital.'

I had never seen him before in my life. I had no idea who he was. I had no idea why I followed him. I dreaded to think how hospital he could be if he turned friendly. We roared off towards Jakarta.

The whole situation was bizarre. Not because I'd been virtually kidnapped by a hospital Indonesian Dutch uncle but because we were able to roar off towards Jakarta. Normally the traffic in Jakarta is so bad the only roaring anybody does is to themselves for being there in the first place.

Jakarta – many Americans make it sound like a Georgian peanut farmer who thought all he had to do to become president was to be a Jimmy – is too big for its own good. With 13,000 islands to choose from you'd have thought the Indonesians had enough space to spread things around a bit. Not on your life. Jakarta is a bizarre rijstafel of a city, but instead of everything being separated into neat little units like a decent rijstafel, it is all piled on top of each other as if served by a trainee anarchist Dutch waiter who has no more idea of the proper way to serve an Indonesian meal than how to survive without drugs for a whole afternoon.

At first you think Jakarta will be, perhaps, a little Dutch. Flying in over Java, the Garden of the East, which is about the same size as England, is like flying over Holland. The wet rice fields, or sawahs, especially around Kindus in the centre of the island, are as neat and square and mathematical as the fields around Schipol. The temples stand neatly to attention at right angles to the roads. Then slowly they begin to change and follow the contours of the map. The water buffalo lounge lazily out of line. Temples stray from their straight and narrow path.

Suddenly you're in one of the mega-cities on the Pacific rim, home to over 14 million people and a regular host for conferences on The Problems of Mega-Cities on the Pacific Rim, which, because of the number of delegates who pour in to debate the problems has all the environmental, ecological, socio-economic and socio-cultural problems the conferences are designed to eliminate.

Jakarta, as a result, is another Taipei or Seoul or maybe Bombay. Without the slums. Well, without the slums you find in Bombay. It has the feel of any Asian city; too many people, too much traffic, too much noise. The roads are crammed from morning to night. The pavements are overflowing. Even in the backstreets where there are no pavements they are still overflowing. In Singapore and Kuala Lumpur in between the BMWs and forty-ton container lorries you see more BMWs and container lorries. In Jakarta you see thousands of tiny death-defying tuk tuks or bajajs, as they call them, and, overtaking them all, millions of wizened old men, sweating under umbrellas and somehow pulling enormous handcarts.

Some of the modern buildings are fantastic. There are ritzy offices and even ritzier shopping centres. Some of the hotels are among the best and most luxurious I've been able to check into anywhere. But to some people, usually the Arabs, Jakarta is a down-market second cousin to Kuala Lumpur, more workmanlike than exciting.

'They've got all the designs we rejected,' a Singaporean property developer once told me.

'They are interesting rather than exciting,' was the down-to-earth comment of a Dutch banker.

But interesting or exciting, with tumbledown shacks propped up by wooden posts peeping out from behind them, the real Asia is never very far away. There are mosques on every block and mini-mosques hidden beneath clusters of red tiles on every street corner. Women wearing the veil drift by. Men in bare feet wander in and out of scruffy offices and warehouses.

Conrad would be lost today wandering around Singapore; in Jakarta, he'd be more at home. Although what he'd do if he ever found out it was the Barbie doll capital of the world – just outside the city is one of the key world production centres for Barbie dolls – I shudder to think. Probably take off for the Heart of Darkness.

I'd no sooner got to my hotel room than flowers and baskets of fruit were delivered. The mini-bar was hastily restocked. The laundry maid arrived and asked if I had any laundry that needed washing immediately, or any suits that needed pressing.

'Now I wait you,' my bodyguard abductor smiled as he bowed slowly out of the room. 'Downstairs I shall be waiting.'

For the rest of my visit he was not so much at my beck and call, he was there before I thought of even becking let alone calling. At first I felt uneasy. Was he a government agent? Secret service? Whose secret service? Why me? Was somebody playing a joke? Was this the Indonesian version of a singing telegram? Who the hell had been sending me 'Wish you were here' postcards from East Timor? Was I going to wake up tomorrow …?

Then I felt guilty. Well, a little bit. Was he trying to shame me into paying him an arm and a leg for services I did not want? Was he really expecting me to take him home with me at the end of my trip? Or his mother? Or his sister? Or, oh no, his whole family? Was he going to get me to swallow a lorry-load of drugs to get them into the UK?

Then I thought, what the hell. I didn't adopt him, he adopted me. I'm his problem. He should do the worrying, not me. But if I was uneasy about him, the hotel staff were certainly jumpy. He had only to appear at the door and everyone sprang to attention. The doorman practically clicked his heels and gave him a full dress regimental salute; the lobby manager oozed an additional slither of charm; the bell captain bowed towards him; the girls at reception giggled and grinned and practically curtsied every time he spoke to them.

I come from the old school that prefers to sneak in and out of hotels unnoticed. Not for me the back-slapping and glad-handing of regional sales managers and conference delegates. But with my bodyguard it was impossible. I had only to think of opening my mini-bar and I was glad-handing everybody in sight: cleaners, lift attendant, maintenance man, the girls behind reception. If I had been running for election against J. Carter himself – I would never dream of running against Suharto and neither would anybody else – I couldn't have shaken more hands. Once I swear I shook hands with the entire East German navy arriving at the hotel on a goodwill mission to sell the Indonesians their entire fleet, although goodness knows who they thought I was.

Jakarta was certainly being very hospital and I felt very hospital as well. Throughout my stay, my mysterious guardian angel took command of my life entirely. If I wanted a newspaper, he would get me one. If I wanted to send a fax he would send it. Had I as much as hinted that I wanted to ship home the year's production of Sumba's famous blood soup with pig fat he'd have fixed it. He negotiated with drivers: I paid less than half what they demanded.

Towards the end he even got me my own personal driver, for next to nothing. Trouble was, he had a pigtail. Pigtails don't normally bother me; nowadays lots of men have them. But this one was, I'm not kidding, hanging from his chin. Naturally I didn't stare, and naturally I didn't let on for one second that I noticed the slightest hint of anything unusual. But I ask you, his chin. I promise you it was a long, thin, jet-black pigtail; not a few spindly strands of hair, but an honest-to-goodness pigtail. Hanging from his chin, almost as far as his waist, with a tiny little band wound tightly round the end of it. Not that I noticed anything, of course. It took all the little power I have not to look at it dangling down in front of him. Even now I don't think about it. Honest.

When he opened the car door for me it took all the energy I had not to gather it up and tuck it in his jacket pocket, to stop it from getting caught in the door. I mean, imagine slamming your pigtail in the door and walking away. You'd leave half your face behind banging on the car door.

Just once I nearly came to grief. I usually keep my briefcase and all my reports and papers with me all the time. It's not that they are worth anything, even as scrap paper; it's just that it has invariably taken so much blood, sweat, agony and tears to produce them that I can't face going through it all over again if they are stolen. One morning I was off to see some officials at the Sake Bank. Just as we were driving away I saw an old Unilever hand I knew from the Netherlands. He'd emigrated, he'd told me, because of taxes and the time he'd spent 'knocking at preferment's door'.

I offered him a lift. Pigtail jumped out, grabbed my briefcase and papers off the back seat and put them in the front. No problem about that. The old Unilever hand jumped in. We were off. Down narrow little roads we went lined with tiny houses with corrugated iron roofs. Along by overflowing sewers, through what looked like building sites. We dropped him at his home near the university. It was a neat, red-tiled bungalow hidden behind a wall of secondhand car tyres. The windows were lined with houseplants. The garden looked a mess. We agreed to meet that evening, said Tot siens, and we drove off.

When I reached my meeting, I jumped out of the car, turned to grab my – then it happened. Pigtail picked up my briefcase, no problem. But as he turned to grab my papers they fell against the front seat. He stooped to pick them up and in doing so caught his pigtail up in the middle of them. He turned to me. There were my papers. And there, wrapped around my reports and proposals, was his damn pigtail. If I grabbed them and walked away, I'd tear half his face off. If I noticed the pigtail, we'd spend half the morning unwinding it from my mass of papers and the other half winding it up again.

'Sir. Good morning, sir.' My bodyguard arrived out of nowhere. 'Quick, sir is late.' He clapped his hands and shouted at Pigtail. 'Take his papers inside. Quick, quick.' He turned to me. 'I vice you everything,' he smiled. 'With me, no problems. Everything very hospital here.'

In many ways, Indonesia is what India should be today. The largest country in South East Asia, it stretches 5,000 km from east to west, the distance from London to Chicago. It has virtually the same mix of rajahs, holymen and temples. It has more Muslims than any other country: over 85 percent of the population and growing. It has a handful of Christians in East Timor, the former Portuguese colony, and they're not growing. It has naked primitive tribes in Irian Jaya in the east. And it has even more naked primitive people struggling to survive in all the luxury hotels in Bali. Unlike India, however, it doesn't have poverty.

'So how come Indonesia has done it and India hasn't?' I once asked another Dutchman who had left Holland because he said he would be killed either by Dutch taxes or by the Dutch decision to legalize euthanasia. We were in a bar somewhere near a ritzy shopping centre called Centre Point. I had just bought him his seventh whisky.

'Suharto,' he slurred. 'Suharto.' Then he paused. 'And I do in truth believe it.'

In 1970 when Suharto came to power, over 60 percent of the population were living below the poverty line. Indonesia was the world's largest importer of rice. Today, like Mrs Suharto, who once spent thirty-six days in the slammer for slashing a fellow partygoer with a glass at one of those elegant aprés-ski parties they have at Aspen, Colorado, Indonesia is a little tiger. For the last twenty years growth has averaged 6 percent a year. It is one of the top fifteen oil producers in the world, but oil accounts for less than 40 percent of export earnings. It's into aircraft, shipbuilding, munitions – and monkeys. Indonesia is a major exporter of *Macaca fasciu-laris* for medical research, especially Aids research.

Foreign investment has come pouring in: over $35 billion in the last five years alone. Over the next ten years they are planning to spend over US$30 billion on building up their national grid to ensure, unlikely nearby Kuala Lumpur, they are never short of power for future growth. Average income has soared from US$70 to $600. Less than 15 percent of the population are now below the poverty line and they stopped importing rice a long, long time ago.

Normally, nowadays, when I'm on a trip and I hit a new town or city, I'm immediately into what I call my BBC programme. I grab the first cab I come across and I'm off checking out all the Bars, Bookshops and Churches. Of course, when I was younger it wasn't always the Bookshops.

In Jakarta, I was stymied. Wherever I went my bodyguard went with me. I was only in the bar being entertained by the Dutchman because I had escaped out the back door from my previous meeting. We'd driven along a narrow lane packed with stalls either side near the back of the university. The car dropped me at reception. As I was waiting I spotted the back door. As soon as my meeting was over I made straight for it. It was my only hope. I jumped in the first cab that came along. 'Bar. Bar,' I whispered at the driver in case my bodyguard heard what I was saying.

What happens? He takes me to probably the only traditional Dutch bar in South East Asia. At first it was as empty as a Dutchman's wallet. Not that anyone has probably ever seen inside a Dutchman's wallet. But it began to fill up. It was the countdown to the most important day in the Dutch calendar: the start of the herring season, which is a combination of

'Beaujolais Nouveau est arrivé', August 12 and Yom Kippur.

The Dutch eat herring all the time. Over a third of all fish sold in the Netherlands is herring. But New Herring Day is unlike any other day of the year. You think the French can be boring comparing different vintages? You haven't heard the Dutch comparing different herring seasons.

'No, no, 1991, old chap. That was the year. The right size, the right fat content. Delicious.'

'No, sorry, got to disagree with you there, old chap. '92 far superior. They were smaller, less fat. More authenticity.'

In Jakarta, it's worse. Days, no weeks before, they are arguing about the merits of different years, psyching themselves up for the arrival of their oak barrels full of herring which, being Dutch, they expect their friends and families to send from the old country.

When I first got to the bar I'd been buttonholed by an old Dutchman who looked like Wilfred Thesiger on heat. He'd come out to Jakarta a million years ago as a junior civil servant and decided to stay – 'just like that,' he slapped his knee in a very old-British-Colonial-office way.

I greeted him using the Traditional Dutch greeting: 'What would you like to drink?'

'What's happened to you British, my boy,' he said in a very colonial accent. 'Used to be very good. Very professional. The best.' He sighed quietly. 'Remember in Malaysia. Soon taught the chaps what it was all about. Pushed the villagers into compounds. Cordon sanitaire between them and the jungle. One hundred percent curfew. Anyone breaking the curfew was shot, no questions asked. Soon cut off their supplies, virtually starved them out. What? Good show.'

He could have been in the Household Cavalry Club or even the Army and Navy Club. 'That's the way to treat them. Soon solved the problem. Reckon that's why they're all so capitalist nowadays. Scared what you would do to them if they turned Communist again, what?'

The British, the French and the Germans I have no problem

seeing as colonialists. But not the Dutch. Somehow to me the Dutch seem to lack the confidence to be colonial oppressors and masters. Or at least today's Dutch; maybe the early Dutch were different. The British you can see marching in their khaki shorts and clipped sentences and taking over as if by divine right. Similarly the French, although they always gave the impression they were doing it by divine right known only to them and their God. The Germans of course, did it because of their links with the Devil.

The Dutch I see being more the diffident schoolmaster, doing it not because they wanted to but for the good of the country and the people and, of course, secretly pleased that it is actually going to hurt them more than it would hurt the country. Some history books, especially Dutch ones, paint a different picture. But I don't believe them. To me its the oh-so-politically-correct Dutch exaggerating like mad to try and restore the balance. It's as if they've been convicted of a single murder but are prepared to confess to a hundred so that they won't look better than all the other murderers.

By now the bar was full of Dutch expats from the Garden of Edam, psyching themselves up for an evening of solemn enjoyment and praying that somebody would soon arrive and buy them a drink. You think I'm kidding. I know plenty of Dutch people who call railway stations all over Belgium for free advice on trains rather than ring their own railways and pay for the call. A Dutch bar, therefore, is the second easiest place in the world to strike up a conversation.

One old man, who practically looked like a windmill, kept telling me, 'I'm Dutch. From Holland.' He had worked for Lloyds in the City of London in the foreign department when he was young. It was his job to read the small print in their policies to ensure that they never had to pay out.

'And did you ever have to pay out?' I asked.

'No, never,' he grinned. 'None of those damn foreigners could read English. They just took our word for it.'

Another Dutchman told me he used to work for Pretty Polly

in Holland, but the company closed down.

'Why?' I wondered. 'Dutchwomen wear stockings don't they?'

'Sure,' he said, 'but their thighs were too thick for the stockings we made. All that cycling.'

He was made redundant. But why come to Jakarta? Dutch social security payments, I always thought, were better than working.

He shook his head. 'Holland is not the Holland it used to be. When I was young, Holland was for men. Now the soldiers wear hairnets. Next they'll be wearing lipstick.' He had decided to leave.

He showed me what looked like a Dutch credit card. 'See that,' he said. 'That is my passport for life. That is what I have to carry if I go to the Netherlands to stop doctors from performing euthanasia on me. You have to have a card now that says, Please don't kill me; a card to tell doctors not to kill you. Can you imagine?'

It was, I agreed, difficult to imagine.

'And this is the country,' he continued, 'that stopped the post office printing Happy Christmas on your letters in case inside was a letter about somebody dying.'

I didn't fancy a fight to the death on euthanasia in the back streets of Jakarta with a whole bunch of Dutchmen. I switched back to Indonesia. 'So what's the secret of their success?'

The Dutchman from Holland thought deeply until I had bought the eighth whisky. 'Consensus,' he said. 'And Berkeley.' A pause. 'And I do in truth believe it.'

Suharto may be a leading member of the exclusive twenty-five-years-in-power club, but in Jakarta you don't have the same happy, relaxed feelings you get in Mobuto's Zaire, Castro's Cuba or got in Kim Il Sung's North Korea. There are few policemen around, and even fewer people mysteriously standing on street corners watching the world go by. People can talk and gossip and criticize freely, even about the President and his family, for while mother is away in Aspen, or maybe just away, for a few weeks, the rest of the family are making it back home. Eldest daughter is running the local construction company; second son is into telecommunications; youngest son is making do with contracting companies.

Even so, 'consensus democracy' seems to work. Suharto is always the only candidate for the top job. He is always elected unanimously, and has been six times. The People's Consultative Assembly has 1,000 members: 500 elected, 500 appointed by the government. Of the elected seats, the ruling Golkar party, which has been in power since 1971 shortly after Suharto took over, controls 400 and the remaining 100 seats are held by the military. It meets only for eleven days every five years to bless the government's programme and vote for the President. The rest of the time they spend in traffic jams in and out of Jakarta because the President's party, the two opposition parties, the military and the provincial representative always agree. Even the tiny opposition Christian Indonesian Democrats party refuses to disagree with anything anyone suggests unless, horror of horrors, they actually have to have a vote on it.

'But it works,' he slurred as I went for the ninth. 'And I do in truth believe it.'

Berkeley is Berkeley, California. Practically every Indonesian economist who cannot add two and two together seems to have earned his degree there. Known inevitably as the 'Berkeley mafia', they believe in all the right things American economists used to believe in: deregulation, exports and a balanced budget. All the engineers, however, seem to have studied in Germany – they are known as the Aachen mafia – and they believe in the things German and Japanese engineers used to believe in: big state industries, strategic industries, long-term planning. The result is that not only are they outstripping other still developing countries – in ten years Indonesia has increased its cocoa production 100-fold while Africa's has virtually collapsed – they are also beginning to compete head on with some of the so-called developed countries. They are even, heaven help them, buying steel mills in Scotland.

'Mamma's still there?' Another Dutchman, also from Holland, broke into the conversation. He was tall, slightly stooped, bald.

'Mamma, who's Mamma?'

'Mamma's Bar, in the centre of Amsterdam. Best bar in the world.'

'Mamma's Bar? In Amsterdam?'

'Sure,' he grinned. 'If you're going to be late you ring up lady wife. Then before she answers you switch on one of the background sound effects. Airports, railway stations, that kind of thing.'

'So she thinks you . . .'

'And you can stay there all night. Only thing I miss.'

It turned out he was also working for Unilever and had been in Indonesia, which he called, somewhat elaborately, 'an archipelago of little islands linked by sporadic communications', for nearly ten years. A relative newcomer.

He went on and on about soap is not soap. The Filipinos like it one way, the Thais another. Everybody, however, likes ice cream although it has to have special secret ingredients to make it survive the tropics. Then he went on about something called Rinso Ultra. In Jakarta, Rinso Ultra is sold in giant Western-size bumper packets. In Ujung Pandang, the capital of Sulawesi, it is sold in one-ounce packets at 30 cents a time.

By now I had no money left. I was down to my last Venezuelan ten-bob note. Obviously, nobody was going to offer me a drink; instead everybody was going along the bar emptying the dregs from all the bottles that were left into their glasses. Typical Dutch.

I left my small change for the barman, which was probably enough to enable him to retire, and stumbled outside. Nobody had offered me a lift. I had no idea where I was. There were no cabs in sight. How the – A car suddenly swung round the corner and stopped right in front of me. Out jumped my bodyguard. 'Very nice evening, sir,' he smiled. 'Very hospital place.'

'How did you know I was here?' I gasped.

'The barman, sir. He is my cousin. He tells me you are here.'

Arguing with hotel porters, fighting with taxi – oops, I mean teksi drivers, being forced to buy twenty-three more batik shirts when I only wanted seventeen; my bodyguard protected me from all the joys of foreign travel. For the first time in my life, I got to the meetings I wanted to go to, at the time I wanted to arrive. What's more I went by the quickest, most direct route, not via the house where the driver's brother-in-law's cousin's wife lived. If I was going out to dinner, we drove straight to the restaurant, and not to a better restaurant down an alleyway next door to the local mortuary owned by the hotel porter's little brother. When we went to government offices, we went to government offices. Not to see a cousin selling a million cups and saucers made out of coconut leaves at a very good price. When I wanted to change money I actually went to a bank which gave me a very good rate. But what not even my bodyguard could protect me from was their famous traffic jams; Muslim traffic jams.

Many people, and especially Americans, see Islam as the 'new enemy'. In their sophisticated analysis of the world, it's simply a case of goodbye Communism, welcome Islam. Everybody needs an enemy. These guys with tablecloths on their heads will do very nicely, thank you, as the new enemy. Going around the US and talking to Americans during the Gulf War, it was fascinating to hear what a fantastic job their boys were doing against that old nutcase Hussein. No mention of their Muslim allies and what they also were doing against Hussein.

To me the Muslims are no more the 'new enemy' than Luther, Calvin and all the other liberals were enemies to established society in the sixteenth century. The Muslims are almost a Christian people. Their basic wishes, aspirations and intentions are, let's be honest, Christian; or, if you must be pedantic, Christian-like. The problem is that Islam today is going through its own equivalent of our Reformation. Some want to stick to the fundamentals: if that's what it says, that's what I believe. Others want to adapt to the present day. Some want to debate by textbook, others want to get violent. Some want a broad church, or rather mosque; others want a small, tight-knit believers' club.

Some believe the faith is supreme. Mosques are not just places of worship, somewhere to pop in once a week, avoid the collection and get out again as quickly as possible. They, like the early Christians, believe places of worship should be the centre, the heart and soul, of the local community; places also for meetings, discussion, exchanging information; places for education. Mosques should run their own religious classes. They should help the poor and needy, just as the early Christians used to help the poor and needy. And Islamic courts, fundamentalists believe, should hear family disputes, although what constitutes a family and what constitutes a dispute are two of the biggest disputes anyone, Christian or Muslim, could face.

Like the problems confronting the Reformation, these are not easy problems to solve. As with the Reformation, when it is finally sorted out nobody will agree with the results.

Many Westerners point to the tensions. Some people told me about the number of churches that have accidentally caught fire of their own accord, and the leaflets distributed in downtown Jakarta claiming the Koran is only really a junior edition of the Bible, so why can't the Christians agree with the Muslims and be done with it. The other two signs I was told to look out for were the number of Muslims in the cabinet, and the number of women wearing the veil.

Indonesia is 88 percent Muslim. Most cabinets are around 66 percent Muslim, and growing, so it looks as if the government is also aware of the tensions. As for women, certainly an awful lot are wearing the veil, but from what I was told they seem to be happy with their lot. They are not demanding to take a more active part in mosque affairs, unlike in some countries.

On one trip to Kuala Lumpur, for example, I turned up in the middle of what was obviously the All Islam equivalent of the Eurovision Song Contest, complete with a bearded Terry El Wogan as compère. Because more and more women were now taking part in mosque affairs, for the first time women were allowed to come as equals with men and chant their favourite verses from the Koran. The winner presumably had the privilege of waking everybody for morning prayers all over the Muslim world which, you've got to admit, is a little more positive than sending everybody to sleep with some inane song about a puppet on a string.

But for me the biggest tension is the Muslim traffic jam. Especially when you're trying to get through Jakarta on a Friday lunchtime during Ramadan.

During the week traffic is bad, if not unChristian. But on Fridays when everyone, apart from the women, heads for his local mosque, it's positively unMuslim.

Imagine East River Drive into New York at four o'clock in the afternoon. Imagine the autostrada into Milan with everybody going in to be fined for corruption. Imagine the Heathfield Country Show after three days of rain, not a tractor in sight and the same old Special Constable on the gate deliberately sending the traffic off in the opposite direction to which it wants to go. Well it's worse than all that put together and multiplied by a hundred.

In Europe and the United States over the last ten years the number of cars per 1,000 population has remained pretty steady. Not so in Asia. There it has doubled and, according to some research firms, it will double again in the next ten years. On Fridays in Jakarta you see it happening.

The jams are so total, so solid, so unmoving, it practically makes you wish you were a Christian. At least Sunday is a sensible day to go to church. The shops are closed – well, most of them. The offices are closed – well, most of them. The roads are empty. Well, early morning, unless the sun is shining.

The Muslims, however, have to be different. On Fridays everything shuts down so that everyone can go and pray. Not at the mosque nearest to their office or shop or market stall; that would be, well, Christian. They all insist on going to the mosque near where they live, which is decidedly unChristian. During Ramadan the government helps by cutting the number of hours in the working day to enable everybody to do his duty.

One Friday I got caught. It wasn't my bodyguard's fault. We'd left in plenty of time. I got to my meeting on time. The guy I was meeting, however, wasn't there. He was stuck in the traffic on the way into Jakarta. On Fridays, because everyone wants to go to their local mosque, they come in by car, which makes everything a thousand times worse.

When he came, I just couldn't – I just couldn't help – I just couldn't help noticing – I mean, as if the driver with the pigtail wasn't enough, this guy had, had, had six fingers on his left hand. Six fingers. Whatever he did, whatever he said, I just couldn't help noticing them.

'Six fingers. He had six fingers,' I just couldn't help telling my bodyguard as soon as I got back to the car.

'Six fingers,' he said very solemnly, 'are a sign of good luck. He is very lucky.'

Apparently, in Indonesia many children are born with six fingers. To the Arabs it's a sign of good luck. Others think the opposite and break the sixth finger off shortly after birth.

After that, of course, we had nothing but bad luck. We hit the traffic jam. It was solid. Some people say it is possible to get caught up in a Jakarta traffic jam never to return, like a Muslim Bermuda Triangle. We edged forward an inch, maybe two inches. Then we sat for hours. You think I'm kidding.

214

Because the jams are so bad and because it's so hot you stand more chance of getting cholera in a traffic jam in Jakarta in Ramadan than you do travelling through the jungles in the far away islands. Then it suddenly struck me. Nobody was smashing their head against the steering wheel; nobody was cursing or mouthing obscenities through the windscreen; there was no baring of teeth, no slow shaking of the head, no sweaty palms. I bet even their corticosteroid levels were constant. This was a civilized, cultured, pre-Reformation Muslim traffic jam. Instead of pumping adrenalin everybody was sitting back and thinking of Mohammed.

In front of us a broken-down bajaj tried to squeeze between one of the old blue double-decker buses and a forty-ton truck. There was no room for a cholera bacterium to breathe but they managed to let him through. As if that was the key, everything started moving again, straightaway. The solid mass suddenly swung into top gear and we were all hurtling down East River Drive into New York at a thousand miles an hour.

We swung round a tiny mosque. People were gathering outside, barefoot on the pavement. Some were already kneeling down. Then out from a side road like a rocket shot a woman, glasses, moon face, a light blue veil, driving a clapped-out old banger. Pigtail braked sharply. I grabbed the edge of the dashboard. What did she do? Well call me Abdul Aziz, this gentle, peace-loving, completely unveiled new Muslim gave me the bird, bone, expressway digit, or to put it bluntly, the one-finger sign.

Which, I suppose, proves that women drivers are women drivers the world over.

It was time to leave. My bodyguard and Pigtail took me back to the airport with its Pizza Hut roofs. It was a Sunday so the roads were empty. We drove through the centre of town, past the enormous luxury Mandarin Oriental. Even now there were small boys out selling bottled water. Okay, I thought, here it comes. The pay-off. Him, his wife, his thirteen children, all want to come and live with me. Past the turning where we took the man from Unilever, past what looked like the street with the Dutch Club.

Suddenly, out of a sidestreet shot another Muslim woman driver. This time no traditional Muslim greeting. Maybe they have rules about that kind of thing on a Christian Sunday. Quickly I asked my bodyguard about Muslim women. How many wives has he got?

'Four,' he says.

'Can all Muslims have four wives?' I wondered.

'Sure,' he grinned, 'providing you can afford them and providing the first wife agrees.'

Keep him talking. Maybe that way he'll forget to ask about you-know-what.

'Does she always agree?' I continued.

'Sure,' he grinned. 'Why not? She is my wife.'

'So are you going to get more wives?'

'More wives.' He slapped his forehead. 'What's better than a new young wife? A car?' He shrugged his shoulders. 'You Canadians.'

Now we were passing the rather sedate, clean-looking shanties on the edge of the airport road. Still no word. Finally, we're at the airport. We draw up by the departure gates and out jumps my bodyguard. Okay, I'm thinking, here we go. Out jumps Pigtail. This is it; the big pay-off. What the hell are they going to . . .?

'We thank you very much, Sir,' says the bodyguard.

'Thank you, sir,' says Pigtail.

'We hope you had a hospital stay in our country,' says my almost ex-bodyguard.

'Well, yes, I have,' I begin.

'We are pleased we vice you on everything,' he continues.

'Yes, you certainly—'

'Now we say goodbye.' He puts his hand out. I shake it.

216

'We say goodbye,' adds Pigtail as he also puts his hand out. That I shake too.

Then they're gone. They're in the car and roaring back to Jakarta. No requests, no favours. They didn't even want my home address.

Not, of course, that I expected anything else.

Bombay

'Quick, lock the doors.'

I was in the back of a sweaty, prehistoric taxi. All I could see were levers.

'That one. Pull it up. Pull it up.' The driver leant back across the front seat pointing at the top one. 'And make certain windows are closed.'

Most Bombay taxis I find are normally as dangerous as a king prawn biryani. But this was worse. Bombay was virtually at war with itself. Over 500 people had been killed in the previous five days. Nearly 400 more had been injured. Hospitals were overflowing. The city was running out of blood, or that's what the doctors and surgeons kept saying, although judging by the streets there seemed to be more than enough around.

The army had moved in, with nearly fifty columns deployed throughout the city. India's famous Rapid Action Force was on its way. The whole city was under curfew.

I had just arrived at Santa Cruz airport from India's Silicon Plateau. I had already waited nearly two hours. There were hardly any taxis, and those there were didn't want to go into town. 'Trouble,' they grunted, and took the people behind me in the queue who, of course, wanted to go in the opposite direction. As two, three families at a time climbed into Bombay's ancient black-and-gold taxis and chugged of into the suburbs, I waited and waited and waited. Santayana had not prepared me for this.

Finally I hit lucky. Normally the journey from the airport to the Taj Hotel is a bed of nails. It can take easily one, maybe on a bad day nearly two hours. That day we drove straight there in twenty minutes without stopping once.

We swung out on the Western Express Highway, normally jammed with traffic. All along on both sides it's packed with tiny shops and houses, most made of wood and every one overflowing with people. In front of them on what pavements there are, on every spare scrap of land, even on top of the earth that has been dug up to repair the road are thousands of tiny tents, boxes and hovels which are even more overflowing with people. In this part of the world, if you have a cardboard box and the chance of a cup of rice every other week you're a rich man.

The guidebooks praise Bombay as a 'quintessential nine-teenth-century British city', and claim that in its semi-Italianate stone buildings they can spot traces of Bath, Manchester, London, even Paris, which has never struck me as a 'quintes-sential nineteenth-century British city'. What they don't tell you about is the crushing, soul-destroying poverty and disease, the babies who never seem to stop crying, the open sewers – to live near even an open sewer is a luxury in Bombay; most people have no sewers. Everywhere there are rats, dead dogs and flies. On everybody: men, women, children, and especially the babies. In their eyes, their ears, crawling in and out of their tiny mouths. And on everything in sight – on fresh meat, dead meat, on dogs, green with rot, that have been dead so long they've become part of the 'quintes-sential British landscape'.

Poverty, disease, hunger I've seen all over the world. Only in Bombay does it seem so overwhelming, so heartbreaking, so impossible to solve. And every day it's getting worse and more impossible to solve. The world's population is going to double to over 10 billion people over the next fifty years. In Bombay you can see it happening in front of your eyes, and the enormous problems it is going to create. Three hundred years ago, people called Bombay 'a poor little island'. It hasn't got any better since.

We've now shot past everything, quintessential or otherwise, at speeds I never dreamed possible for a Bombay taxi, especially with its Victorian meter outside on top of the front left bumper. Past burnt-out cars, still burning, by the side of the road; past buildings still smoking. The road is strewn with rocks and bricks. Trucks appear from nowhere. Soldiers pour from and disappear into what is left of shops and buildings and down smouldering alleyways.

'Trouble, trouble,' grunted the driver. 'I not like trouble.'

We shot past shops and godowns still burning. I could see small groups of people coming out of tents and crawling from piles of rubbish obviously waiting to rush in again as soon as they could. In poor countries, bakeries, shoe shops and hardware stores are the first to be looted; in rich countries, it's hi-fi and video stores and boutiques. In Bombay they loot everything. They can't afford the luxury of choice.

'Because of trouble you pay me extra,' the driver, a tiny little man who looked as though he could hardly see over the top of the steering wheel, turned round and whispered. Here we go again, I thought. 'Not like trouble. It's not good for business.'

'Sure, no problem.'

At least he was taking me to the hotel. We swung off the Western Express on two wheels on to the SV Road to Mahim and South Bombay.

'You also give me present,' he said, 'for taking you. I not like trouble.'

'Sure, no problem.'

'No buses, no taxis, no petrol. I not like trouble.'

I've been through riots and curfews and coup attempts many times in Africa. There, taxi drivers are used to them. They don't usually ask for so much money. But this was my first Indian cultural experience.

Over 20,000 people had already fled the City. Victoria Station, the quintessential British railway station which looks like a cross between St Pancras and a Mogul wedding cake, was choked to overflowing with refugees. The Hewrah Express, the Krishnagar Express, the Howrah Mail and the Minar Express were so full that extra bogies had to be fitted to stop them collapsing.

We were now over Mahim Creek and into Dharavi, which has the dubious honour of being the biggest slum in the world. Smoke was spiralling up in the distance. On a good day, if there is such a thing in Dharavi, it must be one of the worst places in the world. Everything is crumbling to pieces. Everything is covered in grime and slime, and caked in dirt, disease and death. And there are people everywhere: huddled in corners, huddled in boxes, huddled even in holes in the ground, in gaps between buildings, on planks on top of gaps between buildings, on window ledges, where there are window ledges. People are living, desperately trying to live and, of course, dying. Unlike the flies, which never seem to die in Dharavi.

A young man with a filthy, bloodstained bandage round his head was carrying a shopping bag in each hand. His wife was carrying a tiny shrivelled baby. Behind them a boy of about ten had a black plastic sack over his shoulder. The man waved at the taxi.

'Not like trouble,' the driver shouted at him.

We shot past them.

A soldier, a Sikh with what looked like a barbed-wire hairnet over his turban, stepped out into the street which was littered with rocks and stones. We slowed down, but he waved us through.

We were now getting into the centre of Bombay. There were no fires, no rocks or stones in the road, only the occasional soldier. But the streets were still empty. At the windows you could see people looking out. At the occasional door two women would be standing talking. Groups of boys would dash out of one door, race along the street and disappear into another.

People were walking, stumbling, drifting along the streets. An old woman was dragging a straw basket along the gutter, probably everything she possessed in the world. Behind her was an old man whose stump of a leg had formed a kind of pad as a result presumably of being thumped up and down the streets year after year.

We turned a corner. Now I could see the modern tower block of the Taj hotel. Still we were the only car in sight. Still the streets were practically deserted. There weren't even any stray dogs.

'I not like trouble,' the driver said with relief.

I was in Bombay again.

Trips to India are anything but boring. Even getting there is not boring. Especially as they have had seventeen plane crashes in three years, all involving Indian registered planes. Heavy rain; poor visibility; pilot error; they've almost run out of excuses. Three days earlier I had been in Madras where, far from the Madras crowd, poor young Robert Clive, struggling to survive on £5 a year, twice tried to shoot himself. Another plane, a Russian TU-154 on loan from Uzbekistan Airways to Indian Airlines, crashed in thick fog trying to land at New Delhi. It was six hours behind schedule. It had no oxygen masks. The safety regulations were only printed in English. The Indian crew had not been trained in safety procedures. The Uzbeki pilot had been flying for twelve hours. He was running out of fuel. He had already made three approaches, and he couldn't understand the instructions from air traffic control because he didn't speak English. Was it pilot error?

Not at all, said the airline. Only three days before that, the same pilot should have landed at Madras airport but he couldn't find it. Instead he landed at the military airport nearby. Only a professional airline pilot could do that, they said. And to prove how proud they were of his profession-alism, they grabbed the cockpit voice recorder from the wreckage and sent it back to Moscow, obviously to be decoded and quoted in the citation for his next air safety medal. For some reason, therefore, I seem to remember every flight I make in India.

My first visit to Bombay was a few months after Rajiv Gandhi had been killed. His wife, Sonia, had written a book called *My Rajiv* which made me wonder why Jackie Kennedy had not written a similar book called *My John*.

We were scheduled to land at Madras and we did. This was before I started checking the statistics, so I didn't realize how lucky we were. All I can remember now is the smell of curry. I kid you not, there was a thick, steaming, humid curry flavour hovering over the airport, like an old-fashioned London smog. It soaked into my clothes, into my luggage, into my very pores.

For weeks after I got home people would rush up to me: 'Can tell where you've been this time. You don't have to tell me,' they would say.

From Madras I went to Bangalore, and from Bangalore to Bombay. Bombay, or Mambai as it was officially renamed ten years ago although, typical India, nobody took any notice, is the New York of India. It has all of New York's problems, and more: it is four to five times more densely populated. It is the country's commercial centre. It is India's richest business centre and most industrial city. Land prices in central Bombay are as high as in Tokyo. It has over 3,000 companies ranging from the giant US$4.5 billion worldwide, legendary, secretive House of Tata which is in everything from lipstick to cement, steel and chemicals, to Mr Arunchalam's one-man import–export company in the street at the back of the post office which he runs full-time while at the same time working full-time in the Ministry of Finance. Most of them are buried in tiny offices in the back streets. Even the secret House of Tata is tucked away in a nondescript drab brown building. Others are packed on to sprawling industrial estates all around the city. Bombay is one of the largest production centres for diamonds and jewellery, as well as home to the biggest film industry in the world, churning out over 400 1950s-type movies a year.

On top of that, it is home to every colour, class and creed you can think of including Punjabis, Gujeratis, Maharishtians, Zoroastrians, and Parsis who even today insist on feeding their bodies to the vultures on the Towers of Silence on the expensive Malaba Hill on the west of the city.

Just as companies are fleeing New York so they are fleeing Bombay for Bangalore, India's electronics capital, a short air-dash away as the Indian businessman-wallah says. It's practically in the centre of the country; it's easy to get to and from; it's pleasant; it's about 900 metres above sea level; it has the same problems you find all over India but not to the same extent. The weather is about as dry and spicy as a poppadom; It's pretty temperate all year round, and locals say it has an air-conditioned climate. There are parks and trees in the streets. There's even a heavy mist blanketing the city in the early mornings in winter.

The Bangalore rickshawallahs are also famous throughout India. The young ones, the driver-racerboys, wear basketball shoes, Rambo sweatbands and are supposed to give Nigel Mansell a run for his money, even in a Formula One racing car, especially along certain straight sections of Airport Road.

In Bangalore, along JC road, I once spotted a sign on a wall saying, Plaess Urineshould Not Passhere. I mentioned this to a local businessman.

'Too many times have we tried and failed to properly translate English,' he told me.

Bangalore is also much cheaper, and, with the policemen wearing cowboy hats which always impress the Indians, much, much safer. But I admit I still prefer Bombay. Especially the quintessential bits.

And whenever I go to Bombay, I will also admit, I stay at the Taj Mahal. Not to stay there would be a crime, especially as the old wing with its long galleries on either side and the deep well in the centre reminds me of a prison. Trouble is, on this visit it really was a prison, albeit a luxury one. As soon as I checked in to do my luxury porridge, I was told not to even try to escape, I mean, leave the building.

'Because of the situation in the city, the management is advising everybody to remain in the hotel,' I was told very politely but firmly.

'But I've got a couple of meetings. I've got—'

'The management is advising everybody to remain in the hotel. The staff have not been allowed home for three days. It is very dangerous.'

Normally or, I suppose abnormally, I find riots, coup attempts and curfews are the safest time to travel around. Nobody is on the streets, there is no traffic, the police and army are everywhere and all the beggars have disappeared. Not that I have anything against beggars, even Indian beggars, who always seem to have six hands. I can usually do three times as much work during riots and coup attempts, and especially curfews, as when things are normal. Except, of course, you must know the country, the police and how they react.

I survived Africa. I could survive India. 'Yes, of course,' I nodded. 'Very sensible.'

I went to the cashier. 'I need some local currency,' I said. 'Have you got any Swedish kroner?'

'Absolutely smashing,' he grinned.

I unpacked, made my telephone calls and headed for the front of the hotel. The Sikh guards not only looked more military than the Rapid Action Force, they also looked as though they bitterly regretted the day Emperor Ogedei gave in to his eldest son, Kuyuk, and not to Batu, a grandson of Genghis Khan, and called a halt to the Golden Hordes who were massing on the banks of the Danube ready to sweep through the rest of Europe. Personally, of course, I'm grateful. No way would I want to be called Kuyuk Biddlecombe.

225

Anyway, the Sikhs were refusing to let anyone out. 'It is our advice. It is best not to go. Go tomorrow.'

'Okay,' I said, 'I accept your advice. I'll go today.' Which was when I discovered why 99% of the Indian army are Sikhs.

Right, I thought, I'll make for the side door. It was locked. The guard on duty, luckily not a Sikh, told me, 'Because of the situation in the city . . .'

A Dutch woman behind me was describing her latest cultural experience to an Indian woman in a shocking pink sari who was clearly not the type to believe in suttee which, in any case, I've always thought a typical female trick to distract attention from one's husband even at his own funeral. 'His hand was in my bag. There it was, I see it. I go to grab. But it is thin, it goes away,' she said.

Okay, I thought, what about the door in the modern non-prison block? Locked. The door at the end of that passageway? Locked. I'll knot the sheets together and climb out of the window. I was on the wrong side of the building. I was facing the swimming pool. I'll smuggle my way out in the dustbin. I'll dig a tunnel. Hell, I thought, I haven't come all this way to be locked up in a luxury prison. I went back to my cell. All I had left was the Indian hope trick. I called up my contacts.

'I'm trapped,' I said. 'They won't let me out. Can you come to me?'

'Very sorry my dear sir, old chap. Not possible. Out of the question, sir. There are soldiers outside. We cannot come, sir, old chap.'

I telephoned a banker who lived in a large mansion in South Bombay. His son answered the 'phone. 'Very sorry, sir. Papa says he cannot come. There are gangs of hoodlums going from building to building. He can't leave until normalcy returns.'

Normalcy? In Bombay? He'll be there for ever. I didn't fancy putting on the saffron, doing my yoga and singing Vande Mataram every two minutes. So I did the only thing a quintessential Englishman would do in the circumstances. I went down to the Harbour Bar.

'Just like the Blitz,' I heard a cut-glass English memsahib exclaiming as I went in. Not only did she sound as though she'd come straight out of Jennifer's Diary – you know, the type who says Rajah instead of Roger – she looked as though she did as well. She was so thin she'd obviously thrown up everything she'd ever eaten in her life. Even the word bulimia wouldn't stick in her throat.

I ordered a large Scotch. The barman nodded towards the cut-glass accent. 'Comes every year,' he said, 'with Pox and Things.'

Normally I don't drink spirits, but I make an exception in India. Some people say that in very hot temperatures it's an excellent thirst-quencher. I prefer to think of it as my protection for eating chaat, samosas and everything else you're not supposed to eat in the street markets and at railway stations.

Sitting opposite me were two Bombay wallahs who looked as though they were still waiting for the slightest excuse to leap into their shorts in the service of the Empire. Both were wearing sports jackets.

'The new maharajahs of India are still the old maharajahs, what?' grunted the one on the left who looked 16 annas to the rupee.

'More Indians here than there are in Southall,' grunted the other. They looked at each other. 'Maybe not,' they added together.

In another corner a quintessential old-British-Colonial type with a moustache and blue blazer was whispering to his group. 'Good chaps. But don't always think.' They all nodded. Probably without thinking. 'Playing cricket one day with the chaps in the office. Do it once a year. Breaks down that them-and-us feeling, y'know. Old Hancock hits the ball right over the fence. Young Vijay in accounts goes chasing after it. Five minutes, no Vijay. Ten minutes, no Vijay. Wonder where the blighter's gone.' They all shake their heads. Probably still without thinking. 'Go round the fence. It backs on to the toilet block. The door's locked. I go up to the door. Is that you in there Vijay? Yes, sir, he said. Got caught short, sir. Okay, Vijay, I said, but could we have the ball back?'

A typical stressed-out American wandered in with obviously his junior assistant Indian sales manager, who most definitely was not 16 annas to the rupee. 'Wasn't what I was planning,' he said drawling. 'Think I'll have a finger-pressure massage instead. While away an hour.'

Everybody else was talking about the riot, what started it, how it was all going to end.

'In various parts of the city, at Pydhonie, Nagpada, Imamwadi and Mohammed Ali Road, from buses and taxis people are being dragged and asked their religion,' the Dutchwoman I had seen earlier was telling a group around her. 'At best they are stripped and stabbed. The worst doesn't bear thinking about.'

India has enormous, impossible problems. Bombay has more and worse, which are probably even more impossible to solve. First, religion. Muslims are followers of the Prophet Mohammed, a one-time camel thief who suffered a mid-life crisis and came up with the biggest competitor Christianity has ever had, although Salman Rushdie might put it differently. They worship in mosques. They make up 11 percent of the population. In Indian terms that's over 100 million and growing, which is a pretty sizeable minority.

'Hindu' originally meant anyone living around the Indus river. Today it's a lot like the Church of England. It's not really a faith, it's not really a Church. There is no Hindu organization; you can believe this Hindu teacher or that one, worship at this Hindu temple or that one – if you want to go to a temple at all. It seems to be so relaxed that you can be a Hindu and an atheist. Or a Buddhist. Or a Sikh. In fact Buddhism and Sikhism originally came from Hinduism. There are even some Hindus who go to Muslim temples. Hindus make up 83 per cent of the population.

So with 11 percent of the population Muslim and 83 percent Hindu, is India a religious state or a secular state? The answer, like everything in India, is, it depends whom you talk to.

Most Muslims say yes, but it is a Hindu religious state when it should really be a secular state. But Muslims cannot officially agree to India being a secular state because that would give the Hindus more power, which would be more dangerous for the Muslims.

Most Hindus say no, it's a secular state. They don't want to have a secular state, they want a religious state, but they won't fight for one because the Muslims wouldn't like it. So they prefer to leave things the way they are: a secular state, 83 percent controlled by Hindus. If you think that's complicated, try asking a Hindu, what is a Hindu?

Why were we confined to our luxury prison? Officially because of the riots which broke out as a result of Hindu fanatics destroying the sixteenth-century mosque at Ayodhya which, they said, had been built on the remains of a Hindu temple built there originally to mark the birthplace of Lord Ram himself. The Muslims said that the Hindus no longer used the temple as a temple. And if a temple is not used as a temple for so many years, it is no longer a temple.

Unofficially, we were confined to prison because of poverty. The poor are not only still with them, it looks as though they are going to be with them till hell freezes over. According to the Indian government 46 percent of the population, a staggering 361 million, are registered as poor. And this – you'll never believe it – is calculated at the official poverty level of 15 rupees per person per month set down by the national planning committee of the Congress Party leader, Mr Nehru himself, wait for it, based on 1938/39 prices. Of course it has been adjusted for current prices. But the level remains the same. Mohammed alone knows what the figures would be if the level had been increased. And the official number of poor people, the official number remember, is still increasing at the rate of a new Australia of accountants and book-keepers every year.

While the cost of poverty is steadily rising, the number of people able to pick up the tab is becoming less and less. People are not earning as much; more people are evading taxes; and more people are, let's be dishonest, siphoning off more funds. If that's the situation with individuals, you can guess what is happening with companies.

Upstairs in the Sea Lounge, there was a group of old raj-wallahs huddled together drinking tea. Tea! That's a good idea, I thought. I'll have some tea. India was now awash with tea. A democratic Soviet Union had not been kind to them. Under the old Communist regime, non-aligned India had had a cosy relationship with state purchasing organizations. With a word here, a few cups of Assam there, they had no problems getting rid of over half their total production. Now, in a free enterprise world, they were having to fight off Kenya, Sri Lanka, Malawi and the rest. And they were suffering.

While I was drinking my chai-wai/tea, and wondering why they hadn't spotted the signs in all those tealeaves, the old raj-wallahs were going on and on and round and round in circles, discussing the same thing again and again. Which, of course, is typical India. Instead of beginning to solve the problems of poverty like China, Indonesia or other similar countries, the Indians, like all high-minded Fabians, are still setting up committees and talking about it.

As a result, every day the worst becomes even worse and the disasters grow even greater. In many states nearly 50 percent of the population is officially classified as poor. Admittedly the percentage level may have dropped from 56 percent in 1970 to 46 percent today. But in terms of numbers it still means there are today over 50 million more people classified poor in these states than there were before. Instead of improving the literacy rate, improving school attendance and extending life expectancy as similar countries have done, they are still writing reports.

The adult literacy rate is 44 percent. In China it's 72 percent, in developing countries generally, 60 percent. Life expectancy is 59 compared to 70 in developing countries generally. Instead of doing everything they can to stimulate the creation of wealth to pay for everything, encourage individual initiatives, help industry to expand and eliminate corruption at all levels of society, they have introduced more controls, controls and yet more controls. India is still Nehru taking tea with Sidney, Beatrice, RH and all the other Fabians.

While the country crumbles around them they keep talking about principles, processes and practices, bumper capitalism, instruments of governance, worshipping the gods of profit and greed and unbridled pursuit of money. Instead of freedom, they prefer controls to guarantee freedom. Instead of liberalization they believe in conservation to guarantee a liberal society. Instead of accepting reality, admitting they have problems, that they are protected and, therefore, many of their goods are just too sub-standard for the outside world, they insist on setting up more committees, formulating new proposals and demanding quotas for everything.

The result is that India today has the most crushing bureaucracy you can imagine. In triplicate. With each copy signed personally by you, your mother's uncle, your father's third cousin's sister and the local vet. Even to get a cab, you have to fill in three forms. Traditionalists will tell you that the Lord Vishna himself had ten avatars. It is only logical, therefore, that any office worker, manager or special offer at the Sri Rama Co-operative Sugar Factory should also have ten assistants. Progressives, if you can find one in the India bureaucracy, will tell you that's India.

As I was leaving the Sea Lounge the American was coming through the door with his junior assistant Indian sales manager. 'You can keep your finger massage,' he was saying. 'I'm going for a Thai massage next. That's for real.'

I wandered down to the Harbour Bar again. I was beginning to feel like a sadhu, a wandering holy man. Maybe the guard wouldn't be there. Maybe the door was no longer locked. Maybe I could . . .

He was still there. 'Because of the situation in the—'

'I know, I know,' I muttered. 'Prisoner 6-1-4-3-2-1 reporting, sir.'

'I beg your pardon, sir?'

I wandered along to the main lobby. Maybe the Sikhs were no longer there. Maybe I could dash out when nobody was looking and grab a taxi.

'Because of the situation in the . . .' The Taj Mahal's Own Rapid Action Force drew themselves to attention.

'Thank you, men. At ease.'

'Thank you, sir.'

Never one to bear a grudge, I promised to give them all references if they ever thought of leaving the prison service to become cleaners in Terminal 4, taxi drivers in Bradford or worse still, guards with Group 4.

Now I might as well try the Lounge Bar. What else is there to do?

'Of course, dahling Harold was in North Africa. Alamein, you know. Monty. All that kind of thing.' The cut-glass voice had got there before me. 'But we had some super fun. I remember once in Belgrave Square, Mummy and I . . .'

I went back to Scotch. Large ones. I sat at a table with two old Indians wearing grey pin-striped suits and red cardigans and drinking tomato juice. They looked as if they would have been more at home in saffron robes with coconuts on their heads and bunches of rings hanging from their ears.

'To me, *ahimsa* doesn't just mean, Thou shalt not kill. It means, You must not even think it, even in your heart,' said one.

The other nodded, slowly, seriously, and sipped his tomato juice. 'Bhai-chara. That's what Gandhi used to say. Bhai-chara. But nobody remembers that any more.'

'Better one's own bad dharma than somebody else's good dharma. He said that as well.'

'He also said, Better is death in one's own dharma than life in another.'

The bar was filling up. Obviously everybody was making the same trip. An Italian came in, his coat over his shoulders. He was in Bombay, I heard him tell the barman, for a kidney transplant. There were no kidneys left in Italy. The nearest place he could get one was India.

'And what will sir be having?' said the barman.

'A large Scotch, please,' he said.

Which surprised me at first, until I realized that if you know you've got another liver lined up you might as well let the old one go out with a bang.

'Then I met dahling Freddie . . .' the cut-glass voice – who was obviously once the Raj of Belgravia – was throwing up her bulimic memoirs of the Second World War all over the bar.

The American and his junior assistant sales manager bustled in. 'Not as good as in Thailand. But I want to try . . .' He turned towards me. No, I thought. Please not me. That's all I want. Bombay, riots, Sikhs, stuck in here for . . . He continued past me to the two Indians.

'Hey, fellas, let me buy you a drink.' He put his arms around their shoulders. 'Bloody Marys, eh? You drinking Bloody Marys? Barman, two Bloody Marys for my friends here.'

The two looked at each other. They were obviously having trouble with their ahimsas and bhai-charas.

'You can have my chair,' I said leaping up.

'Now can you guys explain to me this caste business?' he said grabbing it and collapsing all over it.

The two saints, or sadhus, gasped at each other. They looked as though they were up the Ganges without a paddle.

'Caste cannot be a class,' said one.

'Because class is antithetical to caste,' continued the other.

'But it is a social class . . .'

The American's eyes were already beginning to glaze over. This was a class – or do I mean caste – Indian Tweedledum and Tweedledee act.

233

'Certainly you can identify castes by referring to class,' said Tweedledum.

'And some castes are socially-backed classes,' added Twee-dledee.

'An occupational group, for example, can be a caste or a class . . .'

'. . . if, in this sense, caste is used as a group/class distinction.'

The American was now sitting there with his mouth open.

'Then when Harold found out about Freddie,' the cut-glass voice was into volume three, 'there was the most awful fuss. But Mummy was wonderful, Dahling, she said . . .'

Please, I thought, please let me get remission for good behaviour. I retreated to my cell to count the scratch marks on the wall until it was time for me to be released.

For two days we were not allowed out. Although I must admit, if you promise not to tell the Governor, I managed to dodge past the Sikhs on the afternoon of the second day. The streets were still empty. The grand ceremonial arch opposite the hotel, built to mark the non-visit to India by Queen Victoria, was deserted. There was nobody along the sea front. At first I thought I'd stroll across to the arch and back just to show all the other prisoners at the windows that Colditz was our first . . . A cab came nervously round the corner. Probably the only cab in Bombay. I ran towards it and leapt in.

'Quick, lock the doors. I don't want . . .'

'I know, I know,' I said. 'You're talking to a professional.'

The driver was another tiny little man, in a string vest, black trousers and sandals.

'Okay,' I said, 'let's drive round. I want to see . . .'

He just stared at me. It was not what he expected.

'Okay,' I said. 'The British high commission.'

I always find that the best way to tour any city is to ask a cab driver to take you to the British embassy or high commission. They never know where it is. They take you to the biggest hotel in town.

'No, that's not it.' We then ask the doorman. He gives the driver directions. We end up at the post office.

'No, that's not it.' A postman gives the driver directions. Which you would think would be pretty spot on. Never on your life.

I've tried it in Africa, Europe, all over South America. Not once have I found the embassy. But I discovered an awful lot about the cities I was visiting.

It was the same this time, and I was able to see the extent of the rioting. In the Worli area, a Hindu district, fires were still burning along Veer Savarka Road, which was virtually the front line. In Mihm, which is around 80 percent Muslim, whole areas had been flattened. Smoke was still billowing up between piles of gnarled girders. Bandra, a Muslim area and the start of one of the big shanty areas, was empty except for an ancient mystic with a long white beard who was pushing an equally ancient bicycle along the roadside. He had probably been meditating so long he didn't notice the violence. In Bandwa, I was told by an Indian businessman, people were so desperate for space that if you left your briefcase on the ground for two minutes a family of seven would move in.

We drove back along the marina, past the mosque. Police and troops were everywhere. The army had moved into the National Sports Club of India and turned it into their depot. Not slow these officer-wallahs. But we weren't stopped once.

Near the port and around the post office there were a few cars. I saw an Ambassador, the old Morris Oxford which, forty years after we stopped making them, is still being churned out in India, something that looked like a Triumph Standard, and a couple of taxis. A few dogs were lying dead in the gutter, but nothing else. There were white flags flying out of windows. A couple rode past on a motorcycle. the woman, in her sari, side-saddle on the back.

On the way back we went to Victoria Terminal, or VT as it is known to everybody west of Heathrow. Gargoyles, turrets, delicate carvings; it's like a mad Victorian architect's revenge on mankind. That grand old traveller, Robert Byron, in that restrained way of his, once called Bombay 'an architectural sodomy'. Which I assume he meant to be taken with a pinch of salt. I often think that if anyone turned around and looked at VT they would be turned into a block of salt. Not immediately, but maybe in three days, because everything to do with Indian railways is running late.

VT was packed with Muslims fleeing the city, sitting huddled around suitcases, bundles of clothes, everything they possessed. There must have been two, three, four thousand people sitting on benches, squatting on the floor, huddled on every spare inch of ground. But it was practically silent. Which, of course, made it seem even worse. An old man with a long, wiry white beard told me they were from the Dock Labour Board Colony in Cotton Green. They were waiting for the next train to Gorakpur and safety. Gangs had moved into their area three days before, attacking them and setting fire to their homes. The police stood by and let them.

'When we tried to stop them, the police fired on us,' he said. His son was trying to buy tickets. His wife was with him. She was nine months pregnant. 'I never want to come back,' he whispered.

On the basis that nobody can resist Carnal Pleasures for long in Bombay, I decided that evening to go to the Tanjore, the hotel's Indian restaurant on the ground floor. Carnal Pleasures is the name they give to their selection of dishes from north and south of the country. Though why Carnal Pleasures nobody has ever been able to explain to me satisfactorily.

First, I thought, I'll try the Apollo Bar on the top of the new wing. It was packed. It looked as though half the Bombay glitterati were there. The other half were probably still guarding their homes. Everybody was talking.

'Even broke into operating theatres where surgeons were operating on victims and stabbed them again.'

'Do you know why we can't get any decent colour film in India?' a long-haired film director type was saying. 'Because only one company is allowed to make the film. And they can't get the sprockets right. The sprockets. The little holes on the edge of the film. That's why our films always seem to wobble. God, if only they hadn't thrown Kodak out in the 1950s.'

'My cousin told me that in Tardeo he saw shops looted and all the clothes, food and electronic goods carried into the local police colony.'

The Dutchwoman was reading a health report on Bombay written in 1867. 'Here it says they calculated two ounces of the stuff per person per day plus forty ounces of urine. It was collected in wooden crates and in baskets which they carried –' she winced – 'on their heads. It was then all loaded on to trains and taken by train to Sion and—' She slammed the book down on the table and fled in the direction of Amsterdam.

Then I spotted the American hobbling up to the bar. 'There I was, lying in this pool of green slime,' he was whispering to his long-suffering junior assistant Indian sales manager. 'They got bowls of boiling water and threw one over my face. Then, I wasn't going to tell you this, they pulled my knees as far apart as they could. I don't know why I'm telling you this. Then they got this other bowl of boiling water and they . . .'

The cut-glass voice pierced the room again. 'Of course, Sidney understands everything. Not, of course, that I would blame him. Mummy always says . . .'

'The Muslims, you must admit, are always quick to take offence. They always start the violence. They—'

'Nonsense, it's the Hindus. People say they are docile and peaceful, but they are the aggressive ones.'

The two old Bombay-wallahs were no longer the peaceful, tolerant, deeply meditative old Indians who had been drinking tomato juice.

'But why should the Hindus always be tolerant? The Muslims are never tolerant.'

237

'It was the Muslims who gave India their language, their culture . . .'

'Nonsense, now you are talking . . .'

Did they really think those Bloody Marys were tomato juice?

'Urdu comes from Iran. India is really part of Hindustan. We were civilized for centuries before the prophet . . .'

'Nonsense,' shrieked the other one, clambering to his feet.

'Pakistan, Bangladesh, Sri Lanka, India, we're all part of . . .'

I decided it was long past time for me to take my Carnal Pleasures. I'd been training in my local take-away for weeks before I came away. I'd survived the vindaloos and biryanis, and graduated to the moglais and masalas. Gosh, I even had a gosht katamassalla and something called a murgh makari. But don't ask me to describe it. I even nibbled a green chilli. The tiniest green chilli you could imagine, but at least I tried. This was going to be the big one.

And it was.

The following morning when I was due to be released I couldn't move. My lust for Carnal Pleasures had destroyed me. Aaaaarrrrrgggggghhhhh. Don't ask me what I think of the quintessential Carnal Pleasures of Bombay.

Colombo

On the beach again? Boozing it up? Lots of lovely restaurants?
And the nightclubs, what about the—?

'No way.' I collapse for the umpteenth time. 'It was
business, business, nothing but . . .'

But I tell a lie; there are some trips that are not all business.
There are those trips where you spend every second of every
waking day trying to get the hell out of the country. Queuing
up for dirty bits of government paper to wave at emigration
officials; queuing up for funny rubber stamps to be slapped on
dirty bits of paper; queuing up for funny stamps for your
passport; queuing up for funny rubber stamps to be slapped
on the funny stamps in your passport; queuing up at the
government office for a voucher for a taxi; queuing up at
another government office to have a funny rubber stamp
slapped on your voucher; queuing up to get your airline ticket
confirmed . . .

'I'm sorry, sir, your ticket is not confirmed.'

'But I booked it in London. Everything was okay.'

'I'm sorry.' Long pause. 'Sir.'

'But I've got a meeting . . .'

'All I can suggest is that you see the manager.'

'Okay, I'll see the manager. Is he here?'

'No.'

'Will he be here later on?'

'I don't know.'

God of Mercy and Compassion. This is like a mantra of desperation on my part.

Sri Lanka is supposed to hold the world record for gone-aways. If a greater proportion of people have skipped this country than any other, you wonder how they did it, and how long it took them. Maybe they heard the Dutch were coming and it's taken then over 200 years to get their tickets to get out.

Dr Livingstone, Mungo Park and all the other great explorers had it easy. I could have done what they did standing on my suitcase. In those days all you had to do was collect a handful of Bibles, a pocketful of shells, and head off for the sunshine. Life was simple. They didn't have to deal with airline tickets, airline staff . . . Anyone on a business trip today has to accept two plain, straightforward facts of life when dealing with airline ticket offices. If you get mad, you get nowhere. Your name will be erased from the computer for eternity. If you stay calm, you'll still get nowhere. But at least your name will still be somewhere, mixed up with the elastic bands, inside their computer. As for death and disease, the great men never had to cope with airline catering either.

It was my first trip to Colombo in Sri Lanka, the land of unpronounceable names such as Anuradhapura, Pollonotuwa and Mrs Noyoucannothaveaticketsopushoff, the royal cities of Parakramabuba and Vijayababu and the spiritual home of Morris Minors. I've never seen so many in my life. Whenever a Morris Minor dies I swear it goes to Sri Lanka where there must be hundreds of little garages and repair shops making all the spare parts necessary to reincarnate them immediately.

I decided to stay calm.

'Okay, thank you very much for your help,' I grovelled. 'I'll come back later.'

Note the deliberate lack of any reference to the manager. Three hundred and fifty-seven years of my life spent in airline offices have not exactly been wasted. Even hint in some countries, of thinking of possibly waiting to see the Lord Chief

Highest Ticket-Issuing Being of All Creation Himself and you're dead. Not only will your name be erased from the computer for eternity but you'll probably never make it past that hooded cobra swaying eagerly at the front door, across the road and into your broken-down taxi which has already been waiting two-and-a-half-hours in a gentle blaze of 107°F.

In other countries it's different, which adds to the excitement of *Airline Offices: The Art of Survival*. Sometimes it is considered simple courtesy to pay one's respects to the airline office manager just as you would to lesser mortals such as the president of the country. In fact, in many countries the airline office manager not only has more planes under his control than the president, he also has a bigger budget. And that's just the petty cash account.

Which approach is best for dealing with which airline in which countries, I'm not telling you. I didn't suffer all this time for nothing. If I tell you, you're bound to be the one ahead of me in the next queue in the next airline office in which I'm having problems. And knowing my luck you'll be the one who gets the last ticket out before everything closes down for three weeks while they celebrate National Urinating against Don't Urinate Here Notices Week.

I was on my way back from a swing through the Far East, or the Orient, as Americans would say. Normally I fly back non-stop. A couple of bottles of champagne, the latest Gerard Manley Hopkins or R.S. Surtees depending on the mood I'm in and I'm away. I don't have any problems sleeping on planes. At least, not so far. This time, however, I decided to stop off in Colombo. An old African hand I knew had fallen on hard times. Colombo, he had worked out, was the cheapest place in the world to live. He reckoned he could have a house, servants and live a fairly reasonable life for a few pounds a month. Whether Arthur C. Clarke, the up-market science fiction writer, chose Sri Lanka for the same reason, I doubt. Either way, it seemed, as they say, as good a reason as any to stop off and look around.

241

The south and west of the island I had been told were prosperous. Deregulation, privatization and willingness to help business had resulted in hundreds of small companies making shoes, toys, clothes, even new Morris Minors. The east and the north, Tamil Tiger territory, were a disaster area. In the old days Jaffna was safe and pleasant. Today there was no electricity, no running water, no sewers, practically no food. The ferry across to India was a long-distant memory.

I checked into the Galle Face, pronounced the English Galle Face as opposed to the French Galle Face, which as hotels go is in a class entirely of its own. Obviously the French don't realize this because the place is full of middle-aged French couples. It's a genuine old-colonial hotel on the beach, just down the road from the State Assembly. It looks as though it's been furnished from the leftovers of a Southall jumble sale in the late 1950s.

Noel Coward, the Queen of Denmark and Bo Derek have all stayed there, which must be about the only thing they have in common. Each floor has its own staff, who are called butlers. It must also be the only hotel in the world where its owner, manager and presiding buddha, Cyril Gardiner, cheerfully admits that his friendliest, most civilized and sociable guests are his beloved cockroaches. So much for the French.

'Cockroaches are the oldest form of life,' he declaims, marching up and down his wood-panelled office, which boasts a fireplace left over from the good old days of the British Empire. 'They are to be honoured and respected. Not destroyed.'

At one time, I was told, the hotel, which has only eighty-five rooms, had over 600 staff, which worked out at seven staff and 85,000 honoured and respected cockroaches per guest. And so honoured and so respected are they throughout the Galle Face that one entire wing has been given over solely to their greater comfort and privacy. Not that they are discouraged throughout the rest of the building. The cockroaches, I mean, not the guests.

The wide, expansive, open-air entrance which welcomed Noel, Queenie and Bo, the hallways, which are long, creaking and echoing, and the rooms, all have wooden floorboards, revolving fans in the ceiling, ancient plumbing and electricity which you can practically see flowing along the outside of what little cable there is.

Along the corridors are the Thoughts of Chairman Cyril: 'Don't smoke in bed. The ashes we find may be yours.' 'Please use the stairs. It's much healthier.'

Do people object? Not on your life. According to a roll of honour in the entrance hall, Noel Coward, the Queen of Denmark and Bo Derek are not the only ones to have stayed at Château Cyril. Sallyanne Atkins (whoever she is), Hirohito, Emperor of Japan, and Gregory Peck have also enjoyed the company of the cockroaches at the Galle Face. Either that or they also had trouble getting their airline tickets confirmed.

I once asked Cyril, as everyone including the cockroaches calls him, why on the Roll of Honour of Famous Guests, George Bernard Shaw appears after Jean Simmons, but he said he was rushing to meet some of his most honoured and respected guests and couldn't waste time chatting idly to me. After just one slightly nervous, scratchy night in the Galle Face, never again would you want to stay in one of those super-clean, modern, comfortable faceless hotels.

In theory, there should have been no problem: a quick flight from Singapore; a few days – and nights – at home with the cockroaches; the next flight to London. No problems. No hang-ups. But I had not counted on the Colombo factor.

Within three hours of arriving, I'm back at the airline office. Again it is full to overflowing with saris and saffron robes, with tee-shirts that have not seen soap and water since they left Taiwan in the Year of the Snake, and creased and crumpled suits, all wondering whether to go mad or keep calm. The place looks like and has that unmistakable sweet odour of one of those modern hippy ashrams. Except we're all chasing something more important than Nirvana.

I take two tickets from the 'Wait until your number is called' machine at the door. I settle down in a corner to wait for the Year of the Rooster. All the time, more saris and more saffron robes keep coming in and taking tickets. I can't make up my mind whether I should give up my seat to a sari or a saffron robe. I decide to do the typical English thing. I look the other way. Eventually my number is called. It's the same sari I spoke to earlier.

'Hullo,' I grovel. I give her one of my tickets from the machine.

'Yes.'

'You said, this morning, that is … Perhaps the manager … it might be possible …?'

Note the deliberate stutter. That's because I still don't know whether Sri Lanka is the kind of country where it pays to see the manager or not.

'That is … if it's convenient …'

'No.'

What the hell! This morning – and I've waited here – Whaddyathink I—

'Oh I'm sorry,' I grovel. 'This morning … you said … I thought …'

'He's not here.'

'When will he be here?'

'I don't know.'

'Will he be here tomorrow?'

'I don't know.'

'I'll come back tomorrow.'

On the way out I sell my other ticket to a Buddhist monk for what I calculate is the equivalent of the average monthly salary in Sri Lanka. Another trick which works in some countries and not in others. I'm still not telling you which. The monk does not seem too unhappy to pay, which either means life on a vow of poverty in a Buddhist monastery in a poor,

244

undeveloped country like Sri Lanka is not too bad or he's made certain my life is going to be hell if I ever reach the Year of the Horse.

That evening the Galle Face (English pronunciation) suddenly becomes le Galle Face (French pronunciation). What seems like un jumbo of French has arrived en ville. A Frenchwoman is a reception creating the typical Gallic fuss. She wants to know where she can buy poisoned raw potatoes.

'Non non non, monsieur,' she is insisting in the traditional Tante Madeleine fashion. 'Raw potatoes. They must be raw and they must be poisoned.'

Poisoned raw potatoes, I ask one of the staff, why does she want poisoned raw potatoes?

'She wants to put them all over the bathroom floor,' He shrugs, 'She says they will kill the cockroaches.'

The following day is a holiday, I discover, as my rocket propelled tuk-tuk screams away from the Galle Face (English pronunciation) at nine o'clock on the dot, shoots along the sea front and spins through a deserted Colombo. It's Duruthu: Full Moon Day. Everybody is preparing to honour the passing of another lunar cycle. In Malaysia, the hereditary sultans, the last of the mega-spenders, blow millions building special mini-palaces in which they can say hullo to the new moon. In Colombo they just stroll down to the beach for a quick shufty.

But why the hell didn't they tell me it was a holiday? The airline office is closed, the shops are closed, the market is deserted. The whole country has shut down. We drive slowly round the old Victorian buildings in the centre of town. Deserted. Even the girl with the cobra has gone. Along past the central post office. Empty. Around the central bus station. Nothing. Past the art gallery, the museum, the university. Zilch. We drive the length of Galle Road, more or less the backbone of the city. With inscrutable Buddhist logic, each time the road goes into another district the numbers stop and start again, so that there are no less than six number one Galle

Roads, six number one-hundred-and-sixes, and six of everything in between. But that's nothing. At least Galle Road is
only called Galle Road. Some roads have two names, their
official name and their everyday name. I decide to make for
Duplication Road, which appropriately is also called R.A. De
Mel Mawatha.

Hey! Wait a minute! What about the airport? Just because the
airline office is closed it doesn't mean . . .

'The hotel. Let's go back . . .'

The tuk-tuk is now a jet-engine, an F-111. Any minute now
we will be flying under the radar straight towards Baghdad.
Within seconds I am at the hotel. I race past the Roll of
Honour. No names have been added while I've been out. I
race up the stairs, past all the butlers, into the room I'm sharing
with the cockroaches.

I call the airline office at the airport. No answer. I call again.
This time I let it ring for seventeen-and-a-half minutes. Still
no answer. Probably dealing with a queue of people. Why
the hell don't I go to the airport, instead of sitting here
discussing Gerard Manley Hopkins's theory of sprung rhythm
with Cyril's damn cockroaches? Quick, the airport number
itself. They'll tell me if there's a flight, if there's a queue, if
there's a chance of . . . No reply. I let it ring and ring . . . Still
no damn reply. What can I do now? Go there? Pack, check
out, go all the way there on the off chance . . . Of course,
air traffic control. If anybody would know if . . . No reply.
Dial again. No reply.

What does that mean? There was a plane, but it's left and
they've all gone home because they know there isn't going to
be another one? Or there wasn't a plane, so there was no point
turning up? Or there is going to be a plane later on so they're
was obviously no point coming in early? But if there was a
plane and it's left, so much for my confirmation. If the plane
has been cancelled, so much for my confirmation. If the plane
is still coming, I'll still need my confirmation. What the . . .!

I slam the 'phone down. So I've given Cyril's damn

cockroaches migraine for a week. What the hell. Here am I, stuck here, nobody answering the 'phone, no way of knowing whether I'm ever . . . Might as well go and have a drink.

I ask the big chief head butler on the door for a typical Sri Lankan restaurant. Might as well drown my sorrows with something hot and spicy. Tante Madeleine is studying the Roll of Honour, obviously amazed that there could be such a thing without any French names.

'Got rid of nos petits amis?' I enquire.

She stares at me. 'Oui, monsieur,' says the husband. 'But now we're overrun with ants instead.'

The tuk-tuk swerves, skids and rockets along Galle Road. And, of course, the restaurant is closed. It's a holiday. So why didn't he tell me? Because I didn't ask. All I asked was the name of a restaurant. My fault. Again. I'm about to climb back into my tuk-tuk. The manager comes running out.

'You are looking for the restaurant, sir?'

'Yes, I was. But I see you're closed.'

'It is a holiday, sir.'

'I know. I didn't realize.'

'We're not allowed to serve any food or drink in the restaurant today, sir.'

'Yes, I realize. I'm sorry.' I turn back to the tuk-tuk.

'But we have a room at the back of the restaurant.'

'Where you are serving food and drink?'

'Yes, sir.'

'But if it's a . . .?

'The law says we are not allowed to sell food or drink in the restaurant.'

'It doesn't say anything about the room at the back of the restaurant?'

'No, sir.'

The room was packed. Half of Colombo was in there eating, drinking, having a holiday. I had learnt something else for my next visit. But I'm not telling you that either.

Back at the hotel, full of lamprai and beer, I notice the

middle-aged French couples suddenly all have pretty little Sri Lankan babies.

'Fast workers,' I mumble to the butlers. 'Typical French.'

Typical French! I discover that French and German couples regularly fly down to Colombo for – babies. They have money but no babies. Sri Lankans have babies but no money. A perfect match. Around the corner, down the road, I discover there is a roaring market in babies.

'Sure, you can buy babies,' I was told in a very matter-of-fact way. 'You want a baby?'

For US$13,000 you can have a real-life, bouncing Sri Lankan baby. What the mother gets is around $500.

'Why not? They have a better home than if they stayed in Sri Lanka. They will be loved and cared for. They will have everything they want.'

'But . . . but . . . but . . .'

Many countries have baby rackets or adoption services, depending on your point of view, run not quite in accordance with the old-fashioned way we do things in this country.

In Madras, you see white cradles outside all the hospitals and clinics.

'Why are the cradles outside and not inside?' I naturally asked.

'So nobody is embarrassed,' I was told.

I confessed I didn't understand.

'So the mothers who don't want their babies can just leave them there and walk away. No questions, no problems,' a gentle old Indian nun spelt it out for me as if it was the most obvious thing in the world.

'And you then look after them?'

She nodded wearily at such an obvious remark.

It's the same in Cambodia where children's homes are only too happy to sell babies for any price you care to name. They call them deathrow babies, because if nobody takes them they'll just be left to die. I mentioned this to an Indian doctor I met in Bombay.

'For God's sake,' he exclaimed, 'what do you expect? These people have nothing. Before the hospital took the babies in, they were just killed and buried. What do you expect them to do?'

I had no answer then and I have no answer now. All I know is, all over the world babies are subjected to the most horrific treatment.

In Naples, one of the favourite tricks of the gangs of women and girls begging on the streets is to actually throw their babies at you. Instinctively you drop your briefcase and try to grab the child before it smashes on the pavement. Immediately they surround you, hugging and kissing you and thanking you for saving their baby – and, of course, lifting your wallet, your credit cards, your watch and anything else you've got worth stealing. What can you do? You can't let the baby smash against the ground, can you?

In the Far East, they will drug babies and throw them at your feet in a desperate attempt to get you to put your hand in your pocket. In Senegal, they've taken it to the most horrific extremes I've come across. In some outlying villages, if they see a tourist driving a car, they will actually throw their babies under the wheels to claim the insurance. Better a dead or crippled baby and some money in their pocket than a healthy baby and no cash.

The only good thing about the baby business in Sri Lanka was that the French were not German, and the babies were not six- or seven-year-old boys with bright red lipstick. Which, I discovered, is a quite different service available in Sri Lanka.

The following morning I was back at the airline office. The tiny girl with the enormous cobra in her basket was now installed on the pavement outside. Everybody, me included, rushed past, whether because of the girl or the snake I don't know. The office was packed. I snatched my usual two tickets from the machine and headed for the only available ... 'Mr Bidkum,' Mrs Noyoucanthaveaticketsopushoff shouts across at me.

Bidkum. Must be a Sri Lankan . . .

'Mr Bidkum,' she shouts again. 'Your confirmation.'

Me? Bidkum? How in a land of such unpronounceable names as Mrs Noyoucanthaveaticketsopushoff can they get my name wrong?

'I have your confirmation,' she says waving a piece of paper at me.

Confirmation? For me? Without having to ... It can't be possible.

'Me?' I mutter.

'Yes,' she says. 'You Mr Bidkum.'

'Of course,' I say doing a right turn on the spot and stumbling up the steps to the counter. 'But I thought the plane had already . . .'

'But here I have your confirmation,' she says waving the piece of paper like you-know-who back from you-know-where.

'Fantastic.' I collapse into the chair opposite her. 'When does the plane leave?'

'I don't know,' she smiles sweetly. 'It hasn't been decided.'

'It hasn't been decided?'

'It could be tomorrow or it could be the day after, or . . .'

'Or . . .?'

'Or the day after. But at least we have your confirmation.'

Fantastic. I have an official, rubber-stamped, triplicate confirmation for a flight that will take off sometime now or sometime never. What the hell does that . . .?

'Thank you very much,' I mutter. 'Very kind. My confirmation. Yes. Fantastic. Thank you very much.'

Foreign travel. The joys of lying on beaches; boozing it up; lovely restaurants; nightclubs. I had been in Colombo exactly forty-three hours twenty-seven minutes. I had spent forty-three hours twenty-six-and-a-half minutes fighting to get my confirmation. Now I had it, nobody could tell me which flight it was for, nor when or indeed if it would leave.

I now had a choice. In spite of its being fairly Catholic in and around Colombo, there was an acute shortage of shrines to St Dymphna, the patron saint of lost causes. I didn't fancy the Dutch Reformed Church in the Wolvendaal area of Colombo, abandoned long ago to the Tamils. (The Dutch in Sri Lanka had apparently adjusted so much to British rule that they even fought on the British side against their fellow Dutchmen during the Boer War.)

The only possible alternative was Buddha; maybe he could be generous and put in a word for me. Or I could forget the whole thing, go into town and sweat my guts out indulging in a traditional Sri Lankan oil herb massage. Everything was spotless, I was told. Whatever anybody said there were no risks whatsoever. It was just that they used the same flowers in the water again and again because of their perfume.

No way am I scared of a few little flowers so I decided on the less risky alternative; I would throw myself on the mercy of the Buddha. But which one?

Sri Lanka has more shrines than Venice has cornettos. It even has complete ancient Buddhist cities like Anuradhapura or Polonharuwa which should in all fairness rank alongside the pyramids as wonders of the world and be buried in tourists and UNESCO grants. Instead they are crumbling gently into the forest.

In the end, because all I needed was a short, sharp miracle and I didn't want to be away from the airline office too long, just in case, I opted for the great Temple of Buddha's Tooth. If anything could help me it was the Tooth, the whole Tooth and nothing but the Tooth. The other thing in favour of the Temple of the Tooth was that it was just over seventy miles away in Kandy, which is practically in the centre of the island, easily, well fairly easily, accessible by train and, because of its height, has a totally different, relaxed, cool climate than hot, sticky, sweaty Colombo.

If the Tooth was going to work wonders it would, knowing my luck, probably have a pretty quick use-by-date, but the train would get me back speedily to Colombo and the airport.

Getting back from any of the other temples would probably take at least 2,000 years, miss not only the replacement aircraft but the one after that and the one after that.

Colombo railway station was just like home – old, Victorian, crowded. And it boasted about as many turbans. The ticket office was pure, or rather impure, British Rail; old, out-of-date and crowded. The staff were also British Rail. In fact I swear I recognized many of them. The only light relief was a notice in front of one ancient ticket desk which said, 'Please use alternative widow'. But they did know their business.

Once I asked the ticket office at Buxted, my local home station, for a return ticket to Stoke-on-Trent. They couldn't find it in their ticket book. Trying to make it easy for them, I asked for Birmingham, but Birmingham, they said, wasn't in the book either.

Everybody in the ticket office at Colombo looked as though they would know the fare off by heart. Including the alternative widow.

The train was about as modern as the train I catch most mornings from Buxted. If it's too hot you open the windows. If its too cold you close them again. Unless, of course, somebody is using the you-know-what, in which case you keep them closed and put up with it.

Immediately outside Colombo the scenery was uneventful, but gradually the countryside opened up and we were rattling through palm trees, flame trees and even paddy fields. Water buffalo and cattle were grazing by the track. We passed lonely suburban Buddhist temples, chugged through more deserted British railway stations, which they probably bought as a job lot from the government in the run-up to privatization – 'It'll help you create the image of a dynamic economy, old chap.' 'Thank you, sir, very much. I'll have twenty.' The announcements for each station I understood as clearly as those on British Rail.

A man wandered along the train selling rolls and cakes out of a greasy plastic bag. Babies started crying, probably because they had been left behind in Sri Lanka and not flown out to a life of carefree luxury on the Côte d'Azur. Old ladies started opening their flasks of tea. Somebody wanted the window open. Somebody else wanted it closed. It really was just like home.

If Sri Lanka is supposed to be the cheapest place on earth for down-and-out expats, Kandy, the last of the ancient Sinhalese kingdoms to fall to the Europeans, is the ideal place to live. It's high up in the hill country, and the weather is warm and pleasant, like spring all year round.

Surrounding it are nothing but tea plantations with such typical unpronounceable Sri Lankan names as Glenloch, Wavendon, even Rothschild. Originally they had all been state-owned and run and losing a fortune. Now they are run by private managers who are convinced that, according to the tea leaves, the industry has a bright and profitable future. In the old days they were producing less per acre than India or Kenya, which are no way their smartest competitors. Now that situation is improving, thanks to the Russians. In the old days Sri Lanka's biggest customer was Iraq, but the Gulf War put paid to that. For two years they hit big problems. Now their big customers are Russia and many of the old Soviet republics. Their samovars do not want the good stuff. They only need the common-or-garden teas, which is exactly what Sri Lanka produces. Determined never to put all their tealeaves in one pot, they have also started producing what the rest of the world wants, as opposed to what they want to produce.

'So what does the rest of the world want?' I asked one tea expert.

'CTC,' he said – cut, tear and curl tea which now accounts for the greater part of world tea – 'and scented teas.'

Growing tea and growing grapes for wine are very similar. Both depend on location and climate. The hills around Kandy are supposed to be one of the best tea producing areas in the world. Quality is vital. With tea, only the top two leaves of the plant are picked for quality. The rest goes into the run-of-the-mill teas. Similarly with grapes: in every vineyard there are certain vines in certain rows that every year give you the ultimate. The rest go into general production.

'Cinnamon,' he said. 'That's the big giveaway. If you taste cinnamon in tea you know it's a cheap tea and the only way it could be sold was to add cinnamon to disguise the taste.'

'What's the most profitable tea you produce?'

'Teabags,' he grinned. 'In the old days all the dust in the mills was just swept up and thrown away or burnt. Now, we put a little into every teabag. It gets rid of the rubbish. It also makes good money.'

He could still remember the day teabags were invented. To him it was probably as important as the day they smashed the atom and Desert Orchid won the Cheltenham Gold Cup for the last time.

'Immediately, the dust was worth money. We were all rushing around sweeping it up as quickly as possible. It was like making money from nothing.'

But my sole objective was not tea. It was to visit the Temple of the Tooth, the final resting place of just one of Lord Buddha's teeth. If I was there hoping to get help with my airline ticket then practically half of South East Asia was also having problems with their airline tickets. The place was packed.

Outside the station, you couldn't see anything for tuk-tuks. The road was crammed. It was like Derby Day at Epsom. The place had a British feel to it; there were lots of old shops; the market stretched to two storeys; the main hotel was definitely Victorian and probably packed with expats trying to survive on next to nothing in a little bit of style.

The temple itself, I thought, would be Karma. But it was like St Peter's on a Sunday morning. People were everywhere: marching briskly into battle with the spirits, wandering along with friends and relatives, all pouring over the open courtyard leading up to the temple.

In the centre of the crowd was the new temple elephant.

Three thousand years ago King Solomon was sending Sri Lankan elephants to the Queen of Sheba as jumbo tokens of his affection. Which has always struck me as the ultimate gift that nobody actually wants. I mean, what the hell do you do when you unwrap it and there, standing on the carpet at the foot of your bed, is a five-ton elephant? Gift horses, I've always thought, should be called gift elephants. You can do something with a horse. But an elephant? Still, elephants have been highly honoured members of society ever since.

The famous old temple elephant had just died, at eighty-four years old after fifty years' faithful service. He was being stuffed and put on display in the temple museum. His replacement was attracting almost as much attention, although what effect he would have had on the Queen of Sheba is difficult to judge.

Buddhism, which has been the religion of Sri Lanka for over 2,000 years, always seems to me to be a gentle, relaxed religion. Low on specifics, high on attitudes and feelings and commitment. Inside the Temple of the Tooth, however, there wasn't too much of those. First we shuffled up the ramp to get inside; then we were all subject to the Watching Eye, temple attendants whose job it is to make certain all legs and arms are covered. The world being what it is today, most of the people being stopped and urged to cover their limbs were men.

Once inside we shuffled along through the ground floor, up the steps, along a balcony and into the tiny circular temple library where the sacred manuscripts are stored. From there along another balcony, through a door and into the outer area housing the Tooth itself. Here people were kneeling and sitting on the floor. Some were getting quite carried away.

Visiting the Tooth was like inspecting any relic of any religion anywhere. We queued up again to shuffle into a tiny chapel, where in what looked like a tabernacle on an altar was the Tooth itself. Sometimes it was on display, sometimes it wasn't. This time it was.

As on any pilgrimage, everybody was there for their own

reason; young people with their hopes for that evening, young families with their hopes for a little further into the future. And, of course, the old. Any religion, they say, is comforting to the old. Many of the old faces and withered, fragile bodies around me looked as though they had had no comfort for hundreds of years. They were all searching for their personal nirvana. Me? I was probably the first person in 2,000 years of Buddhism on the island who was looking not for Nirvana but for an airline ticket.

Was I going to achieve my enlightenment? It didn't look hopeful. Almost as soon as I had seen the tooth the whole tooth and nothing but the tooth, the skies came over dark and it poured like mad. If the trains are like British Rail then Kandy tuk-tuks are like London (or Buenos Aires) taxis. You can never get one in the rain. I had to walk all the way back to the station.

On the train on the way back, I'm sitting by the window wondering like hell if the Tooth is going to work its magic for me. A girl wearing the traditional costume gets on just as we're about to leave. She sits down next to me. The train moves away slowly, then very quickly gathers speed. Suddenly, just as we pass the beginning of the long perilous drop from Kandy to the plains, she jumps up, runs to the carriage door and flings it open. She stands there on the edge. She's not, is she? She comes back and sits next to me again.

Why me? I thought. Why do I always have to get them? On planes, it's fat ladies and babies. Now this, on the train. I try to read my book on Gerard Manley Hopkins, but it's no good.

'My boyfriend has just left me,' she suddenly blurts out.

'Really. I'm sorry.' I go back to Gerard Manley.

'My father has just died.'

'I'm sorry.'

'. . . and the astonishing thing about Swinburne is not his presence but his uselessness, as the admirable thing about Hopkins is not his presence but his use.'

'My mother wants me to come home, but I don't . . . She

pours out a long story. She was born in Entebbe, Uganda. When Amin seized power, the family lost everything but managed to escape to Kenya with the help of friends. They were Israelis. Her father had been very strict, but her mother understood everything. Her boyfriend was from Kandy. She had just been up to visit him. It was the first time she had seen his family. They were nice. But he was different; he wasn't the same as when they first met. They had a row. She walked out.

She uses long, old-fashioned phrases as if she'd been brought up on the Third Programme. Instead of saying Amin seized power she says he 'created grave injustices'. Instead of saying they escaped with the aid of friends, she says her father approached 'some bribery sleuths engaged in malpractices and offered them a gratification'. And instead of saying she'd walked out she kept talking about 'reformulating anew her consent'.

'Really,' I mumbled.

Life was not worth living. Should she go and see a fortune teller? Or should she . . .?

So I wanted to listen to her problems? I had enough of my own. 'What does your mother say?' I grunted.

'I can't reach her.'

'Why? Where does she live?'

'In Maida Vale.'

Which obviously accounted for the strange vocabulary.

Now it's Sunday. The hotel is quiet. Even Buddhist cock-roaches have a day of rest. I clamber out of bed, stagger across the wooden floor and pump the brown water into the chipped basin. I do my best to shave. It's not easy. Maybe that's why they all have beards and let their hair grow.

Wait a minute, is that a coach outside? I race to the window. The French are clambering aboard, with all the babies they've bought from the baby farm down the road. Except for Tante Madeleine who wanted the poisoned raw potatoes. She is hobbling with a stick, her leg wrapped in bandages. She obviously skidded and fell on all those potatoes.

Does this mean there is a flight? Have they heard something I haven't heard? Typical flipping French! I race back to the bathroom and half-finish my half-shave. I throw everything into my suitcase. Within forty-one-and-a-half seconds I'm packed, I've said goodbye to the cockroaches, I'm down the stairs, past all the 'Don't breathe', 'Mind the elephants', 'Be kind to the Cockroaches' signs.

I've paid. I'm into a taxi and we're zooming through Colombo to the airport. There is the occasional buffalo cart. A few cattle are wandering over the road fulfilling Shiva's divine mission to block passing traffic. Two or three bicycles are out for an early morning constitutional. A tuk-tuk tuk-tuks along. The place is practically deserted.

Now what happens? I kid you not. The driver can't find the airport. He's only just started. I'm his first trip to the airport and he can't find it. I'm leaping all over the road asking everybody in sight. It's straight ahead. It's to the left. It's second on the right. Nobody knows where the damn thing is. Suddenly another taxi comes swerving round the corner. I leap back inside. 'Follow that cab,' I scream.

We're caught up in the slip stream. Within seven seconds we're there. The French are streaming out of the coach. Hell, if there's only one plane and they've got here first what hope have I . . .? I grab my suitcase, skid through the entrance, race up to the check-in desk. I'm the only one there. The whole place is empty. Empty! How come it's empty? I thought all the planes had been . . . I kept telephoning. There was no answer. And what about all those years I spent at the . . .? The check-in girl ambles along to the desk.

'I don't know if my ticket is confirmed or not,' I blubber, 'but I gather there is—'

'No problem,' she smiles that serene Buddhist smile and glances at the computer screen. 'Your ticket. Your boarding pass, sir,' she smiles once more. 'Have a nice flight.'

'You mean – you mean—'

'The flight is scheduled to leave on time, sir.'

'You mean—' I turn towards the security check at customs.

'By the way, sir,' she leans forward. 'If you're in town and you ever want to get your ticket confirmed, you know the flower shop by the Holiday Inn?'

'Yes.'

'Go in there, buy some flowers, then ask for the manage- ress.'

'Yes.'

'Tell her you love the flowers, then ask if she can confirm your ticket. Her husband is always upstairs. He's a director of the airline. He'll do it for you straightaway. Have a nice flight.'

Lomé

I must have been buttered – beurré, as the French say.

I can remember picking up the minister and the other officials at their hotels. I can remember driving through Lomé, which at the time was famous dans certains quartiers in Africa for its douceur de vivre or, in English, its dolce vita. I can remember us all tumbling into this fantastic French restaurant on the beach road, a stone's throw from the border with Ghana. And I can remember telling everybody in my bad French – 'Je parle français sans aucun accent ... français' – about my adventures in francophone Africa. After that things get a bit hazy.

We were attending the Lomé Convention, the EC's regular hand-out of funds to third world countries, at the thirty-five-storey Hôtel de 2 Fevrier in the centre of town, which most people said was their favourite hotel in the whole of Africa. Delegates from all over Africa, the Caribbean and the Pacific were there, eating, drinking, talking, laughing, even dropping into the actual conference from time to time to find out how much money they had been voted as a result of their intensive lobbying at the dining tables of Europe.

Over lunch, a group of us had been telling stories about francophone Africa – the 60 percent of the continent which is virtually unknown to the English-speaking world, not to mention to the Caribbean and the Pacific – while tucking into the most delicate chateaubriand I have ever been privileged to taste. Which proves the second Biddlecombe Law of International Conferences: Poor countries always serve rich food. A minister from Burkina Faso, or was it Niger, or maybe Mali, asked if I knew anywhere we could get a good meal in Lomé. The whole table exploded. Plates and glasses leapt in the air as everyone banged the table with laughter. A good meal in Lomé? Lomé's famous throughout French Africa for its restaurants, the quality of its cuisine, the standard of service. It's the best kept secret in Africa. Apart, of course, from the name of that bank in Zürich.

Everybody confuses Togo with Tonga. Well, maybe not everybody. Witty, intelligent sophisticates who have read a certain book on French Africa whose name I can't recall just at the moment, know that Togo is the Dom Perignon of West Africa. Tonga, on the other hand, is where great big Queen Salote came from to sit in the rain and wave at the crowds back in 1952 on what must have been the only really happy day our own Queen has had in the last forty years. The occasional few even remember Noel Coward's remark when somebody asked him who was the little man beside Queen Salote. 'Her lunch,' he replied.

Togo is the old Togoland, the famous model colony of the Germans. Dr Nachtigall, Bismarck's special envoy, ordered a gunboat to anchor off the coast way back in 1884. The next day, July 4, he signed a treaty with King Jlapa III. Togo was German. The following year it was rubber-stamped at the Berlin conference. Today old Togolese around Togoville and Anécho, where the deed was done, will tell you the Germans were tough but fair. They built three railway lines, a road system, a big church, put in telegraphic communications, a direct longwave contact with Germany and constructed three landing jetties, two of which have been washed away. The remnants of the third are still there.

Come 1914, Togo was the site of the first battle of the First

World War. The Germans proposed it should be neutral. Their proposal was rejected. British troops marched in from the left, from the Gold Coast, today's Ghana, and French troops from the right, Dahomey, today's Benin. They had a brief scuffle over the radio tower at Atakpame which was linked directly to Berlin. Within days it was all over. The Germans surrendered.

In 1919 the allies divided Togo (nearly two-thirds to France, one-third to Britain) without of course bothering to ask the Togolese what they thought. Togo was then placed under French mandate by the League of Nations. Between the two wars Lomé enjoyed many special advantages as a result of the landing jetties and the modern railway system. In 1946 the League of Nations mandate was replaced and Togo became a trusteeship territory of the UN. In 1956 the bit of Togo under British administration was annexed to the Gold Coast, which became independent in 1957 as Ghana. On August 30, 1956, the other bit became the first autonomous republic of French-speaking black Africa. On April 27, 1960, independence was proclaimed and the Republic of Togo (not Tonga) came into being.

So, I can remember everybody collapsing around the long table reserved for us hollering, 'Bring out the champagne.' 'I'll have Laurent Perrier.' Such are the pressures on delegates attending international conferences.

The champagne arrived, perfectly chilled. We toasted each other; everybody at the conference; those who got their embassies to register for them and had not bothered to come but were still collecting their daily allowance; those who registered but had not been seen since 11.15 p.m. on the first evening, when they left the downstairs bar with someone who was obviously a very close friend; those who couldn't come because they'd gone to an even better conference; everybody in the restaurant. Nobody thought of proposing a toast to the tax payers of the EC who had made the whole thing possible.

The conference was over. All the decisions had, or had not, been taken. We were ready to celebrate – to continue celebrating. Everybody wanted lobster. We ordered the biggest they had. 'Anything else, messieurs?' said the maître d'hôtel.

'The best French food you have', everybody shouted, in the first unanimous decision of the conference.

We had pâté de foie gras from Israel and Hungary; truffles from Spain; frogs' legs from India and Pakistan; snails from China and, would you believe, Britain; raspberries from Chile. And, of course, the lobsters. From the local fishermen. In Ghana.

'And more champagne?' asked the maître d'hôtel.

'And more champagne,' we all replied.

Then the minister from wherever piped up. 'Pour Moi, Beaujolais Village,' he said solemnly. 'Frais.'

The glasses were refilled; we drank, and ordered still more. We were doing everything we could to help the French, if not the African, economy. Except the minister from wherever.

'Excusez-moi, monsieur,' he said. 'This is not properly chilled. If you would be so kind . . .'

When I first went to Lomé, it was a mini-boom town. Offices were going up all over the place, factories opening, foreign investors moving in. With Nigeria falling apart and problems beginning to affect Côte d'Ivoire, it was one of the cleanest, safest cities in Africa.

The whole country was in a class of its own. While the rest of Africa was struggling to survive, tiny little Togo was humming with a quiet, well-oiled efficiency. People had enough to eat; it was self-sufficient in basic foodstuffs. Most children went to school, most people had some kind of work. It was safe; you could wander all over the place at any time of the day or night without the slightest worries. People were genuinely friendly and polite. It was small enough to feel at home in. It was also small enough to be at home in. Within a few days you knew virtually everybody in town, where all the ministries and offices were, and, of course, where all the bars and restaurants were. It was practically the business, banking and trading centre of West Africa.

In fact, it was so tranquil that I can remember being in Lomé one December morning when the main headline news on the front page of their only national newspaper announced, 'Noël est demain'.

The President, General Gnassingbe Eyadema, set the pace. He was at his desk every morning at four o'clock. By five the presidence was humming; telephones were buzzing, telexes rattling away. Bleary-eyed Western diplomats who didn't realize the world existed at such an hour were being ushered in to see him. Ambassadors were queuing up outside. Ministers were at their desks by 6.30. Meetings were usually arranged at a moment's notice. One minute you could be talking to a minister in his office, the next he was dashing across town to the President, which kept everybody on their toes.

'In the Marines we always hit the ground running,' a US diplomat based in Lomé told me once, 'but this is the first time I've seen a whole country hit the ground running.'

The Grand Marché in Lomé was the number one market in the region thanks to the famous Mama Benzes, or the Mamas, who went around in enormous chauffeur-driven Mercedes Benzes, hence the name. One of the oldest and best known Mamas, Madame Essie Veinyo Adabunu, the eldest of eighteen children, was selling firewood, bananas and corn by the time she was six. As a teenager she graduated to selling cigarettes. By twenty-two she had enough money to buy soap and cushions and take a stall in the marketplace. As times became harder in Togo, she went to Ghana, then the booming centre of West Africa. Within a year she had turned £15 into £300, enough to start buying and selling cloth. She became a cloth merchant, and has never looked back. For, rich or poor, every African woman buys six yards of cloth at least once a year to make her traditional dress. Two yards she wraps around her waist; another two she uses to carry a baby on her back or just drapes around her hips; the rest she makes into a blouse. Richer women can have hundreds of these outfits.

At the time, Madame Adabunu lived in a big house in Lomé, where all the furniture came from Paris. People said she was a millionaire. They also said that the Mama Benzes owned all the taxis in Lomé, a large proportion of the country's truck and lorries, and a growing number of shops. But there was nothing on paper.

'Why do I need paper?' she asked me. 'I can keep everything in my head. If you can't, you are not a good businessman.' And most of the business was done in cash. It was not unusual to see Mamas buying cigarettes by the container-load at the port and paying up to £30,000 in cash on the spot.

The Grand Marché was so famous, traders came from the Côte d'Ivoire, Mali and Niger to buy cotton from the Mamas; they came from Burkina Faso and Benin to buy sugar and rice; they came from Nigeria to buy cigarettes and whisky, and they came from Ghana to buy everything. Even the British high commission in Accra sent a truck every week to buy everything, including the basics, which they couldn't buy locally.

But the Mamas didn't just stay at home. Catch any plane from Lomé to Nigeria, Cameroon, or even Congo or Gabon, and you saw Mamas – many of them occupying two seats at a time – going out to do business. Between them, they were probably worth far more than all the pinstripes on board.

With most people, the Mamas did a straightforward deal – a set price for a set quantity of goods. But to others – the mini-Mamas, the girls who wanted to become businesswomen like Madame Adabunu – they would ask only half the price and take an extra commission when the goods had been resold. This benefitted the Mamas two ways. First, they were guaranteed extra sales outlets for the future. Second, it enabled them to pass on goods they couldn't sell. Each mini-Mama would be given cloth or food that the Mama couldn't sell and wanted to replace. The mini-Mama walked the streets maybe for months until she sold everything, then came back for fresh supplies. This combination of good judgement, good management and pyramid selling Africa-style enabled the Mamas to buy ten containers at a time knowing that they would be able to sell everything.

Many husbands found it difficult living with a successful Mama and went back to their villages. Madame Adabunu's husband left her when she started getting successful. Others stayed. The husband of one successful Mama was still an ordinary schoolteacher. One or two had established companies of their own, but none had come near rivalling the success of the Mama Benzes of Lomé.

'Men are too lazy,' Madam Adabunu told me. 'They just want to wear shoes and a tie, work in an office and be a consultant. They don't like buying and selling and doing business.' She laughed.

Today, however, Togo has big problems. Shops are empty. Those that are not empty are locked and barred. The Grand Marché is deserted. The factories are empty. Foreign investors have fled. The streets are piled high with rubbish. People are frightened to go out. They are barricading themselves inside, desperately trying to get a guard dog. Togo has even had its first bank robbery.

At the dinner, I was sitting next to an official from Guinée Conakry which is famous for gold smuggling. 'I remember what you said about Zaire lunchtime,' he said as we toasted each other. 'I was in Kinshasa last week. I met my friend who is a director of the PTT. I said, Why are you still here? Haven't they made you an ambassador yet? Do you know what he said? He said they wanted to, but he asked if he could stay on another year because he hadn't stolen enough money yet.'

The table exploded, as another bottle of Beaujolais Village arrived.

'Je suis desolé, monsieur,' said the Minister for Serving Wine at the Correct Room Temperature in a Continent Where How Many Millions are Dying of Poverty and Starvation Every Day, 'but it is still not properly chilled. If you would be . . .'

'That's nothing,' I said to the official from Guinée. 'I know one francophone ambassador who'd got a big, impressive official residence in London. But he doesn't live there. He lives in a tiny house in Grays in Essex.'

'Jamais,' he said, staring at me.

I told him about how the ambassador had invited me to dinner and sent a gold-edged card, copperplate writing, my name handwritten in italic script. But the address of the ambassador's residence in one of the most expensive parts of London had been crossed out and another address scribbled in in biro. It was a turning off the High Street in Grays. It took me ages to get there. The house was tiny, but the meal was enormous. We had mountains of smoked salmon. The cook obviously thought it was like any other fish and piled it on. When I judged the moment right, I asked why he preferred a terraced house in Grays to a London mansion.

'Money,' he said. 'The London house is very impressive, but the government don't give me enough to live there. If I lived there, I would have to spend my own money to look after the place. Why should I do that?'

'Prestige? Protocol?' I suggested.

'Yes, when the government pays. Not when I have to pay. So the money the government gives me for the residence pays the mortgage on my little house and', he added, gulping down another half kilo, 'it enables me to eat smoked salmon whenever I want to.'

'Bravo, bravo. Formidable,' everybody cried as yet another bottle of champagne arrived together with yet another bottle of Beaujolais Village. We splashed the champagne in our glasses, toasted each other yet again and . . .

'But monsieur,' the minister sipped his Beaujolais Village, 'I explained I like it chilled. This is . . .'

The maître d'hôtel ran back into the kitchen. We tried to carry on chatting, but it was getting difficult. Suddenly the kitchen door burst open and out came the maître d', the owner's wife, the owner and another bottle of Beaujolais Village. The whole restaurant went quiet. The bottle was opened ever so slowly, with all the precision of dismantling a nuclear bomb. The wine was poured into the glass. The minister picked it up, studied the colour, put it to his lips and . . . 'D'accord,' he whispered. 'Not exactly how I like it.' We held our breath. 'But it will do. Merci.' Everybody collapsed with relief.

So how come Togo is in such a mess?

'Democracy,' a weary government official, one of the few who survived the problems, told me. 'People think democracy means better days. It doesn't.'

As the fashion for national conferences and transitional governments began to grow throughout Africa in the early 1990s, Togo also had its national conference. At first the President was against it, but as demands grew from more and more civic, religious and political leaders, he gave in. The national conference opened at the Hôtel de 2 Févier. At first it was supposed to be advisory. Government representatives sat down with opposition leaders to try and work out a new system for running the country. Then suddenly the conference decided virtually to seize power, appoint its own prime minister and cut short the President's term of office. There was uproar.

'That's not what we agreed,' the survivor told me. 'It was outside the terms of reference of the conference. One day, they agreed the terms of reference. The next day they ignored them. Even a national conference should abide by its own rules.'

Supporters of both sides took to the streets. The army began getting fidgety. Diplomats began cabling home for guidance. Foreign investors started making enquiries about flights home.

Eyadema was summoned by the national conference to attend their closing ceremony. He pleaded a diplomatic sore throat. But he agreed to recognize their new prime minister as well as the new Supreme Republican Council appointed to run the country while plans for municipal, legislative and parliamentary elections were drawn up for the following year. He rejected out of hand, however, all the charges made against him of embezzlement, corruption and violations of human rights and called for an international inquiry to establish his innocence. The uproar got worse – more marches, more demonstrations. The military took to the streets; some said, to restore order, others, to cause trouble. A new constitution was to be introduced, new constituencies were to be drawn up, new elections to take place.

There were more demonstrations, more strikes. The army for a short period took matters into its own hands. Eyadema was written off. He'd been stripped of almost all his powers. If he wanted to use the presidential 747, he was told, he could, providing he paid for the fuel. Before, he had used it all the time; now he went everywhere by car. The end, everybody said, was in sight.

Foreign investors began packing their bags. The last thing they want is political uncertainty. Some just disappeared, leaving the keys of their factory behind the clock on the mantlepiece. With the front door wide open. Others left with a flourish, calling down hell and damnation on the new transitional government. Some foreign investors found they were even pursued to the airport by their employees.

'You mean, workers were out for their blood?' I asked the survivor.

'No,' he grinned. 'They wanted to persuade them to stay. They knew that once they left, they couldn't run the factories themselves. Everything would grind to a standstill. They would lose their jobs. They would have no money.'

Which, of course, is what happened. More strikes took place. There was more uproar. Lomé was crumbling into dust.

Then came one final, beautiful, Machiavellian twist. Joseph Kokou Koffigoh, the man appointed Prime Minister by the national conference and who had probably done most to discredit Eyadema, was dismissed by the conference. But immediately – are you ready? – he was reappointed by Eyadema in the interests of national unity. At a stroke, Eyadema was once again top dog. Nobody could criticize him; he was following the original wishes of the national conference. Nobody could criticize Koffigoh. He had been appointed Prime Minister by the original conference, and was reappointed in the interests of national unity. Nobody could breathe a word against national unity. Eyadema also said that if the national conference couldn't organize elections, he would. Once again a brilliant ploy.

Lomé today, as a result, is nothing like the Lomé of old. Instead of being at the top of the class, it is near the bottom. Instead of being a growing business area, it is virtually empty. Foreign investors have gone. Factories are closed. Unemployment is way, way up.

Instead of being a friendly, safe town it is riddled with violence. People are frightened to go out. Muggings are commonplace. Bank robberies no longer hit the front pages. Bombs go off outside government offices and even the occasional French restaurant.

Who's to blame? Obviously we all believe in democracy. But talk to Koffi Hongbegnon. Does he believe in democracy? Under the old system, when I first met him, he was happy with his 200 grams of corn, 200 grams of flour, 30 grams of vegetable oil, 20 grams of meat and 20 grams of dried peas a day. He was one of 8,000 people being resettled and rehoused in one of the biggest work-for-food programmes ever launched in

Africa, as a result of the construction of Togo's giant US$140 million Nangbeto dam.

With his wives and children, he was helping to build not only a new house for his family but a new village of Adigo as well, which meant much-needed work and food. For with their help he had been bringing home two sacks of flour, one sack of rice, fifty cans of sardines, four cans of cooking oil and one-tenth of a sack of dried peas a month. Today the programme has more or less come to a standstill. He is lucky to get 100 grams of corn.

Talk to Madame Yacoubou. Does she believe in democracy? Under the old system she could afford to feed her children, look after her mother and father and buy a roll of material for a new dress at the end of the year. Today she can still feed her children, but only just. They no longer have milk. For some reason even the free milk powder donated by the EC is no longer getting through to the people who need it. She can't remember the last time they had orange juice. Every day they have rice. If they're lucky they might have fish once a week.

Talk to Togolese businessmen like Mr Eklo on the Boulevard Circulaire, the central ring road in Lomé. Under the old system, business was not exactly booming; business never exactly booms for African businessmen; it booms only for African businessmen with the right local agencies and the right local contacts. But he was happy. Each year things were getting better: he was expanding his premises and taking on more staff; he was making three or four trips to Paris. Even his wife went to Paris to do her Christmas shopping, thanks to a cheap ticket from Air Afrique.

Today, he is practically back to where he started. Business has collapsed, and what business there is, is dodgy. He might get paid, he might not. All his staff are gone apart from Koffi, his old retainer, who will never leave him. His premises have been attacked and looted so many times he has lost virtually all his stock. His extension is in ruins. He operates out of one tiny room. Paris is gone forever. He can hardly afford to cross the street. As for his wife's shopping trips, they're just memories.

When I first met Mr Yao, he was the parson's nose king of Togo. Today he sits in a big, dusty, empty office tucked away in a sidestreet by the hospital. At one time it was the centre of an empire. Container loads were shipped in every year from Europe, even from the United States. Parson's noses were rated a delicacy; everybody ate them, they were a sign of good life. Today it's just a small family business.

'Years ago we made a lot of money out of parson's noses. We couldn't get enough. We had contracts with all the big poultry suppliers,' he reminisced, 'in France, in Britain, even in the States. Our big problem was spreading the supplies. In Europe you eat turkey at Christmas so we would get all our supplies about November, December. But we couldn't sell them all then. We had to build cold stores all over the country.' He thumped the fan on his desk to get it working again. 'Now you are eating turkeys all year round, but nobody here has much money, nor in Benin and Nigeria and Ghana. We don't sell so much any more.'

Downstairs the freezers were practically empty. The warehouses contained one or two boxes and rows of empty shelves. People were sitting by desks, looking out of the window or reading the papers. Parson's noses were obviously not what they used to be.

'I've diversified. I had to. First there were problems with Nigeria, then with Ghana. Business was very hard,' Mr Yao told me he had a small hotel in Lomé which is a home from home for the US Peace Corps. He lets out his cold stores to other companies. He still has his food trading and distribution operation, but it no longer runs in overdrive. I asked about all the people sitting around his office.

'They are friends,' he said with a big smile. 'I can't send them away. They have been working with me for years; we shared the good times, now we are sharing the bad times.'

What about the Great Survivor?

Lomé

'Do you believe in democracy?' I asked him over dinner one evening in the Hôtel du Golfe, a wonderful old-fashioned hotel in the centre of town.

'Democracy,' he laughed. 'What is democracy? Democracy is the freedom to make mistakes.'

The lobsters were massive. They practically covered the table, never mind the plate. We dug into them with relish. The minister was quieter than at lunch. Then, of course, I realized. He was not only eating the great chunks of lobster, he was eating the shell as well. First the legs, which I admit I didn't think much about. It's a bit of a drag trying to get the meat out. But then he sliced through the body and started crunching slabs of shell.

'You should (crunch, crunch) if you have (snap, crunch, crunch) after all (munch, crunch) Africa (crunch),' he said across the table to me.

'Oui, c'est vrai,' I mumbled. I could not understand what on earth he was saying. The crunching of the shell was making more noise than a pneumatic drill. In any case it never does any harm to mutter 'c'est vrai,' I thought. The French do it all the time.

'Une bonne idée,' said the chef du cabinet. 'The English don't know anything about francophone Africa. Nearly half of Africa is francophone, but when I first went to London people asked me why I was speaking French. They thought I came from Martinique or somewhere.'

'They think you've got to have two phones for Africa,' said the post office official. 'A francophone for French Africa and an anglophone for . . .'

'Or they think we're some kind of chasse garde for the French,' said the directeur-général.

'But I noticed *Le Chasseur Français* is on sale at the hotel,' I said.

'Voilà, he's the man to do it,' they all cried. 'You must!'

273

'Sérieusement, monsieur,' crunched the Minister for Lobster-Eating Shells and All, 'you must (crunch, munch, crunch) as soon as (snap, crack, crunch) très impératif (crunch) le contexte (crunch) d'accord (swallow).'

'D'accord, si vous voulez,' I mumbled. Another handy all-purpose phrase.

'And it's much better being francophone than anglophone.'

'You can drink champagne and eat . . .'

'And the Code Napoleon; don't forget Article 340.'

'La recherche de la paternité,' they all chanted, 'est interdite.' More laughter.

'Even the anglophones don't know anything about francophone Africa. A Nigerian came to see me last week. First thing he asked was what time the water and electricity were cut off.'

The minister's plate was now empty. The whole lobster had disappeared – legs, shell, all those funny green bits inside. Even the head, and the eyes. Nobody said anything. Maybe they were too polite. Maybe it was another one of those francophone African traditions: on the Saturday after a conference the senior minister present eats the lobster shell. Or maybe I'd drunk too much. Champagne poisoning, I remember thinking, can do funny things. If I'm ever lucky enough to get it.

Then zock. Memory goes blank. Well, almost.

I can remember suddenly sobering up when somebody said, 'Do you have any cheval blanc?'

'No, monsieur,' replied the maître d' thankfully.

'In that case I'll have some camembert,' said the directeur-général.

I can vaguely remember somebody telling a story about going on a delegation with their president and the president calling him at 3 a.m. to get a chateaubriand for his dog.

Then somebody else told a joke. 'What's the difference between God and President Mobutu?'

'I don't know,' I stuttered. 'What's the difference?'

'God is everywhere. President Mobutu is everywhere – except in Zaire.'

Then over the coffee and digestifs there was lots of laughter because the directeur-général said he once got a plane from Dakar to Abidjan. When they arrived the pilot proudly announced they were bang on time, then paused and said, 'Bon sang de bon soir. I forgot to land in Conakry.'

The chef du cabinet then mentioned a front-page headline in their national newspaper saying 'Police arrest 21-year-old white Irishman', which brought the house down.

I can even just about remember leaving the restaurant, and saying to my friend from Guinée Conakry, 'The minister seemed quiet this evening.'

'Don't worry about him,' he said, giving me his business card. 'His daughter died last night. He's just heard.'

'I'm sorry,' I mumbled. 'I didn't know. How did that happen?'

'She was being born,' he said, scribbling his home number on the back of the card.

'Being born,' I exclaimed, opening the car door for him. 'That's terrible. How is his wife?'

'Oh, she died as well,' he shouted out of the window as he disappeared into the night.

The following morning I got a letter from the minister congratulating me on my decision to write a book about francophone Africa and wishing me every success. He signed it, 'A White Irishman'.

Cotonou

Okay, I admit I don't reckon all this, well, kissing. It's not that it's not, well, y'know, interesting; although of course, that depends on the other person. It's just that I feel there must be some other way of doing things. I mean, it's not exactly hygienic, is it? Kissing men, that is.

Shaking hands, even holding hands with men, I'm used to. My dear, you do it all the time in Africa. Sometimes even in France. And once, but only once, in Italy; at a machine tool exhibition in Milan of all places. But actually going around – mwah! – kissing other men has got to be different. At least for me it is.

French Africans hug and kiss each other all the time. It's their understated way of saying, Nice to see you again, old chap. It's one area where French culture and manners match perfectly with African culture and manners: warm, human, friendly; a natural intimacy. No English sang-froid for them. But when it happens to me, it's different. Dammit, I am after all British. Well, mostly British. My mother was Irish. But the Irish don't believe in kissing much either. Apart, that is, from dogs, horses and any old cheap plastic statue of a saint.

Which is probably why I always remember Cotonou. Many is the time on foreign trips I've been met at airports. But the airport at Cotonou was the first time in my life where I was met and hugged and kissed. In public. By men. Not just one, but a long row of ministers and government officials. All –

mwahhh! – slobbering all over me and handing me great big
smackeroos. One after the other. After the other. After the
other.

Not being one of nature's luvvies, I nevertheless did my best
to respond as warmly and as naturally and as genuinely as I
could. But neither my chromosomes nor one hundred and
seventy five years plodding through the bland, indifferent, icy
warmth of English society had quite prepared me for the
event. By the time I got to the end of the line I felt as though
I had been sandpapered by a Black and Decker drill in the
rain. For their part, the Beninois seemed quite pleased with
my performance, especially the Minister of Commerce,
because after giving me a pretty powerful lustful Beninois
embrace he just wouldn't let go of my hand.

In France it's different, because you know they do it –
mwah – one-two-three, left-right-left, all the time as if they are
on automatic pilot. It's routine, almost meaningless. A bit like
the way Americans always seem to want to punch me on the
shoulder when I meet them. At the end of a trip to the States
my right shoulder is so sore I have to carry my briefcase in my
left hand.

French kissing is a subject which deserves a lifetime's study.
I honestly don't feel I've had enough experience but, for what
it's worth, I would propose the following:-

Friends:	One	Two	
	Left	Right	
Real friends:	One	Two	Three
	Left	Right	Left

New friends who are dyslexic:

	Three	Two	One
	Right	Right	Left

Enemies, colleagues or members of the family:

	One	Two	Three	Four
	Left	Right	Left	Right
or:				
	Right	Left	Right	Left

depending on their political persuasion and how much money they are likely to leave you.

Real, real friends who have a good lawyer:
Forget the whole thing and read a book instead.

But be warned. That is only half the story. There is the question of quality control. A more mature secretary of a more mature MP told me that as far as she was concerned this came under the heading 'All work and no foreplay'. There is also the question of intent. A Togolese minister of foreign affairs once told me, 'The French are capable of kissing you on both cheeks and hating you at the same time.'

The English can't seem to get the hang of it, wherever they are, whatever the time of day, whoever it is. Especially in French Africa. Some English businessmen I know who regularly visit French Africa really enter into the spirit of the thing. They are patting backs, hugging shoulders and slapping great big wet kisses all over any minister, government official or even temporary chauffeur who is sent to meet them. One banker I know – vaguely, don't forget vaguely – positively relishes it. Even buys his aftershave in Paris in order to create the right impression. It seems either to remind him of those long lost days at public school or give him a taste of what might have been.

At the other extreme, some British diplomats make you positively want to curl up and pretend to be North Korean. I don't mean the usual election-time baby-kissing and the let's-all-join-in-the-traditional-folk-dancing stunts for the cameras, although that's bad enough. I mean throwing handfuls of coins and making children scramble in the dust for them. Or during official banquets grabbing the microphone and singing – or trying to – 'When the Saints Come Marching In'. (I kid you not. I was there.) Or even speaking bad French. I remember one memorable occasion when a British diplomat got up after a government reception where we had all been royally entertained. Not only was he, as they say, very tired and emotional, but he insisted on referring to the dancers as 'Les petites jeunes filles' which means something completely different in francophone Africa from what it does in a language laboratory in the House of Commons. Then to everyone's amazement he insisted they all lined up in front of him and, like a reincarnated George Brown who had been preserved in alcohol, proceeded to go down the line hugging and kissing each in turn.

Then there are British Members of Parliament. One occasion I shall never forget however hard I try. I was with an MP on a mission in francophone Africa. We wanted to visit farms, research centres, hospitals and clinics in the north of the country. I stayed in the capital to work.

'Why don't we meet him at the airport?' I said to the minister who had made all the arrangements. 'We could get the press, radio and television and make it a big event. You could get mileage here, I could get mileage back home.'

He agreed. Telephones leapt off his desk as he summoned secretaries and chauffeurs, dragged the director of television back from a late lunch, scared the hell out of the assistant director of radio – the director was in Hastings brushing up his English – and ordered the director of civil aviation to open the VIP suite and put the whole airport on full alert. Twenty minutes later we were watching the plane taxi along the runway. Everything and everybody was in position. The plane came slowly to a stop. As it did, ground staff pushed the giant steps trolley towards it and caught the door which looked for a couple of seconds as if it was going to snap off its hinges, if not be twisted out of recognition for ever. Nobody seemed worried about it and eventually the steps were in place.

'Okay,' I shouted to the television crew. 'Lights.'

As the platform was bathed in light, out on to it stepped the MP – in a pair of swimming trunks, flip-flop sandals and a straw hat. Alongside him, almost wearing what must have been his Hawaiian shirt and a smile was obviously his new young secretary, whom he had met and appointed during his tour of research centres, hospitals and clinics, and who looked more than keen to help him improve some social skills more than others. I froze.

The MP, who was obviously fast picking up the local customs, stepped promptly to the edge of the platform, raised his hat to the light and shouted, 'Fabulous country. Fabulous. The best country in the whole world.'

It was perfect. The minister was delighted, the television crew cheered. The MP and his new young secretary were led off to the VIP suite and interviewed and wined and dined. They were treated like visiting royalty. The Beninois were even too polite to ask if they wanted any clothes. They must have thought that because the British rarely have anything worth promoting in Africa, when they do have anything worth displaying they want to display it. Gone midnight I saw them, obviously extremely tired and emotional, wandering through the hotel. The MP was still undressed in swimming trunks, flip-flops and straw hat, his secretary still almost wearing his Hawaiian shirt. 'Fabulous country. Fabulous. The best country in the whole world,' he waved across to me. His new young secretary looked as though she was about to take down whatever he asked her to.

For me, of all the social courtesies rife throughout French Africa, I prefer shaking or, if I must, holding, hands; although I will sue if you tell anyone I said that. But as I quickly cottoned on in Cotonou, everyone does it all the time. There, shaking, or holding, hands is not only a mark of respect or courtesy, it is a sign of genuine affection and friendship, in spite of what James Joyce said when an admirer asked if he could shake him by the hand: 'You don't know where it's been.'

In francophone Africa, you shake hands when you're introduced; when you leave; at the start of a meeting; at the end of one. You can even stand up halfway through the meeting and shake hands with everybody. And you do it again and again and again. Nobody thinks it odd; it's as natural as being overcharged in the hotels. You shake hands with your friends as often as you shake hands with complete strangers. or vice versa. I've been in meetings in the Ministry of Foreign Affairs in Cotonou with people who have known each other for years, who've worked with each other every day of their lives, and they are still shaking hands with each other all the time. And not just the men. The women shake hands just as easily and freely. It's nothing for a woman to come up to you and shake hands.

Shaking hands is one thing, but sometimes, as I discovered at the airport, the shaking becomes a holding. You start shaking. It's a normal introduction. You feel maybe it is a particularly warm handshake. You're flattered and pleased. Then you realize you're still shaking hands. If you're English, a momentary panic grabs you. Maybe a second hand comes out and you're trapped in a strong grip. You look over your shoulder, hoping no other Englishman is watching. Then the second hand falls away and you're still being held by the first hand. You shuffle. You try to sneeze, so that you have to break off in order to grab your handkerchief. But nothing happens. Then you relax and enjoy a genuine African handshake.

If it's not a formal occasion, or you're not formally friends but genuine friends, the hand breaks away and you try to break each other's fingers by somehow trying to click them together.

Men can shake hands, stand holding hands in hotel lobbies or ministry waiting rooms, or even walk hand-in-hand along the tarmac from the plane to the airport or along the road outside without anybody taking any notice. And without any sexual implications. At least, that I know of. I find that, when in francophone Africa, I can easily join in and shake hands four or five times during a meeting, no problem. I can even hold hands with the best of them. Forget the knighthood, I reckon if anyone deserves a Holding Hands in the Course of Duty medal, I do. But when I come back to England, for the first few days I have to be careful to remember where I am.

A few years back I had a bit of a problem with one especially civil civil servant luvvie in the Foreign Office in Whitehall who kept inviting me around for soirées after, I swear quite by accident, I must have shaken his hand a fraction of a second longer than I should have done.

Oddly enough, French Africans don't seem to have the same enthusiasm for kissing women. They tend to give them the limp handshake and a quick, 'Bonjour, madame, comment ça va?', or maybe a quick air-kiss.

'You know its funny', a big US columnist told me once, 'I've been all over the Far East, to China, Korea, Japan. There you smile at people, they smile back. The wife of the US ambassador in Peking, the first Chinese American, she told me, Whatever you do, smile. But I go around Cotonou smiling – some people smile back, some people don't.'

Admittedly not all Africans are friendly – neither are all Europeans, and definitely not all Americans. That aside, I still think there is a natural friendliness in most people in francophone Africa. The comparison with the Far East is interesting. There, I think, the courtesies are between equals. The junior managers at Mitsukoshi, the big store in Tokyo, might bow low when the senior manager comes along. Similarly in francophone Africa. An attaché du cabinet will always defer to a chef du cabinet, and a chef du cabinet to his ministre, and a ministre to his president. Part of it is, of course, role playing, just as a junior British civil servant will defer to a senior. At least to his two faces. But the greater part, I'm convinced, is a mixture of respect, honour, status and maybe a dash of fear; something which the British, and especially the Americans, can hardly appreciate. This was brought home to me vividly whenever I took a francophone African minister or diplomat to the Commons to see Mrs Thatcher firing on all six cylinders during Prime Minister's Question Time.

'Are they allowed to talk to her like that?' a Beninois minister asked me, wide-eyed with amazement, during one particularly stormy session.

'Sure,' I replied. 'It's part of our tradition.'

'To be rude? To your Prime Minister?' he said, obviously baffled by our traditions. 'And she is a lady as well.'

I mumbled something about accountability and the right to question the executive. The question of whether she was a lady or not was not something I wanted to get into.

'But they don't have any respect,' he said. 'They are not serious. You must respect your prime minister. We do not treat our chief of state like that.'

In Cotonou, *they* might not treat their chief of state like that, but other people do. A few years back the *International Herald Tribune* came out with one of their regular surveys, on Benin. On the front page was a photograph of President Kerekou. It was nothing but a thick black square. The Benin government confiscated every copy: it was disrespectful to their President. Which just goes to prove how wrong you can be. I thought it was enormously respectful. Trouble was, from the picture they printed I couldn't tell which part of the President it was.

In francophone Africa there is also more sense of deference. They have behind them centuries of respect for village elders and tribal chiefs. That's difficult to shake off, especially for older people. Then, of course, there is more of the master-servant relationship in Africa than in Europe. You've only got to earn a few dollars more than the basic minimum wage and you can afford a big house, cars, servants. Chances are, the people who don't smile back at visiting American columnists are the houseboys and servants. Either that or people who don't like what they read in the *Wall Street Journal*.

*

Cotonou, the capital of Benin, the old Kingdom of Dahomey, is one of my favourite French African cities. The others are all the rest. In fact, it's no way a city. It's more like a village, huddled on the edge of the coast alongside Nigeria, trying to pretend it's a town. It has one or two modern buildings. Well, I say modern. Probably the last decent building to be put up in Cotonou was the Benin Sheraton which was built back in the 1980s for two reasons: first to host a giant Organisation for African Unity conference and second to bankrupt the country – that is, the parts which were not already bankrupt. Since then I doubt whether five buildings have even heard a rumour of, let alone seen, a tin of paint.

Most of the roads are still sand. Admittedly solid sand. The houses are practically all made of homemade bricks dried in the sun. Cotonou has few of the services or facilities you would expect. The ministry buildings are all dark, decaying, dusty old French Colonial buildings, which have probably only remained standing thanks to the stacks of unopened files inside propping up the ceilings.

Office buildings are few and far between, apart from those in the port, which has not had a busy day since Nigeria was on a roll during the oil boom in 1970s. Few have telephones, fewer have fax machines; fewer still have any work to do. Instead people sit around all day waiting for their disconnected telephones to ring. Secretaries dream of having enough money to paint even one fingernail.

Except for one office near the French embassy which I visited once. It was buzzing: telephones were ringing, telexes coming in, messengers were flooding the city. Government ministers dressed in their smart new military uniforms were dropping by all the time for an aperitif. An aperitif! In Cotonou! In one of the poorest countries in the world!

'You're doing very well,' I muttered to the président directeur général, a Frenchman naturellement, running the show.

'The President's niece,' he nodded towards the supermodel in the Armani suit.

284

The next time I went, the office was the same as all the others. The French PDG had disappeared. So had the supermodel. Into a French prison. She'd been caught trying to smuggle drugs through Charles de Gaulle airport.

Yet places like Cotonou and Ouidah, the old slave port further along the coast towards Togo, once had the potential. In the eighteenth century they were major trading centres with European warehouses and storage facilities. Trouble came to a head when the local king, Agaja, wanted to cut out the middlemen of Ouidah and sell his slaves direct. They refused. Agaja hit back by invading Ardra and Jacquin, two prosperous slave ports. In 1727 he invaded Ouidah. The Europeans stuck with the old coastal states and the old rulers appealed to the Yorubas, another peaceful tribe, for help fighting Agaja. Virtual guerilla warfare continued for twenty years until everybody patched things up.

In 1737, John Atkins, a ship's surgeon whose crew died on him, described Ouidah as the greatest slaving centre on the West African coast. With up to one ship a week handling slaves for the French, Portuguese, British and Dutch, they were shipping out more slaves than all the other ports put together. The reason was not the ruthlessness of the shipping companies or the brutality of white hunters. It was all due to King Agaja. In order to protect his people from the Yoruba, he needed guns and gunpowder. His solution: to sell his people in order to protect his kingdom.

Before long he had too many guns and not enough people. But instead of calling a halt to the sickening business he started conquering other tiny kingdoms along the coast to keep up the supply. 'If he cannot obtain a sufficient number of slaves,' wrote Atkins, 'he marches in an army and depopulates.' Once, however, he did try to break out of the system. He sent an English captain, Bullfinch Lamb, whom he captured on a raid, back to England with 300 lbs of gold and 100 slaves. He wanted him to negotiate a deal whereby he would continue to sell slaves to the traders but the traders would not ship them out. They would be used inside the country to develop huge plantations. Lamb, surprise, surprise, never arrived in England. He disappeared with the gold, no doubt selling the slaves en route. Agaja went on selling slaves and buying guns. Now don't you think that's interesting?

In 1750, Birmingham was supplying no less than 100,000 guns a year to dealers like Agaja even though the Dutch had previously warned that it was giving them 'a knife to cut our throats'. The British continued on the old, old basis that if they refused the French would step in; if the French refused, the Danes would do it, and so on. If all the governments refused, then private dealers would take over. And so Birmingham continued to prosper, which made their decision just over 100 years later to refuse to finance Stanley unfair and illogical.

'There are forty million naked people beyond that gateway,' Stanley told them, 'and the cotton spinners of Manchester are waiting to clothe them. Birmingham's foundries are glowing with the red metal that shall presently be made into ironwork . . . and the trinkets that shall adorn those dusky bosoms; and the Ministers of Christ are zealous to bring them, the poor benighted heathen, into the Christian fold.' But they still said no. Which immediately opened up the market to Hong Kong, Japan, South Korea and whoever else has got the money for a knitting machine.

Worst of all the slave traders was probably Gezo, who became king of Dahomey in 1818. He faced big problems. The British had abolished slavery ten years earlier and were trying to persuade everybody else to follow suit. For Dahomey this meant disaster. Gezo decided to act.

Since the early part of the eighteenth century and the rise of the Dahomey empire they had been a dependency of Oyo, the great Yoruba kingdom, and subject to its laws and taxes. They were forbidden to do this or that or use certain materials because only Oyos were allowed to do so.

The Oyos also saw the Dahomeian army as part of their army, at their beck and call. The Dahomeians were tough, proud people and all this rankled with them.

If the British were going to stop them from exporting slaves, they had to start growing crops. But their territory to the west and north was dry and unsuitable for crops. They needed somewhere more fertile. And, more important, because the British had put a block on official slave trading they had to find alternative sources of supply to provide new customers, particularly the Brazilians, behind the backs of the British. Everything pointed in the direction of Oyo and the Yorubas.

Gezo declared Dahomey independent of the great Oyo empire and immediately occupied land to the east and southeast occupied by the Egbado and Awori Yorubas. The Oyo empire did not fight back. But the Egba did. They had been expelled from their homelands around Ibadan and were now trying to establish a new kingdom. The last thing they wanted was the Dahomeians upsetting their plans. They all then started fighting each other, at the same time helping the Egbas and Awomis to protect themselves from each other, if you're still with me.

The battle of Ilaro in 1844 was particularly bad for the Dahomeians. The Egba attacked them as they were about to raid Ilaro. King Gezo lost his royal umbrella, his royal stool and his royal war charms. Four years later he attacked and destroyed Oke Odan. Two years after that, Egba attacked Igbeji. In 1851 Gezo invaded Abeckuta, but lost most of his army in the process. He pledged retaliation but died in 1858. His son, Glele, wouldn't even think about his coronation until he had achieved his father's ambition. But he too was defeated, largely because of the British and the missionaries. The latter regarded the Dahomeians as devils; the Egba had to be helped. The Lagos government in Nigeria was, therefore, encouraged to supply the Egba with guns and ammunition and to train their soldiers to use them. King Behanzin, the last

287

independent king of Dahomey, assumed power in 1888, of a much subdued nation. But even that didn't last long. In 1894 he was deposed by the French and seven years later Dahomey became a French colony. Now don't you just feel your life is much richer for knowing all that?

But why didn't they continue their wheeling and dealing? Why didn't they become traders? Why didn't they carve out a slice of the action for themselves? You can bet your life old King Agaja would have done.

After my unforgettable welcome at the airport on my first visit, I had an equally unforgettable meeting the following morning with the Minister of Commerce who kept wanting to hold my hand.

The Benin Sheraton had just been completed and was now officially open for business. The previous week it had been the venue for a summit meeting of the Organisation for African Unity. It had been packed with presidents, presidential advisers and ministers, directors of protocol, chefs du protocol, private hairdressers and personal chefs. Today it was empty – apart from 23 tables, 47 chairs, 15 ashtrays, 7 large African carvings and 5 large plants in the reception area, me and about 4,527 staff.

As we kissed each other goodnight at the airport the Minister of Commerce said he would drop by my hotel at 9.00. It was now 11.00. But in Africa time doesn't matter. People turn up late and say they have been kept waiting by the President much as we blame British Rail. I was prepared to wait all morning if necessary. I wanted to see the Minister. He had agreed. What's more he said he would come to the Sheraton. In any case, so far it had been a good day. I had discovered that I could still buy cheap airline tickets.

Buying tickets in London to Cotonou, or Lomé, or most other places in francophone Africa, costs around £1,250–£1,500 return. In Paris they cost around £1,000. But with Babatunde, one of the chauffeurs at the Sarakawa Hotel in Lomé, they cost me only £500–£600. At one time he was even able to get first-class return tickets for the same amount, which was fantastic. The trick was to say you wanted to go via Lagos. That way I bought the tickets in Lagos, and the Nigerians are nothing if not flexible. It was marvellous. But the Nigerians had now said you could only buy tickets in Lagos if you were resident. I had thought it was the end of my first-class tickets at tourist-class prices.

'Not at all,' Babatunde had just told me. 'We just have to pay my brother a little bit more. He will still sell them to us. You are his friend.'

The problem was that the tickets were unchangeable. Or at least, supposed to be. If you took them into a travel agent, he was supposed to be able to spot some secret coding and refuse to alter them. But I got round this by changing my booking by phone. When I arrived at the airport I was usually given a ticking off, but I always got the plane.

In an effort to cut my travelling expenses, for a time I even travelled backwards and forwards as Dr Ranbir Saran Das, Professor Solanke Onasanya, and once as Tariq Husain. I met a travel agent in Dordrecht in the Netherlands who somehow managed to buy the unused portions of other people's tickets, which he resold on a vast international secondary market. With his tickets, one year I travelled all Africa – under African, Asian, Dutch, American and German names. But when I had problems trying to convince Swissair that I was really a Vietnamese clergyman with a Japanese mother living in Ceylon I decided to give it up. In any case the Lagos connection was working again.

The hotel bar facing the beach was now opening. I went in and asked for a large whisky soda. The barman took the order and passed it to his assistant. They studied it intently, whispering quietly to each other. The barman then came back to me. 'We have Gee-Bee. Would you like a Gee-Bee, monsieur?'

I looked at him. 'Non, merci. A whisky soda, s'il vois plaît.'

He and the assistant went into another conference. Then there was much opening and closing of doors, quick dashes into the back room and at least two hurried telephone calls.

'We only have Gee-Bee, monsieur,' he said coming back to me.

'I don't want a Gee-Bee,' I said. 'I want a whisky soda.'

He stared at me and went away.

I called the assistant over and asked for a Coca, the French for Coca Cola. The barman then returned with the restaurant manager.

'Excusez-moi, monsieur,' said the restaurant manager, 'the barman is confused. You ask for a whisky soda. But you do not want a Gee-Bee. He doesn't understand.'

Now I am the last person dans la monde to claim that my French is perfect but I have had plenty of practice asking for a whisky soda all over francophone Africa. And even once or twice in Paris. 'I don't understand,' I said. 'I don't want a Gee-Bee, whatever it is. I want a whisky soda. In any case, I've now—'

'But a Gee-Bee is whisky, monsieur,' he said, holding up a giant bottle of J B Rare. Which was my first introduction to not only the slang but the accents of francophone Africa.

'Je m'excuse, je m'excuse,' I mumbled. 'Je ne comprends pas. Je suis ici pour la première fois . . .'

The assistant was laboriously writing out my order in triplicate on a pad the size of a Gideon's Bible.

'Been here long?' I asked.

'Just started,' he replied. 'Just left school.'

'And the others?' I gestured towards the assistant.

'Everybody. We've all just left college. For the opening of the hotel.'

The assistant was checking the price of a whisky soda against the drinks list.

'So which school?'

'The Hotel Training School in Lomé.'

'C'est vrai?' I tried not to sound too surprised.

I knew the school, the Centre de Formation Hotelière, very well; one of the few of its kind in Africa. Over the years it has built up a reputation for the skills and quality of its graduates. The governments of Cameroon, Gabon, Niger and Congo send students there for training as they begin to establish tourist industries. It is mentioned in the same breath as similar schools in Strasbourg, Munich and Lausanne. It has even attracted the attention of Paul Bocuse, the famous French chef, who during a recent visit compared notes on traditional African cooking with the centre's professor of cuisine, Bruce Ahlin.

The Director, Mr Senyo Nakou, whom I've met many times, has had experience of all aspects of hotel work throughout Europe and speaks English, French, German and Italian. He worked in a travel agency in Naples and as a hotel supervisor in the Belgian national tourist office in Brussels. He graduated not only from the famous hotel training centre in Florence but also from the prestigious hotel management training college at La Baule, France. He only accepts students between eighteen and thirty, or with more than ten years' hotel experience, who are currently working in hotels and have been recommended for further training. They must also understand and speak English.

The assistant passed my order, in his immaculate handwriting, to the man sitting by the till. He looked at the order and slowly and deliberately entered the piece of paper in the machine. The machine whirred and buzzed and spat it back at him. For a few minutes he stared at it as if it was the last thing he imagined a cash register should do. Then he handed it back to the assistant. I wondered whether they had been taught this by Mr Nakou, but decided it must have been their own invention, or another example of the Beninois bureaucracy at work.

'So what did you learn at the school?'

'Restaurant and bar management, monsieur,' he replied proudly.

'And serving drinks?'

'Naturellement, monsieur.'

The assistant was now asking his assistant for the whisky soda. The assistant's assistant picked up a large glass in both hands and held it away from the bar. He then asked his assistant to put some whisky into the glass. That completed, he asked a young girl assistant to put some soda into the glass. I sat there fascinated. I remembered visiting the school and Mr Nakou telling me, 'We are only looking for students who are polite, tactful, discreet, even-tempered and have plenty of energy and stamina. Students study restaurant management, serving techniques, how to discuss the food with the clients, which wines to recommend, which countries produce wines, the different quantities, and so on.'

Outside professors from hotels and universities lecture on economics, law and hotel management, and there was further teaching in French, English and German, but the emphasis was on the practical. 'We are 40 percent theory and 60 percent practical,' he had boasted.

The school ran four courses: restaurant and bar, serving and management; cuisine and pâtisserie, preparation, cooking and presentation; hall/reception, management and accounting; and bedrooms, laundry, dry-cleaning, etc. They had their own reception, restaurant, kitchen and laundry, and students also worked in one of Lomé's five-star hotels to gain practical experience. For part of their final examinations, the cuisine and restaurant graduates had to prepare, cook and serve a series of lunch and dinner menus for eight people every day for a week. Mr Makou once asked me to be an examiner; now, as I waited for my first whisky soda, I wished I had agreed.

Of course, when the girl assistant finally put the soda into the glass everything overflowed onto the carpet. Which, of course, was why the other assistant had been holding the glass away from the bar. Because he just let everything soak into the carpet instead of having to wipe the bar. The sign of a professional. The barman now stepped in; he took the glass from his assistant and put it on a tray. He called for a towel from the storeroom behind the bar and proceeded to wipe the outside of the glass. Very slowly. Very deliberately. Then he gave me my whisky soda.

'Merci beaucoup,' I said weakly, overcome with exhaustion. This might be one way of solving the chronic unemployment or underemployment problem in Africa but it was too much for me. I drank the whisky soda quickly, picked up a newspaper on the bar, made my excuses and left.

I sat in the lobby and opened the paper. There was a big article about 'la sorcellerie, la magie, le charlatanisme et toute autre pratique susceptible de troubler l'ordre public.' The government was trying to stamp out bogus fetishers. Anyone found responsible for 'le décès de la victime' would be sentenced to between ten and twenty years' hard labour. The genuine witchdoctors would, I assumed, be given a knighthood and a house in the country.

It was 11.30. I emptied my briefcase and rearranged my papers. Again. The porter came and gave me an old French newspaper. I read about a fight to the death in some tiny village called Joue-sur-Erdre in the Loire, between two chefs arguing about how much butter to put in some dishes they were preparing. The heading was 'Une querelle gastronomique'.

Now I tried to nod off. I thought it was the only way to pass the time. But the porter woke me up. 'Tired? Have one of these,' he said, offering me a mouldy-looking selection of what looked like peanuts from a crumpled piece of newspaper. 'They'll keep you awake. Very good. I always eat them.' He grabbed the largest nut, squeezed it between his fingers, rubbed it in his palm and pushed it into his mouth.

'What is it?' I asked nervously. Not that I was worried about the nuts. I didn't like the look of the editorial opinions of the newspaper.

'Cola. Have a cola nut. Très bon.' I took the smallest piece on the basis that that was good manners. It also meant there was less chance of being affected, if not infected, by the newspaper's opinions. It tasted slightly bitter.

You find cola trees all over West Africa. Originally they were planted around the edge of cocoa plantations as protection, but now, especially in Sierra Leone and Liberia, they are plantation crops in their own right. Only two varieties produce nuts which are sold and used commercially: *cola nitida* from Guinea down to Togo, and *cola acuminata* from Nigeria through to the north of Angola. The trees are usually around forty feet high, though some can be twice as big. The pods, which remind me of the ones on cocoa trees, usually contain two rows of seeds. Some people say the *acuminata* has around thirty-five seed leaves compared to the *vitida*.

'So why are they good for you?'

'It's the caffeine. Keeps you awake.'

'Makes a change from coffee.'

Coffee beans contain around one percent caffeine, tea-leaves about three; cola nuts are between the two. How much is in Coca-Cola or any of the other cola drinks, I don't know.

'Do you like it?'

'Not bad.'

'Maybe you should have cola chocolate instead, or cola sweets.'

'You make them as well?'

'No, but I know somebody who does. Do you want some?'

I thanked him, but declined the offer. I didn't fancy meeting the minister dosed up to my eyeballs on whisky soda let alone cola.

It was now 12 o'clock. Waiting, I often think, is part of the African way of life: J'attend donc je suis. But waiting so long was a little unusual for a first meeting. Especially as we seemed to be such good friends. Well all right then, kissing cousins. Normally I find francophones very courteous, very formal and fairly punctual, give or take an hour or three. Much more so than the anglophones. Courtesy visits are important to them. If you arrive in town you must visit everybody you know, tell them why you're there and how long you plan to stay. You might share a cup of coffee or even a glass of champagne. You do the same before you leave. They are also very strong on titles and forms of address. Everybody is monsieur le directeur, monsieur le chef de la délégation, or even just monsieur.

Every day throughout French Africa I can imagine servants repeating their own version of the famous reply of Céleste, Proust's devoted servant, when Gide dropped by one morning for a chat: 'Monsieur cannot receive monsieur but monsieur begs monsieur to believe that monsieur is constantly in monsieur's thoughts.'

At 12.15 I wondered whether to order another whisky soda or ask the doorman for a ton of cola nuts. At 12.30 I still hadn't made up my mind. Instead I was wondering whether I should write a book during my spare time in Africa. At 12.45 I thought I would look out of the window. There was nobody in reception. I had the place to myself. I got up, turned my back on the door – and zap – in a split second the door behind me had been thrown open. The lobby was suddenly full of soldiers, armed to the teeth, all with Kalashnikov rifles at the ready, all p-p-pointing straight at m—me.

My life spun in front of me. I was at school. I was at work. I was at home. I was at passport control when I managed to slip in without a visa by talking to the policeman. I was taking a photograph of the president's statue. I was asking a local journalist about the economy. My head was spinning. I could see letters to *The Times*; bland statements from the Foreign Office and the rest of my life behind bars. Then in between the soldiers came the minister I had been waiting for.

'Sorry about all this,' he smiled, giving me another of his big wet kisses. 'Special precautions. You can never be too certain. Hope it didn't surprise you.'

'N-n-not at all,' I mumbled as he grabbed my hand again.

Of course, it had scared the hell out of me. But not half as much as that first big wet slobbering kiss of his had done.

Kinshasa

'Zaire is an arm and a leg country,' an old Belgian business-man wheeler-dealer grunted at me as we bounced through the clouds on our way down to Ndjili airport just outside the capital, Kinshasa. 'If they don't break your arm or your leg, it will cost you an arm and a leg to stay there.'

This was in the good old days when money was money and five million Zaire banknotes was worth as much as US$2 and inflation was running at a mere 7,000 percent a week. Today, of course, it's ridiculous.

'Tell me the problems.'

'First customs. You've got to know how to—' He jumped back sharply in his seat. The smooth, elegant, worldly-wise Zairois in front of him had pressed the button to bring his seat into an upright position then suddenly for no apparent reason had pushed it back as far as it could go knocking the Belgian's coffee and cognac into his lap, staining his trousers in the last area you want stained.

'Don't worry, monsieur,' gasped an elderly Sabena hostess as she panted up to him, 'I'll get you another coffee.'

'On Lufthansa, they would get you another suit,' snarled a German businessman the other side of the aisle through his gold teeth.

Guarding my sang-froid, I continued. 'You were telling me about the problems, with the customs.'

African Customs are rough and tough and can make your

life hell if you're unlucky. I've seen grown men reduced almost to tears by groups of young soldiers or policemen slowly, oh-so-slowly unpacking and repacking and unpacking the same suitcase, spreading everything over dirty tables and benches and examining everything in amazing detail and, what made it uncanny, not saying a single word in the process. I've seen women forced to unpack their suitcases and then, unable to repack them, having to bundle everything into plastic bags and old sacks. And at border crossings, I've seen customs officials forcing drivers to unpack container loads of goods by the side of the road, and two days later I've seen the driver still trying to repack.

'First,' said the Belgian, twisting in his seat trying to hide the stains with his jacket, 'Don't forget Africans want to be friends. So if you're friendly, they're friendly.'

'What do you mean?' I said. 'I should smile and say good morning?'

'Sure, and shake hands. Better still, say good morning, or something – anything – in their local language. Never fails.'

An excuse to practise my Lingala. 'So what's the second trick?'

'Ask them questions. They can usually only think of one thing at a time. If you ask them a question, it throws them off balance. They forget what they're supposed to do.'

We were now coming in low. I spotted some of the big office blocks. In some ways, Kinshasa is one of the most developed and civilized cities in Africa. The best restaurants serve wonderful wines and champagnes and always at the right temperature. But in most other ways, it is jungle: vicious, cut-throat, primeval jungle.

'So what do you ask them?'

'Anything. Ask about the weather. Have they been there long? Is it better than out chasing criminals? Anything. You've got to be friends and you've got to take their mind off things. As it is they're not interested in what they're doing. You can see it in their faces. They're bored out of their minds. They'd rather be in some bar eating fo-fo or just fast asleep under a tree. They're not made for this kind of life.'

'So, how many efficient African customs officers have you seen?'

'Some are very keen,' he laughed. 'For themselves.'

I knew what he meant. The worst case I ever heard of happened to two Birmingham businessmen on their way to Lomé. It was their first trip abroad and they had been to their local Chamber of Commerce for advice. For some reason, they had been told the best route was through Spain and Nigeria. They arrived at Lagos at around three in the morning and had to change planes. As they went through security, a soldier asked if they had any currency on them. They told him they had £20,000 in notes. The soldier then apparently said he didn't know if they could bring so much foreign currency into Nigeria. He asked if he could check the amount with his superior officer to see what the regulations were. They handed the money over to him. He took it, disappeared into a corridor and – you've guessed it – never returned. After ten minutes, they told me, they began to feel uneasy, but guessed things always took a long time in Africa. After thirty minutes they were beginning to get edgy. After an hour they were in a blind panic, and rushed around asking where the security officer was. Of course nobody knew, or cared. They had been taken. And they had only themselves to blame.

But such flagrant disregard for the rules can have its positive side. I was really late once getting to the airport in Cotonou. Normally I check in three or four hours before departure and go into the bar for a drink, or even go back into town. Or I get somebody to check in for me and arrive as they start to board. This time I got there about fifteen minutes before take-off. The check-in desks were empty, the police and customs officers had all gone home.

A taxi driver came up to me. 'Where is everybody? I want to check in,' I said.

'No problem, monsieur,' he said. 'Come with me.' He

grabbed my suitcase and disappeared behind some screens. I followed, into different offices, then along a corridor and on to the edge of the runway. I hesitated.

'Vite, vite, monsieur,' he said. 'You're late.'

Trying to forget everything I had read about airport security, I chased after him. In any case he had my suitcase. We got to the plane as they were pulling away the steps. He shouted at the workers and they pushed them back to the aircraft. I scrambled up, scattering money like confetti after me. I had made it. No one asked for my ticket or anything. I was shown to my seat. We took off three minutes later. And I used my ticket again the following month.

'So what's the third trick?' I asked as the obviously trainee pilot brought the plane down with a heavy thud on the runway.

'Give them something to do. That really knocks them over. They seem to go to pieces, forget themselves, just fall apart. Pretend you've got problems with your suitcase and give them the key to open it. Show them your camera and how it works. Switch on the radio or recorder. Let them play with your calculator.'

'And, of course, while they are doing that they're not searching your suitcase.'

'Sure. You give them a small calculator to play with.'

'And inside your suitcase is a computer.'

'You got it.'

'Or diamonds. Or gold. Or drugs.'

'Sure. It's a cinch.'

The plane screeched to a halt. We all started fighting to stop somebody else from deliberately taking our luggage by mistake.

'But if you really want to live dangerously you can avoid customs altogether,' he continued, pulling duty-free shopping bags out of the overhead lockers. 'Say you're in transit . . .'

'Oh I know that trick,' I said. 'That happened to me once in Abidjan, by chance. I was in Ouagga, going back to London.

But the girl at the check-in said she could only send my baggage to Abidjan. At Abidjan I would have to re-check in my suitcase. I got to the transit desk at Abidjan and they told me to go and get my suitcase. The police and customs let me straight through. Nobody asked for my ticket or anything.'

'There you are. You could then have left without it being checked.'

'Except for the x-ray machine, but nobody takes any notice of that. Everybody just piles everything through it. It's crazy. Suitcases on top of one another . . .'

'And you can still carry something through by hand. Nobody says a word.'

'But I ended up wandering all over the airport, round the back, everywhere. There was nobody on the check-in desk when I got back with my suitcase so I grabbed a porter and we took it direct to the containers they load on the aircraft. It was crazy. No security. I even saw the dogs they were training to sniff out drugs.'

We started fighting our way off the plane, eager for the three-hour battle through customs.

'You go on ahead,' he said. 'I'll see you on the other side.'

Going through customs is a cross between a medical and going to confession. You stand alongside maybe two dozen complete strangers and open your suitcase and bare your soul, the innermost depths of your being, to a customs officer. Of course, everybody is doing their best not to look at anybody else's luggage. And not for one moment is anybody interested in what the customs officer is asking you. Of course not. But, I mean, occasionally you just can't help noticing, can you?

In front of me was a very smart, sophisticated Frenchman. He looked as though he could have been a diplomat or a salesman for a French arms manufacturer. Very discreet. The customs officer asked him to open his three Louis Vuitton suitcases. They were packed with eggs, meat, fish and cheese – no clothing or anything else. The customs officer looked at the mountain of food. The Frenchman smiled and shook him by the hand, I thought, a little bit longer and a touch friendlier than normal. The customs officer smiled back, shut the suitcases and even helped the obviously diplomatic French-man to lock them up again. You couldn't help noticing that, could you?

Further along a similar thing happened. There was another elegant, sun-burnt French diplomat-type, probably a former member of Action Directe. This one had only two suitcases. He opened them up. They were packed to the brim with expensive boxes of Givenchy.

'Givenchy,' said the customs officer. 'Is that soap?'

'Oui, monsieur,' smiled the Frenchman.

He got through without even having to shake hands.

I now got up to the bench and started opening my suitcase. Alongside me was a Belgian: a little man, very pale, big glasses, wearing a hat. He looked like a salesman for carbon paper; old-fashioned and out of place. Inside, his suitcase was like an operating theatre. There were syringes, needles, a thousand little bottles, three big bottles which looked as if they contained blood, two enormous white sheets, which the customs officer draped over the bench, and about ten pairs of gloves.

'Are you a doctor?' the customs officer asked him.

'Non, monsieur.'

'A salesman?'

'Non, monsieur.'

'Then why have you got all this medical equipment?'

'The wife. She's frightened in case I get Aids,' he whispered. 'She makes me take my own sheets. I have to wear gloves all the time. And the syringes . . .'

The customs officer slammed down the lid of the mobile hospital, put his chalk mark on it and darted into his office.

'. . . at one time I even had to do all my own washing. She was frightened I would catch something from the laundry bags.'

Now it was my turn. The policeman started ruffling through my suitcase, asking if I had any currency or other valuables. I was trying to get him talking. All of a sudden, out of sight of the customs officer, somebody slipped a plastic bag into my hand. From where, or who was doing it, I had no idea. I wondered for a second whether to react, but felt it would be too complicated to explain. In any case, I didn't feel like saying I had a bag without knowing what was in it. It was obviously something dodgy otherwise it wouldn't have been given to me. So I carried on talking to the officer, waving vigorously with my free hand, hoping he hadn't noticed.

It worked. I got the chalk cross on my suitcase. I immediately slammed it shut and locked it. Now I had my briefcase, my suitcase and my mysterious plastic bag. I thought of giving it to a porter, but decided against it. If anything was going to go wrong the porter would just point the finger at me. If I had the bag at least I was a little bit more in control of the situation. I got through passport control, then just as I got to the final gate, the policeman called me back. I wondered whether to break down, confess all and be done with it. He told me I had forgotten to walk through the metal detector. I thanked him and did so, plastic bag in hand. No problem. I turned and waved him goodbye. I was through safe and sound.

But what would happen now? Nobody seemed to be taking any interest in me so I called a porter, got a cab and started loading everything into the boot. As I was about to put the plastic bag inside a boy of about ten or eleven came up, took it from me and walked back into the terminal. I was tempted to follow, but decided not to. Half of me wanted to know what I had smuggled into the country, the other half didn't.

I was about to climb into the cab when the Belgian from the plane came running up, his trousers embarrassingly stained. 'No, no,' he was shouting. 'Don't. Come with me' He got up to me, panting and sweating like a cochon. 'No, don't. Come with me.'

'But,' I protested, 'let's take this cab. I've already—'

'No, no. Jamais,' he was shouting. 'Come with me.' And he started grabbing my luggage out of the boot. He thrust some notes into the driver's hand and we started walking back to the terminal. 'Whatever you do,' he said, 'Don't take a taxi by yourself. Try and get one of the hotel buses into town. If you're not staying at the hotel, it doesn't matter. Tell the driver you haven't made a reservation, you didn't have time, but you want to stay there. Say whatever you have to to get on the bus. If they still don't let you on, or if there is no bus, then try and get somebody to share a taxi into town. Split the fare 50–50 if you can. If not, pay the full fare yourself. Do whatever you have to to share, but whatever you do, don't get a taxi by yourself. It's dangerous.'

Most taxi drivers, he said, were pleasant, safe people, if a little aggressive about money; aggressively charging you and aggressively getting paid. But it could be dangerous. 'I've known a number of people who've been beaten up in their taxi on the way from the airport to town,' he said as we piled everything into the car of his friendly taxi driver.

'But if you have to get a taxi . . .'

'Okay, it's not dangerous if you follow some simple rules: sit behind the driver; make certain he doesn't stop to collect anybody else; above all, make certain he sticks to the route.'

The taxi crunched into gear. 'Make a note,' he said. 'You'll know next time.' All I could find to write on was my airline ticket. 'Come out of the airport, turn left and go past the military airport and you're in trouble,' he said. 'Instead turn right on to a dual carriageway. After a few seconds you'll see posters for Avis and Hertz.'

I was scribbling furiously as we passed the signs. 'You're on the right road. After a few minutes you will pass small houses, some shops, a boulangerie or baker on your left and some bars. The driver might want to stop at one of the bars. If it's the Relais alongside the Pharmacie Paco, don't worry. It's a nice little bar. Friendly, maybe expensive depending on who's behind the counter, otherwise you've no problem. If, however, he goes any further, shout and bang on the side of the car. Tell the driver you know the route to town and that you want none of his nonsense. That should do the trick. Otherwise open the door and keep it open. The driver might genuinely be going to visit his sick mother, as he says, but it's not worth the risk.'

Boulangerie . . . Relais, next to Pharmacie . . . sick mother. I was writing it all over the advertisement on the back page and inside in the margin where it tells you how little hand luggage you are officially entitled to take on board.

'Now keep your eyes peeled. You'll pass people walking, dragging trailers, thumbing lifts, maybe even attending a funeral.' Many's the time I've seen hundreds of people gathered outside a house, singing and weeping and chanting at funerals.

'Soon you come to a little chapel on your right, just set back off the road, l'Eglise de la Charité. The sign will be illuminated in red if it's after dark. Continue until you come to a smaller street which forks right off the main road. That's the next danger point. Whatever you do make certain you stay on the main road. Don't let the driver take you down that little road to the right.'

Eglise . . . illuminated sign . . . pray. I was writing it all down.

'Soon you're passing the big memorial to Patrice Lumumba, Zaire's first doomed politician.' The memorial is a mixture of ski slopes and archways and towers. It was started years ago and still hasn't been finished, probably never will be. Opposite on the right is the Institute Lumumba.

'Stay on the dual carriageway, and you'll see one or two buildings, a few houses. In a few minutes you come to a T-junction, on your left, a big cold-store complex. Turn right, and you will see on your left a small military airport. It used to be the airport for Kinshasa, but now it's only used for small planes. You pass some rough scrubland and go over a single railway line. The road now swings left near a big, modern technical college. Carry on. There are blocks of flats on your right, another military camp. You are now getting into the suburbs proper.' There were more buildings, more people, more rubbish and, maybe depending on the season, water flowing all over the road.

'You turn right again at the next corner, under a railway bridge, passed the Bralima brewery on the right and on your left the local Coca-Cola bottling plant, a Peugeot dealer. Soon you come to a mini-junction with a big Johnnie Walker poster in front of you. Another danger spot. You take the road immediately to the right of the poster. If you go down any other road, shout and bang and scream. Stick to the Johnnie Walker road and you can't go wrong.'

Now the road petered out and I began to wonder whether we should have taken another road. But it was okay, we were safe. On the right was a tatty old office with a sign outside saying, Africa Business. Turn right at the junction, then left at the Fanair mille poster and you're on Boulevard 30 June. This is the main street of Kinshasa. Here you will see all the big bank buildings and shops. It's like a mini-Manhattan. Maybe two hundred metres and there are trees either side of the road; a golf course, would you believe, on your left; the old British Caledonian building on your right, and your first set of traffic lights. Over the lights and you're in Gombe, the up-market, expensive end of town with its neat houses and manicured lawns. If anybody is anybody they're in Gombe, unless of course they are super anybodies, then they can have houses, or palaces, anywhere in Kinshasa.

'Now you can begin to breathe easy. If you've made it so far, you're safe,' the Belgian told me.

Past a big poster for Groupe Seibe-Zaire, the big, big conglomerate built up by Citoyen Bemba Saolona, one of Zaire's biggest businessmen. Then turn right and you're heading direct for the Inter-Continental and safety. As you go down the road you can glimpse the Congo river ahead of you; Conrad's brown current running 'swiftly out of the heart of darkness'. The hotel is on your left. You've made it: forty kilometres in around thirty minutes. Or maybe two hours if it's the middle of the day. You've passed your first test with flying colours. You're in Zaire. You've survived the initiation ceremony.

'So how did you get on with customs?' I asked as the porters unloaded our bags and we wandered into reception.

'Easy,' he said. 'I always hang back and try to spot the senior official, then get in the queue for him. That's what I did this time. When I got up to him I made out we were big buddies, had known each other for years. I asked about the wife and children. He loved that. I told him he was looking good; very fit, very strong. I asked how much whisky he drinks every day. Never fails.'

'Never?'

'I told you, first, they love to be friendly. They want nothing but to have a laugh and a joke. They're not interested in work. Second, it gives him a chance to show his staff how he is respected by a European and treated as a friend. They love that. That's why I always go for the big guys. The little guys are more nervous. They are scared of what their boss will think, whether he'll think there is something suspicious going on between them. Always the big guys.'

'So what have you brought through?'

'Oh nothing,' he said. 'Just plastic bags. Like you.'

'Just had a telephone call from the bank. The manager says they've all been called to a meeting at the Central Bank this afternoon. Said expect the worst. This is probably it. He says his wife is already starting to pack.'

Forget everything the Foreign Office says about Zaire being a bulwark of the West, a member of the international community and one of the richest countries in the world with huge

resources of diamonds, copper and cobalt. Zaire is institution-
alized anarchy. It has none of the trappings of modern
government; no blunders, no leaks, no ministers scoring own
goals and blaming it on the Opposition. There is no organization, no administration, virtually no structure; no law, and
definitely no order in Zaire. It really is organized anarchy. It is
no more a proper country with a proper constitution and a
proper government than politicians are members of the
human race. But nobody says so. Foreign governments still
send ambassadors to Zaire. The United Nations still pretends
it's a real country. Zaire is still invited to attend every
international conference.

The only two people in the world, I reckon, who know the
truth are His Excellency President Mobutu Sese Seko Kuku
Ngbendu wa za Banga, the Helmsman, the Great Redeemer,
the Perpetual Wearer of Leopardskin Hats and Polka Dot
Cravats, the Messiah Himself, and myself. And I'm not saying
anything, for obvious reasons.

But credit – if that's the right word to use regarding anything
to do with Zaire – where credit is due. Zaire, which is about
eighty times the size of Belgium, is the only country I know
where they hold special dinners to pay tribute to the honesty
of government ministers. 'Never in the long history of the
second Republic has such an important and honourable event
taken place,' trumpeted the official proclamation for the
dinner. Trouble was, only a handful were invited and even
fewer were present. The rest were otherwise engaged.

Honest or not, ministers flounce around in the finest
Mobutu-styled up-luxury-market Chairman Mao suits, dripping with Omega watches and waxing lyrical about Zaire
being the greatest country in the world. But they have no
power. If they actually pluck up courage to take a decision
about anything apart from which vintage champagne to have
with lunch, there is no way they can ensure anyone takes any
notice. Mon dieu, I've been in ministers' offices where even
the typewriter doesn't work let alone the 'phone.

307

The civil servants are the most civil servants on earth. For that is all they have to do: be civil. You think Sir Humphrey is a professional. Let me tell you, he's a jungle boy compared to the professionals in Kinshasa. But again, outside the ministers' gilded suites and their own less gilded offices, they have nothing. No management chain, no structure, no discipline. No hope of actually doing anything. Zut alors, most of them don't have any money for themselves. I've lost count of the number of Zairean civil servants who've told me they haven't been paid for months. One poor chef du cabinet told me he has to walk twenty kilometres to his rapidly fading plush office every day because he can't afford to squeeze on board the container lorries that serve as buses in Kinshasa.

Now tell me, how can a country even begin to function when nothing actually happens?

I was once with a government minister in the waiting room outside his office – his office was being used by one of Mobutu's sons – and he admitted he spent every morning studying papers, holding meetings and taking decisions that he knew could never ever be implemented. 'I cannot telephone across the street,' he whispered, in case he disturbed Mobutu fils. 'How can I communicate with our offices throughout the country?'

Outside Kinshasa it's the same story, but worse. There are préfets and assistant deputy vice préfets, but none of them has any resources, none of them does anything and none of them is actually told to do anything. If there ever were chains of command they all disappeared – or knowing Zaire, were stolen and resold – years ago. Each préfet is on his own. Most have just given up. Some have walked away; others, with varying degrees of pretence, act the part. A few have become mini-despots of their own little patch of dust, wheeling and dealing, lying and cheating, grabbing whatever they can.

The only government policy I know seems to be: Don't get caught. Major cheating is for the president. Minor cheating is for everybody else. Diamonds are not sold by the handful, but by the billion. Cobalt regularly leaks through the back door outside all official agency agreements and ends up being traded in convenient little 650-tonne lots on the world market.

For some reason I've never understood, the winds around the borders of Zaire, and Zaire is one of the biggest countries in Africa, are so strong they keep blowing planes off course, forcing them to land in neighbouring countries. Sometimes for only a few minutes; sometimes for as long as it takes to unload a 747 at Gatwick Airport. But don't worry, when they finally get back a little lighter to Zaire soil and report to customs all their papers are still in order. All the goods are still there. Why shouldn't they be? Similarly boats laden with coffee leaving Lumumbashi for the 2,500-mile journey to Kinshasa. Somehow they are always caught by the currents, swept onto sandbanks and marooned often for weeks. Yet again when they finally reach Kinshasa, admittedly a few feet further out of the water, all their papers are still in order.

'It's a magical country,' a World Bank official told me one night in a tiny bar in Zone Matonge, the birthplace of Zaire's unique throbbing music. 'Because everything seems to disappear as if by magic: cotton, coffee, diamonds, cash from the Central Bank. Practically every penny that's ever been put into the country just disappears.' Zaire, as a result, is a Mecca for rough, tough, wheeler-dealer businessmen.

Wherever you go, whoever you talk to in Kinshasa, it's always the same story; no organization, no system, no rules. Everybody is on their own. Unilever have a rambling old office downtown and vast plantations out in the bush which they have been desperately trying to get rid of for years. On one visit I had arranged a meeting with one of the managers. Nobody knew where he was; whether he was at home, or out on one of the plantations, whether he'd been kidnapped, killed or was just spending time getting to know the local people. They had no way of keeping in touch with him. Once he left the building, he was on his own.

Smaller companies have the same problem, but worse. Because there is no banking system, cash is king. Whenever one of their managers is out of the office not only is he on his own, he is on his own with their cash. In a country where corruption is more natural than breathing and children are taught from an early age that 2 and 2 make 7, they have no alternative.

'So how do you know you'll get your money back?' I asked the Portuguese manager of one small trading company.

'We know,' he smiled. 'We know.'

Now don't get me wrong. I'm not saying there is no efficiency in Zaire or that there is nobody you can trust. There is. Trouble is it's the crack Israeli-trained Special Presidential division. In other words, Mobutu's Own.

You want the parliament building blockaded with tanks and armoured cars? No problem. You want the whole of the smart Gombe district declared a military operational zone? No problem. You want an ambassador accidentally shot dead while looking out of his office window? No problem. 'Most efficient army in French Africa,' an experienced, much-travelled French military adviser told me once.

They are so efficient that at the slightest one-eyed wink of you-know-who they will hold whole towns to ransom demanding they pay them all the wages the government has not paid them otherwise they will tear the place apart. 'They tell us that either we pay up or they kill us. What can we do?' a Belgian, a director of an international transport company, told me.

In one town, Goma, on the border with Rwanda, he said, the local colonel had openly called the business people, shopkeepers and expats together and told them if they didn't pay up he would let his troops loose. They refused. He set his troops free. In one night they virtually destroyed the place. Shops, offices, bars, homes, everything was smashed and looted. Then after the soldiers had had their way, in came all the destitute and needy, desperately looting what was left. And in Zaire when they loot, they loot. They're not just interested in anything with the slightest possible value, they take the wallpaper off the walls.

'Even the guards at the local prison joined in,' he told me. 'But when they finished and got back to the prison they found that the prisoners had broken out and taken all their possessions.'

Now tell me, how can that be a real country with a real government? The answer is, it's not. Just because the atlas says it's a country, it doesn't mean it is. Just because it has diplomats and is recognized by the United Nations, doesn't mean it's a country. The truth is it's not a country and it's not governable because His Excellency Mobutu Sese Seko Kuku Ngbendu wa za Banga, the Helmsman, the Redeemer, the Messiah Himself, doesn't want it to be a country and does not want it to be governable. It suits him the way it is: a complete mess. He doesn't want order, structure, a proper administration. He doesn't want roads and telephones and telex machines. The last thing he wants is law and order. Mon dieu, he knows that if he had these things he would not be able to do his own thing. He would not be able to run or not run the country the way he has done or has not done for nearly thirty years. More than anything, he would not be able to keep dipping his hand in the till. Some say he is the richest man in the world. Maybe even the richest man that has ever lived. The US State Department estimates that he is worth at least US$5 billion, about the same as Zaire's national debt. He says he is worth US$50 million, which he says is not an exorbitant sum for the head of state of such a great country.

I was having drinks one evening with a group of Belgian expats who had all left, or been expelled or rescued by the Americans during so many riots and lootings and near civil wars that they had lost count. One fragile, bird-like, elderly lady told me the Americans had not given her enough time to turn the bathwater off. But they all came back again.

'It is my home,' the old lady shrugged. 'Go back to Belgium?' Even in the blazing heat of a Kinshasa lunchtime, the very thought made her shiver.

As I was leaving a big, burly Belgian travel agent arrived straight from the office. 'Just met the bank manager. He says the World Bank are in town. They've been negotiating with le Gros Légume.' He laughed. 'Do you know what he said? He said they were with Mobutu for nearly two hours talking about the debt and the need for stricter controls and . . .'

'. . . and other things,' we all joined in.

'And do you know what he told them?' a serious-looking Greek wheeler-dealer butted in. 'He told them he was the first president in Africa who believed in privatization. He went round all the diamond mines saying, That's mine. That's mine . . .'

Everybody collapsed. I never knew Belgians could laugh so much. Actually I don't think I'd ever seen them laugh before.

'And do you know what happened then?' the travel agent struggled to continue. 'After the meeting was over the president said he wanted to show them his latest project.'

'Another model farm?'

'He took the World Bank delegation to the back of his Residence, and there at the bottom of the garden he showed them the new landing strip he's just built . . .'

'Never,' we all chorused. 'And after talking about debts, and rescheduling . . .'

'Spending all that money . . .'

'And the World Bank as well.'

'And you'll never guess what was at the end of the runway.' He paused for effect. 'A Concorde. He'd just leased it for three months . . .' Everybody collapsed in agony, shrieking and screaming. '. . . because he said he had a lot of travelling coming up and he had to consider the prestige of his country.'

'The man must be . . .'

'How does he do it?'

'And to the World Bank as well.'

Mobutu also knows that if Zaire had even the most basic services he would not be there for long.

Ten years ago Kinshasa gave you the impression of being a sensible city. There was a veneer of business activity; the suggestion of business services and facilities; there were rumours that somewhere there was a government and it was functioning. Companies more or less did some business. The Chamber of Commerce was based in a fairly impressive office block along the Avenue des Aviateurs. There were some pretty impressive books and magazines and newspapers in circulation. There was a buzz. The country looked as though it was ticking over.

Not any more. Kinshasa today is full of nothing but its own irrepressible hopelessness. There are few businessmen left. The Chamber of Commerce hasn't functioned for years. There are no longer any rumours of a government, let alone one that is actually doing the things a government should do. It's every big guy for himself. It's like the Middle Ages, with the barons doing their own thing without interference from anybody.

Nobody seems to care. The big commercial barons don't care. They are managing to survive – and quite handsomely. Why do they want things to change? Government officials, those that are left, are surviving. Why do they want change? If things change they might get worse.

The only law seems to be: Don't steal more than the President. As for Mobutu, he obviously couldn't care less. He's still alive. He's still president. He's got his little, medium, or absolutely gigantic nest egg stashed away for a rainy day. What does he care?

Kinshasa, as a result, is definitely not one of the world's most boring cities. Sure, it looks like any other city. It has slums and traffic jams and Japanese businessmen all over the place. But it is no more the capital of Zaire than Zaire is a country. They are both tokens; a token capital of a token country. And whatever you do or wherever you go, there are rumours. Listen, if you promise to keep this to yourself, I reckon Kinshasa is the rumour capital of the world. But don't tell anyone I said so. Especially not the Foreign Office.

'Tried to get a flight out on Sunday. No seats. Something's up. My contact at the ministry says there's a special television broadcast set for Friday. All the ministers have been told to stay in town. Must be something big. Maybe this time he is going to . . .'

'. . . And his wife said he is much better now. But God, they don't want to go through that again.'

'Should think not,' said a junior official at the British embassy.

'Makes you count your lucky stars,' added a gruff Scottish accent.

'Puts everything in perspective,' sighed a rather jolly-hockey-sticks type from somewhere like Virginia Water who had just arrived in Kinshasa with her husband. It was the first time she had been out of England.

'What. Been hunting tigers?' I said, deliberately trying to butt in and pick up the latest gossip.

We were standing on a balcony outside a house on the edge of Kinshasa. It was another of those expat parties. There was a representative from the World Bank, an official from the European Development Fund, his wife who was dabbling in business – in Africa everybody, especially the presidents, have wives who are dabbling in business – and a rather brisk, middle-aged woman who looked like a cross between the chairman of the Cheltenham WI and the devoted secretary of the head of MI5 when the head of MI5 was a man.

'God, no. Worse than that,' said the Scottish accent, which I learnt later came from the local manager of one of the British banks still operating in Kinshasa. 'That would have been a piece of cake.'

'More dangerous than hunting tigers,' I said. 'What was it?'

'Going to hospital,' said the junior official.

'Here in Kinshasa,' added the Scottish accent. 'You should try it sometime.'

'You mean Aidsville,' a Canadian butted in.

'Molly here was just telling us about the Makepeaces. Shocking,' said the Scotsman.

'Why? What happened? I asked innocently.

Molly was another of those tiny, wiry, middle-aged women who spoke with a Roedean accent and looked as though she would never dream of leaving Mummy. Yet here she was in Kinshasa, had been here over twenty years, had seen it all. But still remained impossibly British. Probably knew French like a native but deliberately refused to speak a word.

'Well, I was at a little cocktail party just before Christmas,' she said, taking a deep breath. 'There were about twelve of us. Mostly British, a couple of Canadians. The Canadians have a big mission here, they do a lot for Zaire. Oh, and a lady from the Belgian embassy. We've all been here years. A little survivors' club. We try and keep in touch, compare notes. Well,' another deep breath, 'we had finished the main course and were about to start on the sweet and Mr Makepeace suddenly pushed his plate back, grabbed the table and came over all stiff and shaking. He rocked back and forward a bit. We thought he was coming over faint. A touch of malaria, maybe. Affects people different ways even though they have been out here a long time.'

'Funny thing, malaria,' said the Scottish accent.

'But he seemed to get worse, came over all limp, like a slow collapse. His wife was the other side of the table, she rushed round to him. She'd been a nurse before they came out here so she knew what to do. We undid his tie. He always wore some kind of army tie. We loosened his belt, undid his cuff links, all the things you're taught to do in emergencies. Then we lowered him onto the floor. Our chef came in with the dessert as we were laying him down. He screamed and ran away.'

'Must have thought it was going to be another one of those Happy Valley parties,' said the Scotsman. We all glared at him.

'Mrs Makepeace was very good, but she kept biting her lip and shaking her head. I asked, what is it, my dear? She said she thought it was a heart attack. Not a serious one, mind you, but a small one.'

'What did you do?' I asked.

'She said the best thing to do was to get him to hospital.'

'To hospital,' everybody repeated.

'You mean the SIDA-gogue,' said the Canadian.

'Well we all know what hospitals are like in Africa, but she said there was no alternative. If we kept him on the floor something much more serious might happen. If we took him to hospital maybe they could do something for him. It was, I suppose, the lesser of two evils.'

The rest of the party now gathered around us. This was obviously something that deeply concerned everybody. Even the Scotsman had stopped drinking.

'How on earth could you get him to hospital?' I asked.

'I had a Land Rover. We put him in the back. It was all we could do.'

'And the hospital was open?'

'Not exactly. It was pitch black. The front door was open. I went inside, but I couldn't find a soul.'

'Doesn't surprise me,' said the Scotsman. 'Probably all on strike. Did you see that all 180 doctors at the Mama Yemo hospital went on strike the other day?'

'Sure. Because they hadn't been paid for four months,' I said.

'Ssh, ssh.' said the young wife.

'Know how Mobutu is going to solve the national debt problem?' interrupted the Canadian again. 'He's going to lay off two ministers.'

'Well. Eventually I found somebody. He was an old man. All

he had on was a shirt. Don't know whether he was one of the guardians or one of the patients. We went out of the hospital, round the back to another big building. He told me to wait outside. There was nothing I could do so I waited. About five, six minutes later a man came down. Looked very young. He asked where Mr Makepeace was and what was wrong with him. I told him he was in the Land Rover and we thought he had had a heart attack. I must say he was very good. He ran round to the Land Rover, got the old man to get a trolley and some help and we got Mr Makepeace onto the trolley and wheeled him into the lobby.

'It's all right,' he told us. He was a doctor, he knew what to do. Mrs Makepeace explained she was a nurse. If there was anything she could do. But the doctor said no, they could cope. By now lights were beginning to go on. I must say we began to feel as though everything was going to be all right. They took Mr Makepeace into one of the wards—'

'What about injections? Did you tell them not to—' interrupted the embassy official.

'—and told us to stay outside. They had all the equipment. We felt quite reassured. We went for a walk. It was a bit stuffy inside, and the seats weren't very comfortable. Anyway, I thought it better to be outside. I don't know how long we were out but it was beginning to get light. We went back and settled down in the chairs. They were all broken, but we did our best. There were a couple of magazines about East Germany, Bulgaria, the Thoughts of Kim Il Sung. Then a young girl, couldn't be more than fifte, came shuffling along the corridor. You know the way they do. She came up to me, didn't say a word. I said, 'Yes my dear. Can I help you? She held up this electric cable and said, "Doctor said he can't make the machine work. He wants a plug."'

'My God,' said the Scots voice.

'I can tell you, I went berserk. I said, we've waited all this time. Here is a man with a heart attack. Then they decide they want a plug.'

'What did the girl say?' I wondered.

'Nothing. Just stared at me, you know the way they do, as if I was being unreasonable. She said she came out before but we weren't there. Well, then we had to find a plug. Can you imagine it? An electrocardiograph, and no plug. We grabbed the light in the reception. By now Mrs Makepeace was shaking. I tore the plug off the flex. We needed a screwdriver – no screwdrivers. I used my nail file from my handbag. Eventually I gave the girl the plug and told her to hurry back to the doctor. I can tell you I was hopping mad. I mean, what would have happened if we hadn't gone back in the hospital when we did?'

'She would probably have been wandering up and down for days trying to get a plug,' said the Scotsman.

'Well, we got over that. I thought, Everything is going to be all right now. Mrs Makepeace had stopped crying. We sat down in those dreadful chairs again, but I'd no sooner sat down than in walked Mr Makepeace. I couldn't believe it.'

'Walking. I thought he'd had a heart attack?'

'He had. Apparently a fairly severe one. The doctor wanted to keep him in the emergency ward for two to three weeks.'

'Well, why didn't he put him there?'

'Because it was upstairs, and they didn't have a lift.'

'You mean,' I stuttered, 'you mean patients with serious heart attacks have to walk up a flight of stairs to get to the emergency ward because there is no lift?'

'Well, there is a lift, but it doesn't work.'

There were so many cries and groans, I couldn't identify them all.

'So what did you do?' I asked.

'What could we do? We had no alternative. We got hold of him, either side, and helped him up the stairs. He was heavy. The doctor had obviously given him something. He was very slow.'

'Didn't anybody help you?'

'Not up the stairs. Once they saw us help him, they left it to us.'

'And upstairs?'

'Oh, they were wonderful,' she smiled with relief. 'They were very sweet, very kind. They put him in a small ward. Not very modern, a bit dirty . . .'

'Like Eastbourne General,' said the young wife. 'They are all the same.'

'. . . but everything was all right.'

'And how is he now?' I asked, quickly wishing I hadn't.

'Right as rain. They're up country now, looking at coffee estates. He swears by them.'

'And was it a heart attack?' I wondered.

'Well, the doctor said it was. Mrs Makepeace thought it was.'

'Damned lucky to be alive,' said the military. 'Rather him than me. One of our chaps broke a leg last year. Towards Christmas. Rushed him to hospital. Local doctor set it. Put it in traction. That sort of thing. Thought no more about it—'

'Come and have some dinner, do, please,' implored the Virginia Water accent. 'Everything is ready.' But nobody took any notice. We were all engrossed in another version of the Horrors of Zaire.

'—Went home for Christmas. In the pub talking to the local quack. Quack said he'd like to have a look at it. Served in Kenya. Knew a bit about African doctors. Had a look. Sent chummy off to hospital straightaway. It had all been done wrongly. Apparently a major disaster. Had to break the leg again and re-set it properly. He was none too happy, I can tell you. Had to spend Christmas in hospital, thanks to these Johnnies here.'

'. . . Dinner . . . everything . . . please,' pleaded Virginia Water, but nobody moved. The planter's wife was now telling her story.

'My daughter has just gone back home to college. When she was here she was not too good. We all thought it was the heat. She came out in rashes. Very odd. We took her to our local

319

doctor, a Zairois, trained in Paris. He took a skin sample, said he needed it for analysis. It was about the size of your hand – She suffered agonies. But we kept saying, the doctor knows best, it's for your own good. I've just had a letter from her. When she got back home her boyfriend made her go to the doctor, who took another skin sample. This time it was the size of a pinhead. Can you imagine what she went through here because of that doctor? It makes me so angry just to think about it,' she shuddered.

'. . . Everybody . . . please . . . please,' Virginia Water was crying in the background.

'Up in the mines we've got a doctor that everybody's terrified to see. So many of his patients have died they call him the Murderer.'

'You should see . . .'

We never did go into dinner. Nobody seemed to fancy eating. We all left early and drove home. Very, very slowly.

Saturday came. The streets were practically empty. Everybody was huddled around their television sets. Come the time for the announcement – nothing happened.

'The television station has been taken. It's always the radio and television that are the first to be taken.'

'Get the driver. I'm going across the river to Brazza.'

'Start packing.'

'But they're always late,' I said. 'If they were on time you'd be just as worried.'

'It's all right for you, you're just visiting. You don't have to live here.'

'No children to worry about.'

'You've got a home to go back to. We've spent eight years and I can tell you . . .'

The television screen flickered, then went blank. Everybody stopped in their tracks. I've never seen anything like it.

An old Belgian lady came in. 'Just like this last time,' she

320

said. 'I'm ready. We've had plenty of practice.'

'The governor of the Central Bank said there has been a big run on the bank this week, obviously everybody drawing their money out.'

The tension was now building up. You were frightened to say anything in case ... Again the television set blinked. This time we also got some scratchy military music.

'Oh my God, it's happened. A coup ...'

'Had to happen.'

'So what happens now?'

'We wait. Keep inside. Keep our heads down.'

'Pray.'

'Listen,' I said, 'nothing's happened. Assume nothing ...'

'Now you listen to me. Coming here telling us what to do. Who do you think ...'

The television burst into full colour. Military music exploded all around the room. The camera switched to the Minister of Information.

'Oh my God,' everybody sighed together. The Minister looked the camera straight in the eye, smiled a wry smile and – you'll never believe it – announced that Zaire and Egypt had just discovered a cure for Aids. I couldn't help it. I fell about the floor. It was so hilarious and so typical.

'Better safe than sorry.'

'You've got to be prepared.'

'Never can tell.'

Then everybody started back-tracking.

'The embassy, I blame. They should have put out a briefing.'

'Of course, I knew the attaché was never in the picture.'

'For the sake of the wife. Gets very nervous, you know.'

'When you've been in Africa as long as I have, old chap, you learn to live with this kind of thing.'

'I'm going down to the Kita Kita.'

*

'What. Trying to kill the germs,' the Minister said as I sat down at the bar and sipped my whisky soda. 'Too late now. Probably be sick as a dog in half an hour. Serves you right.'

We didn't agree on drinks, so I asked which were his favourite African foods.

'Never touch it. Can't trust it. Always stick to decent food. Safest.'

'What about lobsters? The seafood is fantastic.'

'Never.'

'Fish? It's fresh out of the sea this morning.'

'That's what they say.'

'Vegetables. There's nothing wrong with vegetables.'

'Don't know how it's prepared. Knew a chap once. Off sick for six months because of something he had at some official business. Can't afford the risk.'

I mentioned fruit. 'The pineapples are fabulous. You must eat pineapples and paw-paw. They're fantastic, and all they do is cut them up and serve them.'

'But who cuts them up? That's the important thing. How do you know who does it?'

'But it's a big hotel. It's a restaurant. Hundreds, thousands of people eat here every year. It's – it's –' I gave up. There was obviously no point continuing. The Minister was on the briefest of stopovers to wave the British flag, but the only thing he wanted to wave was goodbye. We sipped our drinks in silence. I didn't feel any pain. Well, not from the drink. I ordered another round and paid. We grunted 'Cheers' to each other. As we got up to go, a French businessman came up to the bar and ordered a glass of wine.

'It is South African, Monsieur,' said the barman.

The Frenchman shuddered and ordered a mazout, a whisky and Coke, instead.

'Bloody racialist,' muttered the Minister as we walked towards reception. It was his first visit to Zaire. He wanted to get to know 'the francophones, what?', so he had arranged to have dinner with a Canadian with one of the aid organizations.

'Where is your driver?' I asked. 'He should be here.'

'Let him go,' he replied. 'Didn't want him hanging around. Would have meant paying him extra.'

Which put me on the spot. Official cars I am never given. Hiring a car and chauffeur is ruinously expensive. I always take the local town taxis which are inevitably battered old wrecks, with no paint, no springs – and often no brakes.

'We'll never get a chauffeur now,' I said. 'Shall we take a town taxi? It'll be a rough ride, but at least we'll get there.'

'Probably covered in germs as well,' he replied.

It was obviously going to be one of those evenings.

I found a town taxi, which was true to type, and we shuddered and screeched and skidded away from the hotel. Just around the first corner, the driver turned round to me. 'Petrol,' he smiled. 'We need petrol.'

It was the same old trick. Every taxi in Zaire has just enough petrol to get round the corner. Then, of course, they need more. What can you say? Refuse and you risk having to walk back through town. Agree and you're invariably trapped helplessly in a clapped-out old taxi whose windows don't work in the middle of a petrol station at the mercy of every thief, vagabond and gypsy in Central Africa, pushing everything from cigarettes and newspapers to unmentionable items of clothing under your nose and screaming at you to buy them because their mother has just died, their youngest baby has to go to Paris for a hole-in-the-heart operation or their sister is getting married and they have to pay for the wedding and you can come as well if you want. As the distingué invité. The driver, of course, hasn't any money for the petrol because his father has just had a heart attack and he had to pay for him to go to hospital. You protest weakly, but in the end a five-minute journey takes nearly thirty-five minutes and costs anything from £25 to £35.

As if that wasn't bad enough, the driver now kept telling us the latest Zaire jokes: 'Un petit garçon montre à sa mère un billet de banque qu'il vient de ramasser dans la rue.

323

– Tu es bien sûr qu'il a été perdu? elle lui demande.
– Mais oui, répond l'enfant, j'ai même vu l'homme qui le
    cherchait!' He laughed, and swerved all over the road.
'La Maîtresse demande a ses élèves de citer un mammifère
volant. Un élève se leve et dit: c'est l'hôtesse de l'air! This time
he laughed so much we mounted the pavement and practically ran over a guardian asleep outside a house. Trouble
was it didn't seem funny to me.

Finally we arrived. The house was on the edge of town,
surrounded by trees. Outside there was no wall, no railing, no
hedges, which was unusual for expats.

'No security,' I said as we stepped into the house. Then I
saw why. All the security was inside. There were metal railings
everywhere, from floor to ceiling. To get from the front door
into the entrance hall you had to go through a metal cage. To
go from the entrance hall into one of the rooms you had to go
through a wooden door and a metal door. To get to the first
floor you had to open a gate at the foot of the stairs. Then
there were railings between the top of the banisters and the
ground-floor ceiling.

'Diplomacy,' said the Canadian avec un sourire. 'Not good
for the image.'

The Minister smiled indulgently. He had met a professional.

Dinner was great fun. The table looked as though it was
dressée pour un déjeuner de bonne tenue. The Minister took
the place d'honneur. Everybody swopped stories and tried to
outdo everybody else with the horrors of overseas travel.

The Canadian told us about his experiences in Eastern
Europe: 'If the bread is not delivered then the butter is not
delivered either. That's socialist planning.'

The Minister told us about his visits to Japan and the Far
East: 'Frightful, all this bowing. Had to go and see an
osteopath when I got back.'

He even drank three more whiskies – with ice. But I didn't
dare ask where it came from. The food was very British: plain,

simple, not very exciting. Avocado pear to start with, all sliced up, covered with sauce, little bits of lettuce on the side. The main course was like an Irish stew but not so heavy, a nice rich sauce, plenty of vegetables, but with long stringy bits of meat, which tasted as though it had been marinating for a week. Either that or the sauce had started fermenting.

'Problems with the cook,' the Canadian's wife told us. 'One of his nephews has died and he's gone off to the funeral. We had a devil of a job but I managed to borrow a boy from one of the neighbours. Just told him to get on with it. No problems. I think I'll keep him.'

We all agreed.

'Do you have problems getting good people?' I asked.

'Devil's own job, I should think,' said the Minister.

'Trouble is keeping them. Once you've trained them, everybody else wants them,' said the Canadian.

'The EC delegate has just taken my housekeeper. Took me three years to train him, now I've got to start all over again,' added the wife.

Now we were served lettuce, a great pile of it on a plate with lashings of oil. Normally I don't like lettuce but this was crisp and fresh. Vive la révolution verte, I thought. The table was cleared. In came an enormous sickly-sweet dessert and a bottle of champagne, Laurent Perrier Rosé again, which all disappeared within seconds.

'Now, who'll have a digestif?' asked the Canadian. We all nodded reluctantly as if we were really wondering whether to indulge further or not.

'Splendid meal,' said the Minister, gulping back his digestif in one go. It was the first positive comment, let alone word of praise, that I had heard from him since he arrived in the country. 'Splendid,' he burbled again as he pushed his glass forward for a refill.

Then, inevitably, came the reminiscences. 'Ghastly this nouvelle cuisine,' he said. 'Nothing to get your teeth into. No taste. Typically French. All those sauces. Had dinner with the

French ambassador before I came. Couldn't tell you what we had. Tasteless.'

'Give me a good old-fashioned roast-beef . . .'

'. . . burnt to a cinder . . .'

'. . . lashings of gravy . . .'

'Yorkshire pudding as big as a football.'

'And spotted dick afterwards.'

'Or jam rolypoly. A really good rolypoly.'

'Like they used to make at school.'

'Fantastic,' we all sighed together.

'But I liked the meal this evening,' I said.

'We do our best,' the Canadian's wife sighed gently.

'Liked that stew,' said the Minister. 'Whiff of old England. Smashin'.'

'What was it?' I asked. 'Beef? Didn't know you could get beef like that out here. Or maybe oxtail, or bush chicken, like you get in Nigeria. Tough and stringy.'

'In Ghana they call them chicken spare parts,' said the Canadian.

'Wasn't beef. More like venison,' said the Minister.

'Can't be venison, not here. Probably antelope.'

'Nonsense. You can tell antelope,' the Minister said convincingly.

'All right then,' I said. 'What was it?' I looked at the Canadian's wife and wondered why she didn't put us out of our misery.

'I don't know,' she said weakly. 'I left it to the cook. But I thought it was venison or antelope. It didn't taste like beef to me.'

'Let's ask the cook,' said the Minister. 'Call him in. Settle it once and for all. Bet you it was venison.'

The Canadian rang a little bell and the cook appeared. He was about five foot, a tiny, fragile man, perspiring heavily. He had a pair of dirty grey trousers on, no shoes and a filthy sweatshirt. The Canadian's wife was obviously embarrassed.

'Now, old chap,' said the Minister. 'We enjoyed the meal,

but we want to know what meat you used. Was venison, wasn't it?'

The cook said nothing. He just stared at the Minister. Probably never seen anyone like it before.

'Come on, old chap. No beating about the bush. Tell us. Venison, I say.'

The wife leaned towards the poor helpless cook. 'You hear the Minister. Tell him what it was,' she said.

He murmured, so quietly I almost missed it, 'I don't know.'

'Speak up, old chap,' said the Minister. 'Jolly good meal. Not like that foreign stuff. Thoroughly enjoyed it. Want to know what it was.'

'I don't know,' he repeated a little louder.

'You don't know!' roared the Minister. 'You must know. You cooked it.'

The Canadian went white. His wife started fidgeting. The evening with the Minister was rapidly turning into a disaster. 'Now come along,' said the Canadian, leaping to his feet determined to show who was in charge. 'Pull yourself together. What have you just given us?'

'Please sir,' whispered the poor cook. 'Madame said cook the meal. I saw the meat in the refrigerator. I just cooked it. I don't know what it was.'

'Hilarious,' I said. 'I don't believe it. The first time we've all enjoyed a meal in Africa and we don't know what we've eaten.'

'I'm going to get to the bottom of this,' said the Canadian threateningly. Things were going a little too far. Especially with a British government minister sitting at the table. Even though he was a somewhat junior minister.

'Ask him what we had for sweet,' I said. 'Bet he doesn't know that either.' Then suddenly there was a noise from the kitchen.

'What's that?' said the Minister rushing through the door.

'It's probably our own cook come back early. Leave him. I'll

327

go and talk to him,' said the wife.

'No. I'll go. I want to sort it out,' snapped the Canadian.

The atmosphere was electric. Not wishing to miss a good show I stumbled into the kitchen as well. We all gathered round the two hapless cooks.

'Malumba,' barked the Canadian at his own cook, 'this boy here has given us some meat and doesn't know what it is. Now I want to know what it was. That can't be difficult.'

The cook looked uneasy and turned to his stand-in. 'Where did you get the meat from?'

'From the refrigerator. On the top shelf.'

'On top of the vegetables? On the side?'

'Next to the juice.'

The Canadian interrupted, 'So what was it then?'

'The mystery is solved,' I said.

'I bet it was venison,' added the Minister.

We all looked at Malumba. 'So come on, man. What was it?' said the Canadian.

He looked at us all in turn. 'Le chien,' he whispered. 'You ate le chien. I got it for my father in his village. It was for his birthday.'

'Oh my God', shrieked the wife.

The Minister went white and slumped in a chair.

The Canadian just stared and opened his mouth.

I went back into the dining room and poured myself another digestif. I wasn't so much worried about les délices de la haute cuisine Zairois, I was scared in case any of my dogs back home found out what I'd done.

It was late one evening; I had had a drink in l'Atmosphère and watched Tom and Jerry on the big screen above the dance floor. I came down to reception. Just as I asked for my key, the front door swung open. Staggering in came an elderly man, covered in mud, blood running down the side of his face and wearing only his underpants. He was sobbing and crying. The reception staff rushed up to him.

'The taxi,' he sobbed. 'The taxi . . . It was the taxi driver . . .'

Ouagadougou

Forget Hong Kong. Forget New York. Forget even Paris. The best place in the world for restaurants; for the range, for the quality and above all, for the price (after Lomé) is – wait for it – Ouagadougou, the capital of Burkina Faso, perhaps the poorest country in Africa.

Famine, disease, drought, even tourism: Burkina Faso has suffered the lot. If anything could go wrong, it has gone wrong. Half the population is under fifteen. Half the children under five are malnourished. One child in seven dies before it is one year old, one in six before it is five. Infant mortality is as much as thirty times greater than in the United States. Life expectancy is just thirty-three years.

'That's nothing,' an American banker told me once in Paris. 'If you want to see real poverty you should go to Brownsville, Texas. There they fight over rubber bumpers for their cars.'

Wagga, as we old Africa hands say, is on the edge of the Sahara where the sand turns to sand and scrub. Or at least, it should be. Every time I go back there the sand has moved relentlessly further into the back streets and along the one or two open, tree-lined roads. The town itself is tiny. There are probably only two or three concrete roads. The rest are sand. Hard sand. Most of them with enormous potholes, some the size of an olympic swimming pool. Most buildings are tiny, single-storey shacks. Leaning precariously against most of them are even smaller shacks made up of leaves, branches,

330

sheets of corrugated iron, old cardboard boxes. Everybody is as thin as matchsticks apart from the children and, funnily enough, most government ministers. They all have great swollen bellies although I doubt if it is for the same reason.

Nevertheless, tell anyone on the circuit you're going to Wagga – don't say Ouagadougou or they'll immediately know you're an outsider – and the advice will be the same. Buy, beg, steal or borrow a copy of the – I kid you not – *Guide Gastronomique de Ouagadougou*. If in one of the poorest countries of the world you want to study 'la scéne gastronomique de Burkina Faso' this volume is as important as serving Dom Perignon at exactly 9°C.

You want a French restaurant which serves civet de canard done to perfection? You must try le Silmandé sur la route de Kaya. La qualité of the cuisine is incontestable. They are also famous for their avelines d'agneau. And their crêmes soufflées en dessert are positively out of this monde.

An Italian restaurant? Le Belvedere in Koulouba, the third street on the left after the Hôtel de l'Indépendence, is the numéro uno. Their pizza carbonara is legendary. The service is très agreable. And you can dine dans la cour ou dans le restaurant climatisé.

You feel like a Spanish meal? There's none better than at le Patio, not far from the airport at the start of Avenue Yennenga. The Paella comes highly recommended, as does gaspajo, la soupe espagnole. But be warned. It is sometimes difficult to trouver du vin.

Can't make up your mind? In Wagga, there are over fifty proper, professional, quality restaurants, including Lebanese, Vietnamese, Chinese, Austrian and even one New Caledonian restaurant. Not to mention goodness knows how many 'maquis', the unofficial, everyday restaurants which can be anything from an oil stove and paraffin lamp next door to a petrol station, to a giant bowl of rice beside an open sewer.

These are the cuisines typiques burkinabées. Take my word for it, the Don Camillo in Gounghin near the big stadium serves les merveilles de la cuisine burkinabé. There is even a Hamburger House, 'un symbol de la culture américaine: un restaurant fast food' serving 'variations de l'hamburger traditionnel'.

They are all lovingly described in the *Guide* by its editor, a German technical adviser who spent three years advising the highways division of the local town council by day and by night eating and drinking his way round all the bars, restaurants and nightclubs in town. Which must have been pretty tough. For not only did he force himself to visit every single bar, restaurant and nightclub deux fois au moins, he also insisted on subjecting himself to everything from des spécialités locales to la grande cuisine française as well as, poor man, tasting everything from Dolo, the local traditional beer made from fermented millet, to the finest bordeaux and burgundies. Each bar, restaurant and nightclub he then categorized as either acceptable, bien, très bien or excellent, and wrote a graphic Michelin-style report on every single one, handing out an étoile here, a compliment there and un peu de criticisme wherever he felt it necessary.

The result is the most fascinating good food guide ever written on one of the world's poorest cities. You want the perfect salade? There's only one place: le Vert Galant behind the commissariat central. The best restaurant for fish? La Toque, opposite the airport. Their capitaine is out of this monde. You've a weakness for pâtisserie? The OK Inn on the boulevard circulaire. You won't want to leave the place. Wines? You want to find the best selection of wine in the whole Sahara desert? There's only one place – the famous l'Eau Vive opposite the market, which is run by a group of Belgian nuns who definitely do not believe in serving loaves and fishes. They have a cellar which is 'bien garnie'.

Eat your heart out Egon Ronay. What else could anyone possibly want to get one's teeth into in one of the poorest places on earth than a guide gastronomique?

On one trip to Burkina Faso, I was with an American. The usual thing; the embassy in Paris had heard he was interested in investing in Africa and wanted him to come to Wagga. They had asked me to brief him about their country, the opportunities for investment, government assistance for major new projects, and so on. Almost from the moment we met I suspected they had the wrong man. He said he was from Tucson, Arizona and was big in oil. He was supposed to have construction interests around the world. He had completely captivated the first secretary of the embassy, a jolly lady who was supposed to be a niece of the President but seemed to know nothing about embassy affairs, let alone business. I told the American all about the country, painted it in the most attractive colours I could. But he kept telling me not to bother. They were all the same. He had been round the world more times than Neil Armstrong. There was nothing I could teach him. When I mentioned the country was in the CFA franc zone, he laughed and said it was the same as all the other soft currencies. Which rather confirmed my suspicions although, of course, I didn't try to correct such an expert. As we walked down the embassy steps into the grey Paris drizzle, he asked me to join him later for dinner.

'That's very kind of you,' I said. 'Where are you staying?'

'At the George Cinq the fifth,' he said.

On our first evening in Wagga I decided to take him to l'Eau Vive. It somehow eases the conscience to eat superb French food and drink superb French wines in a desperately poor country if the restaurant is run by nuns. Well, that's my excuse.

The taxi dropped us by the market square opposite. As soon as I got out an old man came scampering across the road on all fours. He was horribly twisted and had sandals not only on his feet but also on his hands. He swung himself down on the side of the road, took a small tin out of his pocket and opened it up for me. I didn't know how much to give him. As little as possible, you're always being told. It's the gesture that counts. Anyhow, lots of them put it on. But somehow he seemed to deserve more than a gesture and I was pretty certain he wasn't putting anything on. I compromised. I didn't give him what I thought I should have to make up for his condition, but I gave him more than I had even given a beggar before.

'Merci beaucoup, monsieur,' he said with a smile and a wave, 'très gentil.' His broad smile revealed a row of gold – were they really gold? – teeth. I thanked him and continued, my conscience easy for a few minutes.

As soon as you go in the Eau Vive, you wonder whether you should have tried the outdoor bar down the road instead. It looks and feels, well, homely. There are religious posters all over the place. Outside in the courtyard is a statue of the Blessed Virgin. There's a slight smell of incense about – either that or Mother Superior has cremated the chateaubriand. The nuns, who look more like aid workers or nurses than Audrey Hepburn, are brisk and to the point. They are definitely not the type of waitress you would ever dare chat up. Come to think of it, few people would want to chat up any Belgian woman, nun or not. But the food is superb. Fantastique, Formidable. Their phacochère en cocotte, sauce aux champignons, is a miracle. But then it has to be, otherwise nobody, probably apart from the French, would eat phacochère. Phacochère? You don't know what it is? It's warthog. I thought everybody knew that. Their antelope roti au menthe poivrée is a touch more conventional, but still absolutely heavenly.

That evening practically every aid worker, World Bank official and wheeler-dealer south of the Sahara was there. We were ushered to a group in the far corner. I sat under the only non-religious poster in the place. Which, of course, would have to be about Aids.

As we joined them a Belgian aid worker was putting his glass down on the table. 'The secret is to keep calm,' he said.

Everyone around the table added their two francs' worth.

'Do nothing.' 'Wait.' 'Don't get annoyed.' 'Won't make the slightest difference.'

'I remember once' – the traditional opening line for any conversation in Africa where everybody tries to prove they know the continent better than anybody else – 'I was in Abidjan,' a German accent continued. 'At the airport. We were delayed, must have been four hours—'

'Four hours, that's nothing,' interrupted the frail old French poodle sitting next to me. 'I was once in—'

Suddenly through the babble of French – good, bad and Franglais – German, a bit of Spanish, some Lingula and God knows what else, I heard from the table alongside us an undistinguished Canadian accent whispering softly to a soft Irish accent.

'But you and I are ...'

'My boy ...'

'He's yours.'

'... sixteen ...'

'You're sure?'

'... for four hours!' the German drowned them out. 'Everybody raising hell. I ask the guy behind desk, How many times you have these problems? I bet it causes lot of work. To me he starts chatting. Ignores all others. He say he call engineers. Their telephone number he had. His brother is engineer. He rang him. He told him it would be two hours about. Some valve gone. Simple job. Wouldn't take long. He tell me because we are friends.'

'Same as some people go into a restaurant and start shouting, garçon, garçon. Usually Americans,' smirked a German-looking Swede, who turned out to be a Frenchman working with a British company selling armaments to governments throughout West Africa. He was so successful, he told me later, because they thought they were dealing with a French company. When they realized he was working for a British company it was too late for them to change their minds. 'I mean, who says garçon any more? Some people say chef, some say patron. I always say monsieur. It works. If you're friendly, they're friendly.'

Everybody else joined in. 'I always ask about their children, they love that. Never their wives. Some of them can't remember who their wives are. That's always a good one.'

'I find if you can make them smile you're okay.'

'If they don't smile, I always say, why aren't you smiling? Have you got problems? Don't worry.'

Which sounded to me like patronizing Africans, rather than being friendly.

'Do you find it works with the police?'

'And even the military?'

The American then suddenly said, 'You haven't seen anything until you've been along the Mexican border.'

Not that I was listening, but the Canadian and Irish accents were now breathing heavily.

'. . . social arrangement . . .'

'Together. You mean . . .'

'. . . careful. You must be . . .'

'But will you . . .?'

'If I come to a roadblock,' a Belgian-looking Frenchman who turned out to be Canadian with a Swiss mother butted in, 'I always get out and talk to the police. Nobody else does. They cower inside their cars. If you get out, it puts them off. They don't know what to do.'

'And shake hands.'

'And say bonjour.'

'It's also a good way of finding out what it's all about.'

'And where the police are from.'

'And what kind of police.'

'I remember once I was in Congo. There were policemen there from Zaire.'

'But that's an invasion.'

'Happens all the time.'

'Anybody can cross the borders. Leaky as a sieve.'

We all laughed and ordered another round of drinks. By

now the poor nun was being drowned by our smiles and enquiries about her children, how long she had been at work, how long she was going to have to stay.

'You should go there one day,' the American suddenly butted in.

'Where?' I turned to him.

'Along the Mexican border. I tell you . . .'

In the background, I just couldn't help noticing the heavy breathing had now turned to panting.

'But there's thirteen years difference between . . .'

'That's nothing. To me you will always be . . .'

'Well, he did say if anything happened I should . . .'

'How long have we known . . .?'

'But you don't understand. You never . . .'

'I've been in some of their wars,' the German accent drowned them out again.

'Nasty. Was in Katanga myself during the troubles. Messy business,' added the Belgium.

Then as the warthogs and antelopes landed on the table everybody was off again.

'I arrived in Wagga the day of the coup, with the minister of Posts and Telecommunications, a good friend. Known him since before he became Minister. Suddenly I heard gunfire. The Minister said to me, you'd better get back to your hotel. Do you know, I got out just as they were closing the gates, otherwise I'd have been stuck in that Ministry when they came round looking for people behind the coup. That was a near escape, you know.'

'Same thing happened to me when Sankara took over. Nasty.'

'What about Benin? There were rumours about a coup against Kerekou. Let me tell you, they were no rumours. That was true. I was in Cotonou, in the port. I was going back to the Sheraton – you know the one with a London bus parked outside? I got to the corner and you should have seen the military. Everywhere. Absolutely berserk. I thought to myself, this is it. I told the driver, make for the hotel. I've never seen him drive so fast. Got there just in time, I can tell you.'

'But there was no coup.'

'No, but it was a pretty close thing, I can tell you.'

'I always ask them how long they've been on duty. Works a treat.'

'How long have you been on duty? What? Four hours? I bet you're tired.'

'And nothing to eat or drink, I suppose.'

'Must be very hard being a soldier.'

'But you're doing a good job,' we all chorused.

Now the American mumbled at me again, 'I tell you, you owe it to yourself.'

We all looked at him. He nodded. 'I'm telling you, you owe it to yourself.'

I couldn't help noticing that the panting had suddenly ceased.

'I mean, Good God . . .'

'Oh so we're back to that again.'

'It is the same . . .'

'No.'

'You're just like . . .'

'So are we going to or . . . .?'

Then, wallowing in our reminiscences, we all began shouting at the poor nuns for another round of drinks.

'Bet you don't remember when Traore took over.'

'That was a long time ago.'

'Ten, fifteen, twenty years. Easily.'

'Must have been late 60s.'

'64.'

'Didn't think it was as long ago as that.'

'I was there . . .'

'You don't look old enough.'

'. . . right in the middle of it. Nasty.'

'And what about riots?'

'I was in Lagos just before Christmas, driving round town

making some calls. We turn a corner – slap-bang in the middle of a riot,' said the Belgian. 'Banging the roof, smashing the bonnet, all around us. Practically turned the car over. Got as far as bouncing us up and down.' We all leant forward. This was danger at first hand. 'Then somebody said they saw the American ambassador. They all turned and started chasing him. Lucky for us, I can tell you. Nearest escape I've had.'

'What about the ambassador?' the American asked, suddenly very concerned for the safety of his fellow countryman. 'What happened to him?'

'They roughed his car up a bit, ripped the flag off the front, smashed the bonnet. But he was all right. The police arrived in time.'

'Just as well,' he grunted putting his nuclear missiles back in his pocket.

'But you should have seen how they beat up the crowd. Really laid into them. A bit nasty.'

'Did you get out and ask how long they'd been on duty?' I asked innocently. Another round of snorting and laughing and banging the tables.

'Always works,' said the younger Frenchman.

'Excuse me, officer, before you beat that guy's brains out could you tell me how your children are?' said the Swedish German.

'Bet they haven't given you anything to eat either.'

'Best be friendly.'

'Never fails.'

The Swedish-German, who was now looking more Swiss-Dutch, called for more drinks. It was going to be a long night. Then suddenly a tiny bell rang. The nuns handed us printed cards. It was time for their short evening service. As we shuffled to our feet, the elderly French poodle revealed a pair of dirty old khaki shorts – and a shiny aluminium leg strapped to a stump just above the knee. One of the younger nuns sang 'Ave Maria'. We all tried to join in, more in spirit than anything, but without much success.

'How did you get that?' I asked as, the service over, we collapsed back in our chairs.

'I tried to talk my way through a roadblock,' he said. 'In Zaire.'

We finished the meal in silence. So did the table behind me. Except for the odd phrase that I just managed to catch.

'You are without doubt the most . . .'

'Well, I don't think that's . . .'

'. . . demean yourself . . .'

'Okay, you've made your . . .'

As we walked back to the car, a young man in an elegant white suit, his arms covered in chains and necklaces, with a fistful of watches, all genuine Cardin, came up to me.

'You buy watches. Jewellery,' he said.

'No thank you,' I said mechanically.

'Good prices. You like watch. Good jewellery. Real gold.'

'Non, merci beaucoup,' I said.

He stood in front of me. 'You have plenty of money. I saw you give some to that old man with the gold teeth.'

'That was all I had.'

'You've got plenty left. I saw.' He pushed his face right up in front of me. I could see the gravelly, bloodstained whites of his eyes. He was perspiring gently. It flashed through my mind, shall I just buy one of his watches? It probably won't cost much. He probably needs the money as much as the old man. Then I thought, no, why should I? I don't want his cheap watch. Plenty of people try to sell you things and when you say no they go away. Why should he be different?

'Non merci, not today,' I said, trying to step round him. But he blocked my way. I was beginning to feel edgy. I looked around. Nobody seemed to see me.

He pushed his fistful of watches under my nose. 'If you don't buy one of my watches,' he said slowly. 'I'll kill you. And,' he continued menacingly, jerking his head towards the other side of the street, 'you see my friend over there?' I looked. His friend appeared nastier still. 'You see my friend over there,' he repeated slowly. 'If you don't buy one of my watches he will kill you also.'

'Not as bad as Brownsville,' the American said. 'You should see what it's like along the Mexican border.'

Now what shall it be this evening? Indian? Chinese? What about Vietnamese?

Decisions, decisions, it's always decisions in Wagga. Anywhere else, it's simple. If I've plenty of time I head for the nearest three- or four-star. If I've no time I just collapse into the first restaurant, hamburger outfit or whatever I come to. In Wagga I always have a conscience, in case I miss out on the best restaurants. Every day, therefore, I try to eat in two if not three different places, drink in three if not four different bars and take in at least one nightclub. That is the only way I feel I can pay tribute to 'les variétés de la cuisine à Ouagadougou'.

Wait a minute, I know where I'll go this evening. I'll go back to the Eau Vive. It will be the perfect end to une journée nonstop de discours.

The morning had begun early. I was up and out before six. The place was deserted; the bars and street cafés were empty. There were no taxis, not even a motorcycle. And if there are no motorcycles in Wagga you know something is up. I asked an old man lying in front of the Air Afrique office if there was another coup or if it was just a public holiday.

'No, no public holiday,' he said. 'Everybody has gone to the railway. They are helping to build the railway.' He rolled over and went back to sleep. But he was right: ministers, civil servants, businessmen, even journalists, they had all gone to lend a hand. Out in the bush, too, people were helping to build a railway.

The reason: more than 600 kilometres away, near Tambao in the far north of the country, are 15 million tons of rich manganese deposits. Sankara wanted to exploit them. The

World Bank and other aid organizations were not convinced. They said it was not a viable project. Sankara told them what he thought of them and decided that Burkina would build it themselves, pay for it themselves, and even extend it to Niger, giving Niamey direct access to Abidjan.

In theory, I reckon rail is always better than road. In just five months in 1897 Kitchener's Anglo-Egyptian army laid 230 miles of track, bypassing a 500-mile loop of the Nile, and completely outmanoeuvred the French at Fashoda. In other words, rail is quicker to build, more economic to operate and better for shifting heavy loads over long distances. The trouble with Sankara's dream of a Saheilian Ouagadougou Choo-Choo is that Burkina is already in debt on the existing 1,199 km stretch up from Abidjan in the Côte d'Ivoire; the new Trans-Gabonese railway cost tens of thousands of lives, which makes everybody a little wary; and there is no guarantee that Burkina can get a good price for the manganese if they can ship it out. The new man, Compaore, has not said anything yet. But the odds must be swinging against the project.

The last time I visited the railway they had built about 50-60 kilometres on their own and were talking about the next phase. I wondered how much it was all going to cost and where they were going to get the money from. But I couldn't meet the director.

'He travels,' said the secretary. The usual excuse.

'When will he be back?'

'He is travelling.'

'I know, but for how long?'

'He is travelling. That's all I know,' she said screwing her face up and waving her arms in the air.

I asked for the assistant director, and was ushered in to see a young man in his early twenties. As soon as he saw me he picked up pen and paper and started writing everything down. What did I want to know? Why did I want that information? What was I going to do with it? Would I double-check everything with him first?

He asked for my business card. Because everyone in francophone Africa asks for your business card, I've developed my own special system. At first, I used to give everybody my card: ministers, government officials, presidents of chambers of commerce, policemen, porters and anybody who asked me the way to the nearest mosque. But I very quickly realized two things. First, it was costing me a fortune. Two days in francophone Africa and I would use up more cards than I use in London in three years. Second, my secretary was becoming a little irritated at the number of cousins of ministers, wives of civil servants and bunches of second cousins thrice removed of hotel porters that were arriving unannounced at the office. It wasn't so much the numbers, although at one point it looked dangerously as though we were consuming more coffee than the Côte d'Ivoire was not releasing on the open market. It was the parcels and shopping bags and cardboard boxes. Clearing the files out of the storage room was one thing, but when the pilipili and tomato paste started oozing out and staining the carpet, and worse still making the cleaning lady hand in her notice, I was forced to do something. I decided I would only hand out my business cards in francophone Africa to key players. To other people I would give somebody else's card.

Admittedly I've had problems trying to sound like a Swede dealing in computers, not to mention a director of a Nigerian merchant bank. And I got some funny looks from a minister in Zaire when without thinking I gave him a card saying 'Madame Danielle Weiss, Marché Tropical'. If there were any repercussions, I haven't heard them, although there was a rumour last time I was in Brussels that Zaire had increased their advertising budget.

On the other hand one or two printers in South London have rung me up to see if I know the Wolof for 'three weeks is long enough. Won't your mother be worried about you?' (I didn't.) My dentist once asked me for the Lingala for 'I don't care if it looks like a rocking chair, I've got work to do.' And on another occasion an official on the Africa desk in the Foreign Office wanted me to correct a series of imperative verbs in Lingala in a cable he was sending to Brazzaville, which I did. I don't know the language at all, but I thought it best to try and be seen to help the Foreign Office; you never know when you might be thrown in an African jail and need their help.

The other variation is to hand out African business cards. Nothing is more calculated to break the ice at a stuffy diplomatic reception in Cotonou on New Year's Eve than to hand the Russian ambassador a card saying 'Baba Traore dit Papa Diop. Chauffeur de Taxi'. I once used a Senegalese minister's card to get a hotel room during a francophone summit in Lomé, when there wasn't a room to be had for love or American dollars. Trouble was, all week wherever I went I could hear people whispering 'Marabout blanc' behind my back. But the best African cards of all to hand out are those belonging to French bankers or aid officials. On the back of every one I scribble 'Any amount of money, please call'.

To the assistant director, I gave a business card for the Secretary for Development Aid, Federal Ministry of Natural Planning in Lagos, which had some kind of effect, for he immediately assigned one of his assistants to look after me.

'So are you going to build the extension?' I asked him.

'It is government policy.'

'But will you be able to implement it?'

He shrugged. 'We have no money. We can't do anything.'

Which seemed pretty reasonable to me. The pity is more people don't realize it, especially as overall Africa's debt burden now stands around US$200 billion and growing. Official and commercial debt rescheduling is probably adding at least an extra US$1 billion a year to the total, about 44 percent on the continent's GDP. Countries like Burkina Faso are running desperately not just to stand still but not to fall still further behind.

'I don't understand it. Twenty years ago in Africa we were earning on average maybe US$100 per person, and we had no debts. Now we're earning twice, three times that amount and we have enormous debts. Before we were told we were rich. Now we're told we are poor. It doesn't make sense,' he said. 'The problem was, the big countries came and sold us very big projects. They were too big, too expensive. We didn't know; we trusted you. You advised us, you lent us the money. We started making the payments. Everything was fine. Then you change the interest rates. You reduce the money you are going to give us for our commodities. It's unfair. It is changing the rules. It's moving the goalposts halfway through the game. You don't want us to win. You always want to win.'

He was right. Wherever you look, whatever indicator you take, it's bad news for Africa. Commodity prices are down and likely to stay down. Coffee and cocoa prices, for example, are lower than they were in 1975. Private sector investment is down. There is a desperate shortage of skilled manpower. Populations are still growing. Food production is struggling desperately to keep up. But some people are hopeful; luckily, the key players are.

As I left he asked where I was from. 'Canada, Sweden, Holland, the United States,' he guessed.

'China,' I said. 'Je suis chinois.'

He stared at me, wondering if it was true. Which tells you a lot about Burkina Faso. When I said I was English, he told me he had visited London once on his way back from Moscow. 'Very old-fashioned country Britain,' he said. 'The 'phones are so slow.'

After I left the railway station I had lunch with a member of the IMF team trying to negotiate the solution to Africa's problems. We went to see la Charmante Dominique at la Chaumière, un petit restaurant typique du Midi, even down to the interior rustique. It's unbelievable. I chose the salade Chaumière, which tells you how good it is. Normally I run a kilometre if anyone even suggests salad to me, and there was

345

practically everything else on offer. Dominique, as usual, was très attentif.

So was there a solution to Africa's problems? Was the IMF man hopeful?

'Yes, I'm very hopeful,' he said. 'First because everybody now accepts there is a problem. Second because everybody now accepts that we must find a solution. This is important because the solution can only be a political solution taken by politicians. I am also hopeful because the timing is now right. In the past we didn't have all the necessary factors in place. Now they are falling into place.'

'Such as?'

'Such as the need for discipline. We always say that Britain has Mrs Thatcher, Africa has the International Monetary Fund. Whatever people say in public – some people say we are the number-one hate figure in Africa – in private we all agree on the need for discipline. Countries, governments, have to be taught the need for financial discipline. It's harsh. It's unfair. All the wrong people, the poor, the innocent, the hungry, they all suffer. But it is the only solution. Next, people, especially the creditor nations, want to see the debtor nations taking their medicine. This is largely psychological; but if that is what they want and that is what is needed to solve the problem then we must give it to them.'

'Controls, checks, balances . . .'

'They are all necessary to make certain it doesn't happen again. We need an independent, professional public admin- istration. We need agreed accounting standards. We need tighter control of banking and banking procedures . . .'

'Anti-corruption . . .'

'Some people say the solution is not more aid, but no aid at all. In the last thirty years Africa has received over US$70 billion in aid. Where has it gone? The problem is not money. There is too much money around. The problem is controlling it. We need more and better accountability.'

'Spending it on the right projects . . .'

'Controlling the expenditure. Eliminating all the waste and inefficiency and . . .'

'Corruption . . .'

'And, appelons un chat, un chat, corruption. We all know the stories about food aid. Food arrives – there are no trucks or ships. It sits on the docks and rots. That's terrible. Big prestige projects, although thank goodness we don't get so many nowadays, are a waste of money. Building railway suspension bridges in countries where there are no railways . . .'

'Yes, but you can't just blame the country. These projects can only go ahead if the banks agree. If the banks don't like them they shouldn't agree.'

'Anti-corruption procedures. These will all take time. But we have recognized the need and we are doing something about it. On the political front, we couldn't do much until the end of the Reagan administration. We needed an administration in Washington that knew and understood the problem. This we now have. Another piece falling into place.'

'The commercial banks . . .'

'We needed the commercial banks to adjust to the situation. We needed a period of calm. We wanted them to start writing off some of the debts and adjusting to the situation so that we could all sit down and talk. And we have achieved this position today without extremes. We could so easily have had an upsurge of anti-capitalism in Africa: thousands of people fired and sent home to their villages. In Senegal civil servants were retrained as farmers. In Mauritania factory workers were sent back to the land. All the ingredients were there. But there has been nothing. Similarly we could have had the Western nations packing up, going home and wanting nothing whatsoever to do with Africa. It was a very dangerous time. But we have eliminated the tensions. Now we can talk. Psychologically that is good.'

'And will you succeed?'

'Of course. All the ingredients for success are there.'

'And the solution?'

'The ADB has proposed some form of securitization. That is going to be the basis of the solution. We still have the details to work out. But securitization will be the basis of the solution, and soon.'

'So what abut the French?'

'The French are very important to Africa. They are le grand frère. But we realize their situation politically. They want to help and they do help. President Mitterand always insists that Africa is not marginalized, but we know that not everybody in France agrees with him. We know many French companies have lost money in Africa, and many have closed down in Africa. So while he is a friend he has more influence privately than publicly.'

For tea I went to Chez Bawa, on the way to the airport, with an official of the Quai d'Orsay who just happened to be in town. The Chez Bawa is a bit heavy on the musique – it is run by a jeune rasta-man burkinabé – but the milkshakes are worth bursting your eardrums for.

'Why is Burkina Faso so important to the French? Why do you take Africa far more seriously than we do?' I asked him.

'You must remember, France has been invaded twice,' he began. 'That's an experience you never forget. After the war we had to decide how we were going to stop it happening again. How to stop a third world war. First, we decided that the more Europe was united the better. That is why we take the European Community far more seriously than you do. So, it costs money; it's cheaper than another war. But we then had to decide what would we do if there *was* another war. We decided we needed Africa. First, as a source of supplies, the same as you had your Commonwealth. Second, as a source of men, again as you relied on your Commonwealth armies. And don't forget,' he said, 'we made these assumptions thirty years ago, not today. Third, as an alternative base for the French government. De Gaulle did this during the last war, but he wasn't the official French government. Our plan was to move

348

the official French government to French Africa and, if we had to, to conduct the war from there.'

'But that's still not official French policy,' I said.

'No, of course not, but that is the basis of our thinking. That concept or philosophy, if you like, affected our thinking for a long time. That's why we paid so much attention to Algeria, why we didn't want to let it go. That's why Burkina Faso is important to us.'

'But why have I never heard this theory before? I've never read about it or seen it in any policy documents or anything.'

'Of course not; to have discussed it openly would have meant the French government publicly admitting that it thought a third world war was likely, when we were doing everything we could to ensure peace in Europe. That would not have been possible. It would not have been politics.'

'And worse,' I added, 'it would have meant that you thought you could be defeated for a third time.'

'Precisely. Which French government would have been prepared to admit even considering such a thought? It would have been catastrophic.'

'And it might even have been an encouragement to somebody to start something,' I said.

'Voilà. Exactement.'

It was an interesting theory. 'But wait a minute,' I said. 'If that was the background, the unthinkable background scenario, how come you made so many mistakes?'

'So many? No so many as you. We still have French Africa. You don't have a British Africa any more.'

'I agree. But you have had your problems. Algeria.'

'I know what you mean. The problem was, that was the plan in Paris, but the people on the ground didn't know that. Some of them were marvellous. Gave their lives for Africa. But some of them started kicking the Africans around. Les vagabonds. Things got out of hand. People remember the bad things, never the good things.' He sighed. 'The rest is history.'

'But why didn't you step in before things got out of hand?'

'Timing. It's always a question of timing. We wanted a big presence in Africa for strategic reasons, as I've told you. We also wanted their raw materials. Their taxes. Their revenue. The people who were kicking the Africans around were usually the men running the countries, producing the revenue, so we had to turn a blind eye.'

'Because the more they kicked the Africans around, the more they increased production, the more revenue for France.'

'Exactement. You are thinking like a Frenchman. And the more they increased production, the more money they could steal and put in their pockets.'

'And the less you had to pay them.'

'Sure. We gave them all big offices, big cars, lots of servants, fancy uniforms. The French love that. They will do anything for a uniform.'

'And medals.'

'And medals.'

This was fascinating. At last I felt I was getting under the skin of the French and discovering how they think.

'So tell me,' I asked, 'why did the French give the Africans the right to be elected to the Assemblée Nationale?'

'We wanted to bind ourselves closer to Africa, but we also had to make sure Africa bound themselves closer to us. Giving them the right to sit in our national assembly was the only way we could do it.'

'I thought it was a great idea. I always wondered why we never did it. We could have let them into the House of Commons, or maybe just the senior politicians into the Lords.'

'And we also did it because we believe it is better to fight somebody in a debate than in the streets. We thought that once somebody came to Paris they would think the French way. They wouldn't be so independent. They would be assimilated, become like all the others. La crème culturelle.'

'So how do you see things today?'

He took out his cigarettes and spent a long time selecting

and lighting one. The prevarication struck me as odd, because the French have fabulous connections throughout franco-phone Africa. First, the currency. Practically every country is a member of the Communauté Français-Africain. In other words they are members of the CFA franc zone which is backed by the French franc. From the French point of view this ties the countries to la France. From the countries' point of view it virtually gives them a hard currency. Talk to a British exporter trying to do deals in niaras, or worst still in cedis, and you'll see the difference a hard currency makes. Second, France has the lion's share of the market. Admittedly they have their ups and downs, but it is still very much their chasse garde. Third, politics; by and large the French and the francophones are hand-in-glove culturally. Y-a-rien à dire.

'I think the relationship is as strong as ever,' he began. 'First, because there are no substantial disagreements between us. We agree on most things. Second, because Africa sees that France is the only major power interested in Africa. If Africa falls out with France, who will represent their interests? Britain? Germany? United States? Never. Then I think there is a cultural link . . .'

'Language. Attitude. Philosophy.'

'It's very important.'

'But French investment is falling in Africa.'

'Of course, because Africa is not so active. The competition is stronger; the type of materials Africa requires at the moment are not made by France.'

'So what about the CFA?'

'You mean devalue it? Never. It is the psychological link that keeps the Community together. We cannot change it because of short-term considerations. Don't forget, devaluation would make our exports more expensive, which is what we don't want. We want the market. Our businessmen are going to find it difficult surviving the European market. The last thing we want is to give them problems in Africa as well. We are doing everything we can to encourage our companies to do more business in Africa: English-speaking Africa, Zaire.'

So what happened? The French devalued the CFA by a massive 50 percent. Which proves that nothing is true until it is denied by a French diplomat.

Dinner that evening in the Eau Vive was fantastic. Everything you could imagine was on the menu: cheese dough rolls, quails' eggs, salad, olives, rare roast beef, filet mignon wrapped in bacon, sliced tomatoes, pommes frites, onion rings, beetroot the size of footballs, palm hearts, Brazilian mozzarella. Don't forget, in French Africa, the poorer the country, the better the food. I'd been in poverty-stricken Wagga for six days and I'd eaten everything from warthog to les avelines d'agneau – or maybe the other way round. I'd drunk everything from jus naturel to Dom Perignon, all served at the right temperature. And my semaine gastronomique had cost me less than US$100.

Now try and tell me Hong Kong, New York or even Paris is better than good old Ouagadougou.

Gao

Quick. Drop what you're doing. If you've been planning to cross the Sahara, now is the time to go. Don't leave it a moment longer. For the Sahara is no longer Sahra, or empty, as they say in Arabic. And it's rapidly becoming less Sahra every day.

The massive rocky Hoggar mountains east of Tamanrasset, the ancient city of the Touregs, the legendary blue men of the desert, now echo to the roar of giant luxury air-conditioned Gelandewagens, Nissan Patrols and Volvo Laplanders instead of the soft pad of camels' hoofs. Sleek Peugeot 504s with their ultra-smooth suspension, Toyota Land Cruisers and the occasional chugging, bumpy Land Rover are turning the fabulous Tenere desert, a neverending sea of spectacular shimmering sand, into a racetrack.

Even the rougher, tougher Tanazrouft, over 1,000 kilometres of flat, empty plains, is not only littered with wrecked trucks and worn-out copies of the latest Tom Clancy or Frederick Forsyth, it is alive with the sounds of Walkmen and sixteen-stone raucous Yorkshiremen learning to ride their first camel.

The centre of Agadez, the legendary desert town on the crossroads of every major camel route in Africa, now has – mama mia – its own Italian ice cream parlour, slap-bang opposite the mysterious Hôtel de l'Air, a mecca for desert travellers from time immemorial. The last time I was there

Théodore Monod, the tiny, wiry, wizened, eighty-year-old French professor, the world's greatest living expert on the Sahara, couldn't get a seat at the bar for Canadian tourists, even though he had just walked barefoot for over ten days across the desert in a camel train from the salt capital of Bilma. Which not only tells you everything about the Sahara today, it also says everything about the Canada of tomorrow.

Pitch camp anywhere in the fabulous, breathtaking sand dunes of Gouloukou or Chiriet or at the foot of Mont Greboun, and within three minutes, literally out of nowhere, will appear three Arab salesmen pushing traditional Toureg flip-flop sandals or soapstone statues of camels.

Once I climbed slowly to the top of an enormous sand dune in the Ain-el Hadjadj Valley on the way to Mali and saw way below me in the delicate, still early morning light a tiny fragile wadi or oasis. Under the palm trees I could see a collection of Volkswagens. But all around the pool, as clear as daylight, stretched out in the vaporous early morning sunshine were, I promise, at least a dozen towels.

If you've got all the tee-shirts, seen everything and been everywhere apart from the Sahara, now is the time to make a Beau Gesture and go before it finally becomes the Great Sands Amusement Park. For the Sahara, ten million square kilo- metres of desert, twice the size of Europe, is not just sand, sand and nothing but sand. It's hills and mountains. The granite hills south of Arak are among the oldest in the world. The Hoggar Mountains, which can rise up to 2,000 metres, are so rocky that the villagers and tribesmen, instead of wearing the usual soft sandals, have made their own special heavier non-slip variety which you don't find anywhere else in the desert.

The Air Mountains are bleak and desolate apart from Adrar Chiriet, a circle of rocky hills which are home to nervous gazelles. Bat an eyelid, let alone switch on a diesel engine, within 100 kilometres of them and they disappear into the rocks leaving just their tracks behind.

The Sahara is also the biggest wildlife park in the world. Lions disappeared in the 1930s; the striped hyena became extinct in the 1980s; but there are plenty of others left. Ostriches, gazelles – not the Adrar Chiriet variety – giraffes, especially near Arly in Burkina Faso, are sometimes two a penny.

Now and then, if you're quick, you can even spot a fennec, the wild desert fox with big ears. Once I was crossing the Sahara with a French expedition and one of the Land Rovers ran over what must have been the unluckiest fennec in the world. Immediately the French slammed on the brakes, leapt out of the Land Rovers and started trying to skin it for dinner.

On the outskirts of Iferouane, where the World Wildlife Fund, with a little help from Bob Geldof, are establishing the world's biggest and probably least known game reserve – it covers 8 million hectares, an area three times the size of Switzerland – if you're lucky you might spot the rare addax antelope or even some barbary sheep.

But if you prefer more urban pursuits, there are plenty of fascinating little towns to explore. El Golea, built on an oasis surrounded by thousands of palm and fruit trees, has to be one of the prettiest towns in the world. Ghardaia is fascinating, especially its secret holy city of Beni Isguen, inhabited by a special Muslim sect, where smoking and drinking are banned and you're only allowed in with a guide.

I always remember In Saleh, a desert town carved out of the sand, because on my first visit I drove the wrong way up an unmarked one-way street and spent six hours in the local police station in the company of the town's solitary secret policeman.

Mopti, I'm convinced, is the straw mat capital of the world, especially the old part of the town; Agadez; Bilma with its salt pans; Zinder, especially on market day; Ayorou where I once bought a camel; even Niamey with its Russian restaurant and Bamako and, of course Ouagadougou, the capital of Burkina Faso: they are all far more fun than Paris, New York and Tokyo rolled into one.

On one trip across the desert, we were getting closer and closer to Gao in Mali. Suddenly in the distance, à travers le desert, we could see four or five buildings. Outside one building was a flag, hanging heavy with sand. I guessed it was the Mali flag and the building was the police station. If you see two or three buildings gathered together in Mali you just know one of them has to be a police station. The others were barracks, or maybe homes.

We swung off the main track and climbed a small incline to the village. We turned into the space between the buildings and – surprise, surprise – there were five or six Land Rovers, three or four police and military vehicles and around twenty people sitting, walking, talking, smoking. It was an international press party touring the country at the invitation of the World Bank. At a glance you could tell who was who. The French journalists all had elegant designer safari suits and matching Louis Vuitton safari luggage. The Germans were wearing khaki and green fatigues. An Italian radio reporter was dripping with gold bracelets and watches. A group of Americans were in Madonna sweatshirts. And there was one journalist with a tie on listening to the BBC World Service who came from you-know-where. We all laugh at *Scoop* but it's as true today as it was then.

A woman came out of one of the houses. She took no notice of all the people and the fuss. Maybe the World Bank ran these bus tours every day. For her, they were just tourists. Surrounded by the Land Rovers, gold Omega watches, designer trenchcoats and battledress tops, luggage splattered with exotic labels, and goodness knows how much valuable camera equipment, she began to prepare probably the only meal of the day for her family. Just one Nikon could have kept her and the whole village in luxury for the rest of their lives. But the equipment was being used to record her activities rather than help her.

She threw a handful of maize into a wooden bowl. A baby stumbled out of the house and waddled up to her. More journalists and cameramen surrounded her and started taking photographs. She now had more press watching her every movement than Lady Di would have opening a home for abandoned wives. The woman picked up a pole and started pounding the maize. A man came out of the building that looked like a police station and saw the throng surrounding the woman. He turned, ran back inside the building and shot out again putting on his hat and carrying a cane under his arm.

'Security. Security,' he screamed. "No photographs. It is forbidden to take photographs. Security.' Everybody fell back in amazement.

'What security?' said a burly French journalist with a beard and Yves St Laurent army fatigues. 'She's cooking. There is no security about cooking.'

'We're just taking photographs of the baby,' said a fierce German woman who looked as though she'd just got back from Alamein.

'Les Africaines, c'est typique,' said another Frenchman lighting a Gaulloise.

The policeman had grabbed the woman and was screaming at her to go back into the house. She was staring at him blankly. The policeman kicked her bowls of food over in the sand and pushed her back towards the building. Other policemen arrived out of nowhere. One came to the aid of his superior, others ambled over, tying on their belts and adjusting their hats. Two started moving the journalists back, as if trying to control a peaceful trade union demonstration on the tarmac at Charles de Gaulle. The leader of the group, who looked as though he'd been through the war in Chad without getting a speck of sand on his Yves St Laurent suit, looked resigned and started walking back to his Peugeot 504. The Germans looked as if they might make a diplomatic incident out of the affair. An American pulled another Coke out of his camera bag, emptied it in one go and threw the can on the sand.

More police were now arriving, and it seemed as if we might really have a diplomatic incident. The leader of the group then returned from his Peugeot with a packet under his arm and beckoned to the screaming policeman. They turned and walked towards the police station. Gradually everybody began to unwind. As they disappeared inside the building a tense calm descended over the village. The French brushed the sand off their designer jeans; the American had another Coke and threw the second can on the sand. Another couple of hours and the village would have been eligible for a grant from the Ford Foundation for an environmental impact study. The English settled down to listen to a report direct from the Conservative Party Conference in Eastbourne. We all waited and waited. Would it be peace or war? Would we all be given 100 lines and told not to do it again? Or would we be thrown in gaol for ever? Then suddenly I heard laughter. First a chuckle, then a deep, rich roar. The leader and the police chief were obviously getting bombed out of their minds on a bottle of Johnnie Walker. Les deux mots de passe nécessaires en Afrique pour tous.

'C'est de rigueur,' the group leader told me afterwards, 'although it plays hell with my liver. If there is ever a problem, especially in a Muslim country, get out the whisky. Never fails. If I'm doing a trip like this, I always take one car full of whisky. It's the only thing they understand, the one international currency. Forget the dollar. A bottle of Johnnie Walker Black Label is like a gold bar. It'll buy anything. It'll fix anything.' He took a deep breath as he slumped into the driving seat of his 504. 'And it'll fix anyone.' He pushed the thing into gear and swung it into the desert.

Everyone suddenly ran like hell, grabbing jackets and coats, cameras and notebooks, and leapt into their cars and Land Rovers in hot pursuit. In two seconds everything was quiet.

The woman came out of the house again. She set down her wooden bowl in the sand and threw her maize into it.

The policeman staggered out of the police station and came

wavering up to me. 'You take her picture now?' he said. 'No problem. No security.'

I took her photograph. Then I took another of her with the policeman smiling weakly in the background. 'Now we celebrate,' he said.

I went back with him to the police station. Under a dusty portrait of the President, alongside a pile of dusty papers – he had none of Richard II's problems – were three large bottles of Johnnie Walker Black Label.

'The press are stupid,' he said. 'They are not serious. They come here, they give me bottles of whisky, they drink whisky with me. They think they can get round me with their alcohol. Then they go away. They think they have bought me. They think a bottle of whisky buys me. They are stupid.'

'But why did you take it?' I asked.

'Because with whisky I can buy things for my people. It is money.'

'But you also drink it,' I said.

'Of course. If I didn't drink it they wouldn't give me whisky. They would give me pencils or pens or papers. That's more important than whisky. We need pens and papers and books. We need everything. But with whisky I can buy what we need.'

He offered me another glass but after what he had said I didn't feel like any more. I was in the middle of a charade, a desperate game between two sides, neither understanding the other, but each benefiting from the other.

'You mean, all this was a game?' I said. 'Just to get the whisky?'

'Of course. I'm not stupid like them. I know when a woman is making food that is not security. But what else can I do? I'm here, in the middle of the desert. How else can I make money?'

The poor policeman, like so many others I have met travelling in Africa, was a victim of la vie nationale. He had worked hard at school. He had been to Abidjan and Paris and to Moscow as a student. He wanted to study to be a lawyer, but he was told that before he could do so he had to be a policeman. For a year he had been responsible for security between Gao and the border with Niger.

'They say it is security but all we do is block the road and make drivers pay us to pass. We do well. At least we make enough to live on,' he said. 'Some people refuse to pay. A German once refused to pay. We made him wait all day and all night. He was stupid. He could have reversed and driven round the roadblock. We wouldn't have done anything. We couldn't do anything. We had guns, but no ammunition. The guns wouldn't have worked either, they were old and rusty. But he waited and waited. We told him it was the rules. The Germans, they're stupid. No imagination.'

'What about the French, do they obey the rules?'

'Jamais, unless it suits them. The French will make up the rules. They will also change them again. We have beaucoup de difficultés avec les français. If you tell a French driver he can't pass, he will say he knows the President, he knows the minister, he knows everybody. They think we're impressed. My brother knows the President, they went to school together. But my brother is in the ministry in Bamako and I'm here. What good does it do knowing the President? But we let them through, we pretended we were impressed. In any case the French always give you money. The Germans, never. We needed the money so we let them through.'

'Don't you get paid?'

'Of course we get paid, but the money never reaches us. If you're in Bamako you get your money. Here, you get nothing.'

'So it's the only way you can get money?'

He produced a bottle of water and a glass, and pushed an opened bottle of whisky towards me.

'Why do you think the press are stupid?' I asked.

'They come here, they spend their time eating and drinking. They go away and write articles about our country as if they are experts. They know nothing. They are not serious. Un handicap majeur pour nous. I've seen the newspapers,' he said. 'They write about unimportant things. They don't write about people starving, people who are sick and dying. They write about films, people on television. They should write about serious subjects. The French newspapers, they write about what the President says, what the minister says, what the Opposition says. That is not important. They always disagree. They should write about the big issues; how people are going to eat; how they are going to be healthy. What a personality says or does is not important.'

'But shouldn't you know both sides of the question?'

'Both sides? What do you mean?' he slurred. 'How can there be both sides? We know we must feed our people. How can you argue about that? We must educate our children: we must have schools and books and equipment. We need medicines and hospitals. We have lots of sick people who must be looked after. How can you argue about that? There is nothing to argue about. There is only one side.'

He had a point. Most francophone African newspapers are largely government run, if not government owned. Some are quite dull, almost like parish newsletters. Others, like *Le Fraternité Matin* in Côte d'Ivoire, are lively tabloids, but even they tend to be newspapers of record, or 'reference newspapers for the action of the party and the government' according to *Fraternité Matin*'s editor-in-chief, August Miremont. A bit like the Tory-worshipping *Daily Mail* rather than investigative, entertaining, independent publications.

Except, of course, in Senegal. *Le Soleil*, Senegal's daily morning newspaper, is a genuinely exciting read: big headlines, lots of photographs. The weekly, *Le Cafard Libéré*, 'journal satirique, vraiment, indépendant', is outrageous in African terms. It criticizes everybody, including the president. Obviously modelled on *Le Canard Enchaîné*, it's a cross between *Private Eye* the week after it's lost a heavy libel case and a redbrick student magazine.

French African news sense is also, I find, slightly odd. They'll run no end of stories about the British royal family. 'Le chien preéféré de la Reine Elizabeth a été mordu à mort,' ran one article I remember, including quotes from 'un spécialiste de psychologie canine'. A few stories about la Dame de fer, but precious little about the British government. It's as if they subscribe to the foreign news service of the *Sun* instead of *The Times*. Similarly they will publish long articles about plans for 'l'érection d'une statue en bronze représentant deux belles de nuit' in Belfast with the support of Rhonda Paisley, 'fille du pasteur Ian Paisley', but nothing about the troubles themselves.

The policeman poured two large Johnnies.

'I agree they are the big issues,' I said. 'I agree nobody wants to argue about them. But there are different ways of solving the problem. These things have to be discussed—'

He interrupted me sharply. 'Discussed? Our children are dying of famine and you want to talk. Our people are sick. Our children want books. There is no discussion, Ce sont less essentielles de la vie nationale.'

'But you've been to France, you've seen the political debate. The government says one thing, the opposition say something else. Don't you think that's useful?'

'Useful? It's stupid. I don't know why they disagree. They are not serious. There is nothing to discuss.'

Looked at from a dirty, stifling mud hut of a police station in the middle of the Sahara, you have to admit that many of our so-called political disagreements are pretty stupid. We'd drunk some more whisky. There was still some in the bottle. He was getting petty relaxed so I guessed now was the time to ask him about censorship.

'Okay, I agree,' I said. 'To keep debating these issues as we do is silly. Now tell me about newspapers. Shouldn't newspapers be independent of the government? Shouldn't the press tell the government what the people think and not what the government thinks?'

'Par ailleurs, the government is the people. The government doesn't need the newspapers to know what the people think, they know already. They represent the wishes of the people. What can the newspapers tell them?' he slurred back at me.

'But not everybody agrees with the government. There are different points of view.'

'There is a child dying of starvation. You want to have different points of view. Me? I want to feed the child.' He grabbed the bottle – literally liquid gold, which could have fed many children had he sold it instead of drinking it with me – and poured again.

'Why do you fill your newspapers with, with ...' He searched the air for the right word. 'With nothing? You write about things that are not important. Our newspapers write about our plans for our country, our hopes, our wishes. They write about the President and the work of the government, how they are fulfilling the wishes of the people. They write about serious things. How can that be wrong?'

I picked up an old dusty copy of *L'Essor*, Mali's daily newspaper, from the table. On the front page was a story about the government. Inside was a story about an Englishman adopting a python after it had eaten some reptiles at London Zoo. 'So is that serious?' I asked.

In another copy I discovered a story about a French couple who had made a fortune in Brittany by visiting priests and begging for money to look after their children. 'Is that serious?' And another story about a Filippino having a cake nine metres high to celebrate his seventy-first birthday. 'And that?'

'No, of course not. But people like to read silly stories.' He pushed the bottle across to me. 'Vive la banalité.'

'Vive la finesse,' I said. I declined, thanked him profusément and staggered to the door. The heat hit me like a sledgehammer.

'Don't forget, we are very serious,' he mumbled.

'What? About whisky?'

He smirked. 'The French said we could be the bread basket

of the region. We have the Niger and the Senegal. We make good farmers. You see, one day ...' He staggered out of the doorway and slumped on a bench underneath the flag.

Mali was once one of the richest countries in the world. In the thirteenth century it was the major trading centre for merchants and traders. Under Mansa Musa in the fourteenth century it stretched from Tekrur in the west to Dendi in the east and from Walata, Arawan and Tadmekker in the Sahara in the north to Futa Jellon in the south. So great and so rich was the country that when Emperor Mansa Musa made his pilgrimage to Mecca he took 500 slaves and something like 50,000 ounces of gold, which he distributed to the poor. Timbuktu and Jenne, which even today boasts the famous Great Mosque, were major centres of study in the Islamic world rivalling European centres of learning.

The tall, majestic Malians were also recognized for their courtesy and hospitality, or karm. When the king sat down to eat, everything had to come to a stop until he had finished. They rang bells and banged drums to ensure that everybody knew the royal meal was about to begin. If you were lucky, or unlucky, enough actually to see the king eating you had to take off your outer garment, wrap yourself up in it, kneel down and beat your breast and scatter dust and ashes all over yourself until he had finished. You think that's bad? Be grateful you never saw any of the king's camels bringing the food to the palace in the first place. The slightest glimpse of a royal camel or of any of the food and you were promptly executed. If, however, you averted your eyes and did not wear sandals in the king's presence – another offence punishable by death – chances are you would be promoted. Being promoted in ancient Mali meant being allowed to wear wider trousers. But never as wide as the king's. Perish the thought.

In spite of this, Ibn Battuta, a fourteenth-century Paul Theroux and one of the Arab world's great travellers, said:

'One of their good features is their lack of oppression. They are the furthest removed of people from it. Their Sultan does not permit anyone to practise it.' He went on to praise the way 'they clap fetters on the children if there is any failure on their part in memorising the Koran and the fetters are not removed till the memorising is done'. He praised them for 'dressing in fine white clothes on Fridays', but was slightly irritated that if he couldn't get to the mosque early, 'you will not find anywhere to pray because of the mass of people.'

But by the fifteenth century things were beginning to fall apart. The Malians were being attacked by Touregs. Surrounding countries started raiding their caravans. Eventually the Great Mali empire gave way to the not so Great Songhai empire, the eastern province which had built up enormous influence thanks to its trading links with the Hausa in northern Nigeria. But the Songhai was even shorter lived than the Mali Empire. Within one hundred years it had been destroyed by Spanish mercenaries hired by the king of Morocco, El Mansur, who was eager to get his hands on the gold. He got the gold, but not the empire. The empire, which continued to crumble, he left to the Malians.

Where is it all today? Gone. Disappeared. A sleeping policeman in the middle of the desert.

Gao is what a desert town should be: a collection of tiny huts and homes huddled together in the middle of nowhere on the banks of the Niger. One tarmac road through the centre, a main square, a big, faded, run-down, French-colonial-style hotel, two tiny market squares selling the basic necessities. A handful of bars and restaurants, lots of tiny children running all over the place, a million flies, blistering heat, up to 130° F. And sand. Sand. Sand. Sand.

Two Land Rovers roll into town and it's the big event of the day. We arrived. It was the big event of the week. Maybe there's a couple of thousand inhabitants. Some people say there's ten, even twenty thousand, which I cannot believe. To me it feels as though there's around 200, if that. There's the hotel, two or three tiny offices, the inevitable police station, a huddle of houses. That's about it. How that can support over 200 people beats me.

For over 1,000 years Gao dealt in gold, salt and slaves. Some people say they are still dealing in slaves, shipping young people and children up from the south to Algeria. But I didn't see any signs of it. All I saw were gnarled old Touregs with their gnarled old camels; Moagas selling salt; Mossi selling cola nuts, the Peules in their traditional conical hats. I also spotted Fool Foolds, Hassanic Arabs, Muslim Tedas and Dogons whose traditional calendar is made up of five-day weeks. I even saw a Japanese salesman in a black suit selling fax machines He was sitting on a box at the corner of the square with a tiny lap-top computer. Standing on a box alongside him waving what I first thought was an upside-down umbrella at the sky, was a tiny Arab boy. The Japanese salesman was sending his daily sales report back to Tokyo by satellite. Maybe the Toureg with the camel, the group of Hassanic Arabs in the square and the Muslim sitting on the banks of the river, are all partners in the world's biggest white slave operation. Maybe the Japanese with the hi-tech umbrella is their banker. Maybe the boy holding the umbrella represents the buyer. How do I know?

Everywhere else everybody is begging for something. Children are begging for bics, young men are begging us to buy everything from genuine counterfeit Rolexes to toilet paper. The old men were just begging. Around the edge of the square the women were looking on, no doubt criticizing and complaining about everything in sight.

On the main square, tucked away behind the camels, is the Hôtel Atlantide, one of my favourite hotels in the world. The Crillon in Paris may have the gold plates, the Hôtel du Golfe in Lomé may have the crispest white tablecloths; the Galle Face in Colombo may have the most sophisticated cock-roaches you're ever likely to meet; but the Atlantide, which looks like a mosque built by a trainee architect who specialized in Turkish baths, beats them all. It's run by an Indian woman with one arm. The rooms are dark and dismal and shabby. The showers rarely work. But the service is out of this world, even though it might not be quite so hot on some of the finer details.

I once had a suit cleaned and pressed in minutes. (I never travel across the Sahara without a suit, otherwise 'Er Back Home might think I was actually enjoying myself.) Trouble was the jacket was folded and pressed like a shirt. For months afterwards I was wearing a suit with razor-sharp creases – down each side of the jacket, across the middle of the sleeves and along the back, where it was folded to fit on to a backing sheet of cardboard and squeezed into a cellophane bag. Would you get that kind of service at the Crillon? Jamais.

You can get to Gao any which way you choose. By plane direct to Tamanrasset – Tam, as we old Africa hands say, Djanet, Mopti, or Timbuktu. But be warned. Their time-keeping is not perfect. Here they measure time not by minutes but by millions of years, a bit like British Rail. And the planes? Now, I'm not saying they are unsafe. But quite often they are so overcrowded, people are sitting down the middle of the aisle. Once we had live goats on board.

You can go by boat up the River Niger. Riverboats slide lazily as far as Mopti, Timbuktu and Gao. Canoes go everywhere. You can go by road, in enormous air-conditioned luxury Gelandewagens, if you insist, or by bicycle. I once met an English schoolteacher in Ouagadougou who had cycled all the way from London. Or you can go by taxi. Agadez has a fleet of big Peugeots. So do most other so-called isolated desert towns. Fares are relatively cheap, considering. From Niamey to Ouaga, for example, a twenty-four-hour drive, costs about £80; similarly from Bamako to Mopti.

You can take a bus. The Algerian SNTV long-distance buses go everywhere. There is a daily service south from Ghardaia, another runs three times a week from Agadez to Niamey, and so on. You could thumb a lift on one of the enormous 300-year-old Mercedes trucks that seem to run on coaldust and belch out huge clouds of black smoke. A good place for getting a lift is the customs post in Tam. It's not allowed, but it's amazing what hard currency will do in a socialist country.

You can even go by train, from Dakar to Bamako, or from Abidjan to Ouaga, which, in the broiling desert heat, is not that much different from Network Southeast in midsummer. And not that much quicker either. Wherever you go by train in the Sahara, it takes twenty-four hours. At least.

Me? I believe in suffering. I prefer good old-fashioned Land Rovers. Although last time I crossed the Tenere – I shall deny it if you tell Thesiger – I succumbed to the much more comfortable Toyota Land Cruisers.

But however you cross the Sahara you won't be disappointed. By the beard of Allah, I guarantee it.

The first thing that strikes you is that the desert, the biggest desert in the world, is not just sand. It's everything else you can think of, plus sand. From Ghardaia to El Golea, its 250 kilometres of coaldust; then from El Golea to In Saleh, it's flat and stony. The gravel plains of the Tanezrouft are so boring the only excitement you'll experience is having lunch with passing Touregs and using some of the larger stones to smash the skull of your cooked goat's head to get the brains out. The goat's, not the Touregs'. Tesalit is surrounded by a mass of grey black slate.

But when you're in the sand you're in the sand. South of Tamn, if you're not another Mark Thatcher, you can drive for days on end through the most glorious golden sandscapes you'll ever see. Vast endless seas of sand; enormous swooping sand dunes the size of the South Downs. In the Ain-el Hadjadj Valley, however, it's a wonderful deep red which glows in the sunset.

The most spectacular sand of all is the Tenere Desert, especially the stretch from Tchou to Mont Agadez. The largest stretch in the whole of the central Sahara, it swoops and swerves, rising to peaks of over 1,000 metres, then it suddenly drops. And the amazing thing is, it's changing all the time. One minute it's deep gold, the next it's salmon pink. Then it's sharp and crisp. Next, it's fuzzy and shimmering.

Look at the desert once and it's sharp and vivid. You think it's remained the same for a million years. Look again and you can actually see the sand blowing from one place to the next, from the top of a dune down to the valley floor.

North of Arak it changes again. For in the Sahara, one second you're driving on glorious golden sands, the next you're engulfed in a thick, impenetrable cloud of fech-fech, a very fine, loosely-packed sand which billows up into enormous clouds as soon as you even think of looking at it.

The first time I hit fech-fech was on the way to Gao. I was driving a Land Rover at over 100 kph, in convoy. Ten, maybe five metres in front of me was another Land Rover, also doing 100 kph; ten, maybe five metres behind was another, going at the same speed. For two hours we zoomed across glorious sand. It was a fabulous, exhilarating experience. Suddenly, in a split second, I could see nothing. It was just black. I was in the middle of a thick, gooey cloud. I wanted to brake. But I couldn't. I was in convoy. If I even gently touched the brakes, the Land Rover behind me, which by now was also driving blind, would immediately smash into the back of me. Then the one behind him and the one behind him and so on. Instead, against all my instincts, I gripped the wheel and kept driving. At exactly the same speed. In exactly the same direction. Luckily, so did all the other drivers. Had one of us braked we'd have been another addition to the piles of skeletons you find everywhere in the Sahara burnt white in the sun.

When we finally reached Gao and the Hôtel Atlandide, did we celebrate? I can remember piling into the big, sprawling bar, which was packed. I can remember the Indian lady offering everybody drinks. I can remember tray after tray of pastis. I can remember drinking toast after toast to what's their name ... to ... whatever. I can remember meeting French businessmen, teachers, garage mechanics, who had just dropped out of the system, headed for the desert, and ended up in Gao. After that, nothing.

The next thing I remember is being woken up in my room by the old man who has become not only my personal valet and bodyguard but my office manager as well. He tells me I'm wanted at the police station. Maybe I had been reported. Maybe I was going to be arrested. Maybe I should have given him more clothes to wash and iron. I took a taxi and went straight to the police station near the Sahel Vert, one of the better restaurants in town. It was dark and slightly chilly after the heat outside, and looked as though it had been built with blocks of sand. On the floor there was sand. On the desk was a thin layer of sand. I sat on a bench in the corner and waited. People kept coming in and out, shaking hands, slapping each other, occasionally snatching a quick kiss. A Belgian came in with a policeman. He came across and we shook hands. He seemed to think we'd met before. Then they went out again.

Eventually I saw the Inspector. We reminisced about Paris and the cold weather and how dangerous it was for Malians to go to France nowadays. Nothing about being drunk in bars. When I left the police station my driver had gone. I decided to walk back across town to the hotel. Just outside the bank I met 207 little Arab boys all wanting a bic and a Belgian who definitely seemed to think we'd met before.

'So how's business?' I asked over the cries and shrieks for a bic.

'Business?' he said nervously. 'I'm not a businessman.'

'Sorry,' I shouted over the screams. 'The only people who come here are on business.'

'I'm a dentist,' he said. 'You don't remember?'

Why should I remember? Being a dentist and a Belgian, I'd have thought, was something you would want people to forget.

'On a health programme?'

'No.'

'On holiday?'

'No. You asked me that last night. Look, I'm sorry,' he said, 'I don't mean to be rude, but I'm looking for a Lebanese.'

'A Lebanese? In the middle of the desert?' I had just travelled thousands of miles across some of the roughest desert in the world. We were surrounded by sand and children. It would probably be another two weeks before I reached so-called civilization. And I am talking to a Belgian who's asking me if I've seen a Lebanese.

'Could you describe him?' I murmured slowly. 'Perhaps I might recognize him.'

'He's about 1.6 metres, grey hair, glasses, gold tooth in the front. Speaks very good French. A gruff accent.'

'No,' I said slowly, 'I can't recall seeing anybody quite like that in the desert.'

He didn't smile. He was deadly serious. 'I must find him,' he said.

'How do you know he is here?'

'He told me,' he said.

'But you can't find anything out here.'

'I've got to find him,' he kept repeating.

We walked across to Le Désert bar followed by the children. I felt like the Pied Piper. We sat on a bench outside.

'How long have you been looking?' I asked.

'About three weeks,' he said. 'All over Mali.'

I was hesitant to ask any pointed questions, in case I'd asked them the night before. But the whole idea of a Belgian dentist scouring Mali for a Lebanese was too crazy for words. 'Why are you looking for him?' I asked point-blank.

He leant towards me. The children stopped screaming. 'Gold,' he whispered.

'Gold,' I said. 'You mean he's stolen your teeth and you want to get them back?'

'No, he hasn't stolen anything,' he said very headmasterly. 'I want him to get me some gold.'

'But how can this Lebanese get you gold?'

'Ssh,' he said.

We started walking back to the hotel. The children had given us up and gone off looking for another potential source of supply.

Mali has enormous mineral deposits. There are extensive gold fields in the south and west of the country, bauxite in Kenieba and Kita and marble at Bafoulat. Diamonds have been discovered in Kenieba. There is manganese at Angongo, and phosphate mines at Tilemsi. The problem is developing and exploiting them.

'So how can this guy get you gold?' I whispered as we turned towards the main square.

'He gets it from Guinea. Very good quality, very good price. Also emeralds and gems from other parts of the region. A lot from Nigeria.'

'But isn't that illegal?'

'Sure it's illegal,' he said. 'That's why I have to be careful.'

I had come across some Americans years ago going round francophone Africa trying to sell gold mines by the cubic metre. The deal was, you bought your cubic metre and any gold they found on it they bought from you at the rate of US$250 an ounce. Which, to me, sounded slightly crooked. I asked them how they were doing.

'Fantastic,' they told me. 'Because anybody who buys a cubic metre automatically becomes a partner in the company and business partners are entitled to visit the States for meetings.'

So they automatically get a visa.'

'Right first time,' they grinned. But they refused to tell me how much they were charging for a cubic metre.

Guinea, I knew, had diamonds. An Australian-run mine in the south of the country, close to the border with Sierra Leone and Liberia, had just discovered a 181.77 carat colour-D diamond almost as big as the Koh-i-Noor, the world's largest, which is mounted in the Queen's royal sceptre and guarded day and night in the Tower of London. In Nigeria illegal mining was also becoming a big problem. Some Nigerians I know take topaz and amethysts with them when they go abroad. It gets round the foreign currency regulations and gives them a big profit. But I couldn't remember anything about gold.

'So how did you get involved in the gold business? I asked the dentist.

What he told me was amazing. 'I live in San Quentin,' he said, 'about two hours from Brussels. My lawyer called me one evening and asked if I wanted to make a million dollars. Naturally I said yes. In Belgium we have taxes up to here.' He waved his hands above his head. 'He told me to come to the Sheraton in Brussels for a meeting. My lawyer was there, and a doctor and two businessmen, all clients of the lawyer. He told us he had met this Lebanese who could get gold out of Guinea. Lots of it. But he needed US$250,000 stake money to pay expenses: his ticket, the police, customs.'

'And how much gold would he bring out?'

'Maybe US$10 million. He said he didn't know until he got there.'

'So you were putting up $50,000 each to make £2 million. How did you know he wouldn't just take the money and run?'

'That's what we said, but the lawyer said we could trust the man. In any case it was a gamble. If we lost, we lost $50,000. He said we could write it off against tax. If we didn't we could make maybe two million.'

'If it was as easy as that, why did the Lebanese need you? Why didn't he just put up his own money and keep everything?'

'We asked that too, and the lawyer said that's what the Lebanese usually does: keeps the money or gives it to his family and friends.'

'So why was he going to share it with you this time?'

'The lawyer said they were friends, and the Lebanese wanted to help him.' It all sounded very suspicious. 'So we gave him the money.' He paused. A camel drew up slowly outside the petrol station opposite the hotel. 'I didn't want to at first. It all sounded very strange. But the others did. In the end I agreed.'

I wondered about the next question. 'And did you get the money?'

'Sure, we got the money,' he replied. 'Two million dollars in a Swiss bank.' He grinned all the way from his left upper molar to his right upper molar. 'Ten million dollars. Just like that.' I breathed a sigh of relief. 'We gave the lawyer the money. Three weeks later I got a telephone call, would I go to the Sheraton? We all turn up. The lawyer tells us the money is in Switzerland. Apparently the Lebanese got into Guinea from Mali. Crossed the border miles from anywhere, met his contacts, got the gold.'

'You mean gold taken out the back door?'

'No, gold from small private mines. The owners don't want to give the gold to the government because they get nothing for it. They prefer giving it to dealers.'

'Which is against the law . . .'

'Which is why he crosses the border from Mali, and brings the gold back into Mali.'

'Isn't it illegal bringing it into Mali?'

'Sure, but once it's in Mali nobody worries.'

'And in any case the Lebanese has paid everybody off. So how does he get it to Switzerland?'

'By plane.'

'You mean US$10 million in gold fits into a suitcase?'

'Look, a million dollars' worth of mercury fits into a tube this big,' he said holding his thumb and first finger about three inches apart.

'How do you know about mercury?' I queried.

'Another story,' he said. Obviously this syndicate of Belgian bourgeoisie was up to everything.

'So how much does he pay the Africans for the gold?'

'About five to ten thousand dollars.'

'But that's nothing,' I said. In January 1980, gold hit US$850 an ounce, although now it's around US$400.

'To them it's millions.'

Which was true. The average income per head of population in Guinea is less than US$300 a year. But this was another example of Africa's famous informal sector at work, making gold production, apart from South Africa, one of the continent's big growth areas of the future.

'And what do they do with the money?'

'Buy new equipment for the mines, videos .... Bring the stuff in across the border.'

'Because otherwise the government would know that . . .'

'Exactly.'

'What happens when the gold gets to Switzerland?'

'You get a couple of banks to analyse it. They give you a price, you take the best price and put the money in the bank. That's it.'

'You mean you just walk into any bank and dump US$10 million worth of gold on the counter and they don't say a word?'

'Apparently not.'

'The lawyer said.'

'The lawyer said.'

We had reached the steps of the Atlantide. 'So you've got a couple of million dollars in a Swiss bank,' I said. The dentist nodded. 'So what are you doing here?'

'Mais enfin,' he said, suddenly turning serious and no doubt putting on his best consulting manner, 'we all told the lawyer we wanted to do it again, but the lawyer said the Lebanese told him he didn't want to do it again.'

'What? Too risky?'

'That's what he said. But we didn't believe him. We said we wanted to ask the Lebanese ourselves. But the lawyer said he couldn't trace him.' He spat into the sand. 'Just an excuse. Didn't want us to see him. Wants to keep him to himself.'

'So you're trying to find the Lebanese so you can cut the lawyer out.'

'Bien sûr,' he nodded vigorously. 'We decided we would give it four weeks. After four weeks . . . .'

'You give up and go back to being a dentist.'

He nodded. 'A policeman in Bamako told me the Lebanese often comes through Gao. He has a big car: two Malians travelling in front, policeman with him in the back.'

'So you are just waiting?'

He nodded.

'It must be better than being a dentist . . .'

He nodded again and showed me two gold teeth.

'. . . in Belgium.'

If the Sahara has one of the best hotels in the world, it also boasts some of the best food, and I don't mean roasted fennec, camel steaks and crunchy black and yellow coleopterans. There's the wonderful Eau Vive restaurant in Ouaga, of course. But the best roast lamb I've ever tasted was in Tesalit, on the border between Mali and Algeria, seated round a campfire and surrounded by howling hyenas. And on the Plateau de Tadernit, just past Ghardaia, are a group of shepherds who serve the best chachumba I've every had.

Not interested in food? You prefer to feast yourself on culture? The Sahara, which boasts 60,000 years of human habitation, is the world's biggest art exhibition and museum.

There are the famous rock paintings in the Hoggar Mountains, in Tibesti, and at Fezzan showing hunting and grazing scenes 2,000 years old. There are rock engravings at Adrar Bous on the Air Plateau. Dinosaur bones litter the sands at Guadoufaoua, west of the Tenere. I once took what I thought was a rare fossil of a fish I found in the middle of nowhere all the way to the museum in Niamey to be told it was of no interest. They already had millions of them. Archaeologists have even found evidence that pottery and the graphic arts were invented in the Sahara.

There might not be any admission charges to the museums

in the Sahara, but even a desert rat like me will admit there are some disadvantages to a holiday in all that sand. First – unbelievably – it's cold. And I mean cold. Whether you're sleeping in a Land Rover or curled up with a camel under the stars. Before my first trip I was told it would be cold at night – because it was so hot during the day; often as high as 50°C. Don't you believe it. The Sahara is cold because-it's-cold. At night, temperatures can easily drop way below freezing. And even though you're wrapped up in your thick woolly djellabah, it still gets through to the marrow of your bones.

Second, it can be dangerous. Especially if you're caught in a sandstorm. My one and only sandstorm, just outside Timeiaouine, lasted maybe twenty minutes. But it's amazing how it suddenly hits you from nowhere, how it roars down and engulfs you, how it lashes and buffets everything quite mercilessly – and how the sand gets everywhere; in your eyes, in your ears. You're even coughing up sand for days afterwards.

Third, it can be – how do you say? – different. I don't want to upset anyone, but put it this way. The first time you have tea with a Toureg and you find a fly in the glass, you ask for another glass; the second time you remove the fly; the third time you drink it, fly and all.

But the Sahara is worth every fly, beetle, cockroach and locust, for no matter how many times you cross the desert, it's always different. Paris is always Paris. Venice is always Venice. Not the Sahara. It's changing all the time. One second you're in the middle of the emptiest place on earth; the next second you're in the middle of 1,000 camels smuggling gold across the borders or carrying blocks of salt all the way back from Bilma. One minute there is a valley here; the next minute it's gone. One day you wake up and find a crowd of butchers at the foot of an enormous sand dune slaughtering camels for the day's market. The next day, the dune has disappeared.

You can marvel at sunsets over the Niger; shelter under the trees at Assamaka, the only shade for a 1,000 miles; join in the

Ghimbala whirling fetish ceremonies, or collapse in tears because your Land Rover has overheated yet again.

There is a million times more sand in the Sahara than you'll see anywhere else on earth – and it's a million times better.

But don't leave it too late. Go now, before every wadi has an ice-cream parlour, and before all the Touregs swop their tins of camel's urine for Del Monte cans of fruit from California and their camels for government-issued prefabs. And if you see a Lebanese with two gold front teeth, tell him there is a dentist from San Quentin who would like to talk to him.

But whatever you do, don't tell anyone you're going. They might want to go as well. Then it won't be Sahra any more.

Flick

ABOUT THE AUTHOR

Geraldine Meade lives in Dublin with her husband
Johnny and their six children. She is a primary school
teacher and has an MA in Children's Literature.
Flick is her first novel.

Flick

Geraldine Meade

Little Island

FLICK
First published 2011
by Little Island
128 Lower Baggot Street
Dublin 2
Ireland

www.littleisland.ie

ISBN 978-1-908195-01-2

British Library Cataloguing Data. A CIP catalogue record for this book is
available from the British Library.

Cover design by Cian McKenna
Inside design by Inka Hagen

Printed in the UK by CPI Cox and Wyman

Little Island received financial assistance from
The Arts Council (An Chomhairle Ealaíon), Dublin, Ireland.

10 9 8 7 6 5 4 3 2 1